# Property
# and Political Theory

# Property
# and
# Political Theory

ALAN RYAN

Basil Blackwell

© Alan Ryan 1984

First published 1984
Basil Blackwell Publisher Limited
108 Cowley Road, Oxford OX4 1JF, England

Basil Blackwell Inc.
432 Park Avenue South, Suite 1505
New York, NY 10016, USA

British Library Cataloguing in Publication Data

Ryan, Alan
Property and political theory.
1. Property – History
I. Title
330'. 17'09033 HB701
ISBN 0–631–13691–6

Typeset by Cambrian Typesetters, Aldershot
Printed in Great Britain by Camelot Press Ltd, Southampton

# Contents

# Preface

I hope that the interest of what follows is sufficient to absolve me from the need to justify my writing it. I am, however, rather painfully aware that a scholarly treatment of even a small number of the subjects on which I have touched would require more time and expertise than I possess, and would result in more volumes than most of us would have time to read. But I hope this rather brisk treatment of some of the issues raised by the writers I deal with below may at any rate induce some of my readers to go and get the same pleasure from them that I have had myself.

In writing this book I have contracted the debts which it is usual to contract: John Dunn, Quentin Skinner, Geoffrey Hawthorn, Steven Lukes and John Gray have raised more awkward questions than I know how to answer; Herbert Hart has for twenty years set standards of lucidity and rigour in the philosophy of law which I make no claim to emulate, but which have made me think it is worth trying to think a bit straighter. The Social Science Research Council awarded me a personal research fellowship in 1974-5; I hope the results justify their judgement.

Like all male authors I have incurred debts to several ladies; Margaret Whitlock typed and retyped drafts of the book at an astonishing pace; my daughter Sadie reminded me that I had owed the typescript to my publisher more years than she had been alive; my wife Kate typed out part of a first draft and told me why so much of it wouldn't do; and Mary Ann Sieghart insisted that if I could explain in tutorials what I was trying to say by way of conclusion, there was no particular reason why I shouldn't write it down. All these have 'mixed their labour' with what follows; the errors are still mine.

# Bibliographical Note

It is evident from the footnotes how heavily I have relied on a number of well-known works; my larger debts and allegiances would make a long list with more of the qualities of a rag-bag than a select bibliography. I should therefore like simply to refer readers to the excellent bibliography of works on property compiled by G. F. Gaus and printed in *Nomos* 22, *Property,* ed. John Chapman and Roland Pennock (Aldine Atherton, Chicago, 1980).

# Introduction

In what follows, I shall be pursuing a familiar story in what I hope will not be too familiar a way. The familiar story is that of the career of private property as a central institution of western society. The unfamiliar aspect is the attempt to concentrate on what a succession of thinkers have had to say about the relationship between property and work. That many theorists derived the right to own from the activity of working is scarcely news; the 'naturalness' of labour as the moral title to what is created by that labour has been a commonplace of political and economic radicalism for three hundred years; and political and economic conservatism has had a continuous struggle to defuse the revolutionary implications of it.[1] But views of what 'work' is have varied a good deal, as have views of what work might become in some transfigured society. Not all theorists have remained so stolidly empiricist as to define work entirely in terms of what the so-called working class spends most of its time doing; not all theorists have been so stolidly empiricist as to define property entirely in terms of those rights which private law recognizes in a given place at a given time Many have seen a significance in the relationship between men and things that would surprise the average conveyancer or practitioner in equity. The exploration of some of these purported insights has rather more than curiosity value, for part of the interest of property as a subject for the political theorist lies in exploring the moral and political universes in which 'it's mine' makes such different sorts of sense.

This has some practical implications: a benevolent but not very imaginative government may be quite at a loss to know why hard-up peasant farmers will not accept new and better land in order that an airport may be built on their present holdings. Even the more imaginative of us who can see that 'this piece of land' can be 'mine' to the peasant in some sense in which the share certificate

[1] Anton Menger, *The Right to the Whole Product of Labour* (Macmillan, London, 1899), is still the best account of all this.

cannot be 'mine' to the rentier, may find it hard to keep the difference in mind. The same thing plainly applies to work: it is usually obvious enough why men on an assembly line or in a motor factory paint-shop do not like what they do. It is more puzzling when men enjoy what to outsiders seems dirty, dangerous or exhausting labour.[2]

The relationship between labouring and owning, though central, is not the only one which even a fairly narrow analysis must look at. Besides the obvious definitional worries – what is it to *own* something, what can and cannot count as working – to which different thinkers have given very different replies, there are, as we have already suggested, problems about what can and cannot really be *owned*. Is anything potentially property, or must some things always be treated very differently from the things we call property? For instance, Hegel suggests that there is a conceptual as well as a moral impropriety involved in slavery: men, who are themselves the sources of the possessory intentions in terms of which he analyses property, already so thoroughly possess themselves that there is no room for anyone else's possession of them.[3] This contrasts with the assumption of legal positivists that if a given legal system recognizes the existence of 'slaves', slaves certainly exist, and men can certainly be owned. Again, where property is important as a capital asset, are all such assets on a par, or is land, say, in some way special? From a political point of view, many further questions arise. We want to know how it affects a person's allegiance to his society to possess or not to possess property; we want to know if the performance of certain sorts of work makes a man less fit to be a citizen, or less able to be one. Not all thinkers about work and property have been concerned with all these questions, but many of the more compelling thinkers certainly have, even where, as in the case of Marx, the concern has been to explode the whole social framework within which the questions have been so posed. So, what follows is concerned to spell out the political theory of property in addition to the moral theory of its justification or critique.

What follows is not exactly an essay in the history of ideas, though I should be distressed if I were simply wrong about what as a matter of historical fact some or all of my protagonists thought or

---

[2] Alasdair Clayre, *Work and Play* (Weidenfeld & Nicolson, London, 1974), pp. 84–7.
[3] G. W. F. Hegel, *The Philosophy of Right* (Clarendon Press, Oxford), §57, pp. 47–8.

meant. What follows belongs more to the realm of the philosophical analysis of ideas than to the tracing of their history.

Their history is in principle a matter of their transmission, of knowing who influenced whom; such questions are essentially causal and empirical, even if they are often impossible to answer in detail because of a lack of empirical evidence about what it was which persuaded an author to think as he did and to employ this rather than that conceptual scheme. Their philosophical analysis is a matter of their coherence and their implications. The tidiness of this line between my aims and the historians' is, however, partly illusory. If a man is trying to follow a rational argument, the historical and philosophical questions of what his assumptions and conclusions were seem to intertwine. The historian can hardly see a move from premise to conclusion as a brute causal connection; the philosopher cannot discover what the premises and conclusions were without finding out what as a matter of historical fact they were.[4] And since words shift in meaning over time, the philosopher who wants, as I do here, to think out Locke's problems with Locke, will find himself in need of some of the skills of a translator. This means that when in doubt about how to construe an argument, some reference to its historical context is inescapable.

The problem, then, is one of how *much* and what context is inescapable. Two considerations press in different directions. The first is that we need above all to be aware of the context in which the ideas were formulated and circulated. This will not yield a complete explanation of the text, since that depends upon what further questions the text raises once it is understood in this narrower sense. But it does yield the basic understanding of the text.[5]

The second direction in which we are pulled is rather different. Once the essay or book in which we are interested has been put before the public, it takes on a life of its own. Whatever the copyright laws, an author has only a limited control over his own writings. What he writes will have implications which he did not see – implications in the narrow sense of more or less logical

---

[4] John Dunn, 'The Identity of the History of Ideas', *Philosophy* 43 (1968), pp. 85–104.
[5] Quentin Skinner, 'Meaning and Understanding in the History of Ideas', *History and Theory*, 8 (1969), pp. 3–53; see too his essay on 'The Limits of Historical Explanation', *Philosophy*, 41 (1966), pp. 119–215 – though I think that there is by now a consensus that this essay sets those limits implausibly tightly.

inferences from what he says to the consequences of what he says. When Locke founded property on labour, a reasonable inference might be that, as St Paul and Lenin agreed, the man who did not work had no right to eat. It is going too far to say that Locke either said or implied in the *Second Treatise* that 'he who does not work, neither shall he eat,' but it is not going too far to say that *what Locke wrote* implied it. Works outlive their authors, and take on lives their writers might be perturbed to see. With some writers this process is so striking that a major historiographical effort goes into making sense of it; the history of how Machiavelli's major works were read, from 1520 to the 1980s, is the most obvious instance.

So we can wonder why Locke or Marx or Hegel or Mill has been read as he has, what was there on the page to provide the material, as well as what was there in the mind of the reader to work it up. And we may become more or less critically embroiled in the process ourselves. It may outrage us that Marx so misrepresents Hegel in the *Economic-Philosophical Manuscripts*, and we may want to rescue something more true to Hegel's intentions than the caricature Marx offers; but we need not feel anything of the sort – we may only wish to see what image of Hegel Marx believed his readers would be prepared to accept, and to draw what conclusions our interests dictate.

This suggests – it comes nowhere near showing – that it is very unlikely that anyone would do well to offer a 'complete' account of any tolerably complex and contentious topic in political theory, such as work, ownership and their political consequences. There may also be an irreducible minimum of interpretative dissensus, as in all philosophical and cultural studies. We can, certainly, expect agreement on the more or less brute facts of the careers of Marx, Comte, Mill or Weber; it is less reasonable to expect consensus on the significance of those careers. This dissensus is all the more likely if we are interested in a strongly present-centred history of ideas. I do not mean by this a didactic history in which we attempt to draw 'lessons' for the future from the record of the past; I mean, rather, a history in which we are selfconscious about what our interests in the subject are, and envisage ourselves as in some measure engaging in a dialogue across time.[6]

[6] The idea that philosophy in general has taken this 'conversational' character is the upshot of the argument in Richard Rorty, *Philosophy and the Mirror of Nature* (Blackwell, Oxford, 1980).

At all events, what follows does not pretend to be a complete account of the *dramatis personae* who appear in it; readers will estimate the extent of the incompleteness by the number of questions they wish I had asked but have not.

Here, the story begins with Locke and ends with us, though the intellectual story may be said to begin with Locke and end with Marx and Mill. I choose these starting and stopping places because the two traditions of thinking about work and ownership and their political implications which I discuss – what I call the 'instrumental' and the 'self-developmental' traditions – can usefully be seen starting in the work of Locke and Rousseau. To put it briefly, my view is that in the work of Locke a tension which generally exists between these traditions is resolved because of Locke's Christian (or at any rate theistic) assumptions. Social institutions such as the institution of private property, and the tasks of everyday life, such as working consistently and conscientiously at our jobs, are instrumentally justified – that is, they are justified because they enable 'all mankind to flourish as much as may be'.[7] But, individuals are not simply instruments of the social well-being of men in general; they have been put on earth by God to do their duty to Him. In doing that duty, they express themselves – to know what God requires and to do it faithfully is what a 'self-developmental' picture of the Christian life requires. So, even though Locke features in these pages as one of the begetters of the instrumental and utilitarian theory of work and ownership which is so typical of British social thought, he also features in the history of the self-developmental theory, too. His example suggests that once God is dead, the choice of perspective on social life becomes harder.

Rousseau illustrates precisely this. Rousseau secularizes social theory; his *Discourse on the Origins of Inequality* is important because it discounts the assumptions about the intrinsic plausibility – indeed, obviousness – of instrumental and utilitarian considerations which Locke relies on, and insists that the crucial question each man faces is about how he himself lives up to his own self-image. But unlike Locke, who could see the proper self-image as being determined from outside the whole social order by the dictates of God, Rousseau sees our self-images set by our social surroundings. In some societies, that image of an acceptable self is so set that we can

---

[7] John Locke, *Two Treatises on Government*, ed. Peter Laslett (2nd edn, Cambridge University Press, Cambridge, 1970), I, §§41–3, pp. 187–9.

readily live up to it. In others, it is so set that constant dissatisfaction is our lot.

After Rousseau the lineaments of modern arguments are easier to discern. In Kant, and after him Hegel, we get a fully developed picture of how the nature of the individual will, with its striving after freedom, requires the existence of a system of private property rights, framed by a suitable political order for their maintenance, and how, within that system, men can work at tasks which will develop their distinct and individual personalities as well as fitting them into an acceptable social order. In contrast, Bentham offers the classical instrumental and utilitarian defence of the institutions of private property in terms of their efficiency as solutions to the problem of scarcity and mutual competition.

And just as Kant and Hegel and Bentham defend the private property systems of their day, though along very different lines, so their successors attack the system of private property as it operated in the nineteenth century and defend some kind of socialist replacement of it. Here I take Marx and Mill as the protagonists of the story – Marx attacking property in terms of those self-developmental considerations which Hegel had employed in its defence, and complaining that work and politics were both realms of something more like slavery than individual self-expression, while Mill turned utilitarian considerations against the unregulated *laissez-faire* system which his father, and to some extent Bentham, had defended.

The conclusion will surprise few readers, though it may irritate a good many. This is that the expectations which fuelled the arguments of Mill and Marx have turned out to be false – not misguided or silly, but as a matter of fact wrong. The world has for all sorts of reasons turned out to be a rather different place from the one they supposed they could glimpse coming into being. My explanation of all this is not particularly original, though my explanation of how it comes about that both the utilitarians and their opponents have come to be wrong-footed is rather more so. But even those readers who think that I am wrong about the causes of the viability of capitalist private ownership and the unattractiveness of socialism, both Marxist and Millian, should find enough in the fact of the unpopularity of socialism to give them pause.

The role of the historical figures with whom I deal here, then, is to support my view that during the three centuries of argument about the relationship between work and ownership and their consequences for political life, two different images of the nature and point of work were at issue, and two different images of the nature and point of property rights went along with them. These I call the instrumental image on the one hand, and the self-developmental image on the other. There is some significance in the fact that the instrumental view is closely associated with British political thinkers accustomed to a form of property law very different from that in the context of which Kant, Hegel and Marx were writing. The English legal system discouraged a question which Roman law encouraged, namely, 'What is it to be the *owner* of something?' or 'How does a thing become Mine?'[8] The English legal inclination to enquire what gave a man good title to possession and no more than that, seems to have diverted a certain psychological or metaphysical interest into other channels.[9] It was left to a different philosophical tradition to enquire into the relationship of owner and owned.

The burden of the case is that the instrumental tradition regards work or labour as a cost incurred by men who want to consume the goods thus made available to them. The natural condition of mankind is one in which the earth will not satisfy human needs save when human beings expend labour to make it do so. It is not an inevitable or logical corollary of this view that men must always prefer less labour to more; it is perfectly possible to hold that some work is much more agreeable than the rest, and perhaps so much so that some work ceases to be a cost incurred in satisfying our wants. None the less, it is natural and usual for this to be ignored, especially since one assumption common to economists from the nineteenth century onwards is that efficiency and disagreeableness increase together, and that the paid labour falling to most men certainly cannot be expected to offer much intrinsic satisfaction.

This view is most explicit in the utilitarianism of the early nineteenth century, but it is foreshadowed by Locke's account of property in the *Two Treatises*. 'Pure' instrumentalism is something of an ideal type; and it will be suggested later that a generally instrumental view of labour is the more acceptable when not too much is made of purely this-worldly or self-centred considerations. The instrumental account of property is in essentials the applica-

[8] Barry Nicholas, *An Introduction to Roman Law* (Clarendon Press, Oxford, 1962), pp. 15ff.
[9] F. H. Lawson, *The Law of Property* (Clarendon Press, Oxford, 1958), p. 6.

tion of the same consequentialist analysis to social institutions. Anyone's property limits the freedom of everyone else to acquire and use what he feels like acquiring and using.[10] It is an institution which therefore requires justification. The justification is that the existence of *some* rather than no rules will aid us to apply labour to the world as effectively as possible. Some rules are clearly necessary if men are to know what they may look forward to using in peace; minimal property rules are such rules. The defence of *private* property in a recognizable form goes far beyond this, of course, but rests upon the same considerations: proprietary rights over non-consumables are or are not justified if they are or are not an effective means to the end of efficiently exploiting the resources of the natural world, in comparison with any other system of rights and duties.

I call this justification instrumental rather than utilitarian in order to leave room for arguments which are not strictly utilitarian; a strict utilitarian would, in principle, though less certainly in practice, be relatively deaf to questions about justice or fairness. Moreover, one instrumental argument for private property – though not one I deal with here to any extent – is that only the social recognition of *property rights* will ensure that people's other, and more important *rights*, to political liberty, free speech and so on, will be secure.[11] As for justice, private property would be *utilitarianly* justified if it were a useful device for maximizing the pay-off from the joint efforts of mankind, even if in the process there was no very exact correspondence between an individual's efforts and his pay-off. This would be a drawback only where it threatened to become a source of inefficiency too. Although Locke certainly employs arguments of a utilitarian kind, and appeals more than once to the goal that 'all mankind should flourish as much as may be', we cannot call him a utilitarian in the nineteenth or twentieth century sense, if only because he never sets out to enquire how distributive principles summed up as 'justice' or 'equity' relate to aggregative principles. As I have suggested, God's plans for the universe play an important role here: when God intends that men should flourish, he does not intend that we should sacrifice some

---

[10] Henry Sidgwick, *The Elements of Politics* (Macmillan, London, 1891), pp. 66–70.
[11] Lawrence Becker, *Property Rights* (Routledge & Kegan Paul, London, 1977), pp. 75–80, 117; I suggest below that although liberty may sustain private property, the converse seems less plausible.

men to the welfare of the whole community. But even the later adherents of the instrumental tradition care more for justice than the strictest utilitarianism would allow; J. S. Mill, for instance, plainly regarded the fact that the hardest working earn least as a powerful objection to existing property arrangements, and it is clearly to the injustice of the fact that he objects, not to the impact on aggregate welfare.[12]

The instrumental view of work and property has a good deal of stamina; it is the commonest view to be discerned in recent industrial sociology, and it is so because it is a widely held view among the workers whom industrial sociologists study. That work is a cost incurred in earning the means of consumption and leisure time activities seems to be the prevalent view among affluent workers at any rate. That there is nothing 'special' about owning or not owning the means of one's livelihood seems an equally common belief. An instrumentally oriented worker ought in principle and seems in practice to prefer to work on an assembly line where this yields him a higher income than, for instance, running a small-holding which he owns.[13] Neither the nature of his work nor what he owns should be an essential constituent of what another tradition would call his mode of being in the world. He will no doubt mind a good deal whether he owns, that is, secures, the consumer goods for the sake of which the burden of work is undertaken, and there are obvious reasons of security of tenure and so on why he may prefer to own a house rather than rent one. Crucially, however, he will not care that he does not own the 'means of production', neither the tools he uses nor the conveyor belt he works beside, let alone the cars he works on.

The instrumental view of property assumes that the only rational mode of understanding work and property from a social standpoint is the instrumental mode, because it assumes that the rational mode of understanding them from an individual standpoint is instrumental. Since ownership or non-ownership has no intrinsic significance for individuals, it must be an instrumental question whether the recognition and enforcement of private property rights

[12] J .S. Mill, *The Principles of Political Economy, The Collected Works of John Stuart Mill*, vols II & III (University of Toronto Press, Toronto, 1965), pp. 381–3.
[13] J. H. Goldthorpe, D. Lockwood *et al.*, *The Affluent Worker* (University Press, Cambridge, 1968), vol. I, discuss those who do have these preferences; G.C Homans, *Social Behaviour* (Routledge & Kegan Paul, London, 1961), discusses some who do not — for instance, French-Canadian peasants migrating to New England.

in land, raw materials and the produced means of production,
yields social benefits. If property rights are an indispensable
condition of a good life, for extrinsic reasons; if only some such
system encourages adequate levels of thrift and effort; or if any
alternative would have appalling political costs, then they are
justified. In this century, most of the arguments about the rights
and wrongs of state ownership have concentrated on just such
points as these; and the result has been to blur the lines between a
fully 'private' and a fully 'socialized' system, as ways have been
sought of escaping the costs of either extreme.

The line of demarcation between the instrumental view and the
self-developmental view is not sharp. Nor does it mark a clear
political division. What follows shows often enough how similar
political allegiances can be defended in either tradition, and how
*some* features at least of working life or of a man's relationship to
what he owns can be favourably or unfavourably characterized in
either tradition. We may, for example, argue on the instrumental
view that it is wise to confine political rights such as suffrage to the
owners of real property of a certain value — on the grounds that
their possessions incline them to moderation, and disincline them
to radical egalitarianism, render them less vulnerable to corruption
and intimidation, and so on. All this may be inferred from Locke or
James Mill without undue violence to the text.[14]

But it is also explicit in Kant's analysis of political rights, though
it there appears as something like a deduction from the concept of
property. A man who possesses property is, and a man who doesn't
is not a *person* for political purposes; not to have property is not to
be, in the appropriate area, one's own man and therefore not to
have a personality to express in the polity.[15] What is packed into
the *concept* of property thus analysed is much the same as what
emerges as contingently, but closely linked to it in the other
tradition. I do, however, want to say that even where similar
allegiances are defended, there will be characteristic differences of
tone, and that these may in the end dictate very different kinds of
politics, a case which my discussion of Marx and Mill will illustrate
and, I hope, support.

[14] James Mill, *An Essay on Government* (Bobbs-Merrill, Indianapolis, 1957), pp. 74–6; Locke,
*Two Treatises*, II, §§140–2, pp. 380–1.
[15] Hans Reiss (ed.), *Kant's Political Writings* (Cambridge University Press, Cambridge,
1970), pp. 77–8.

The self-developmental view is committed to two propositions. The first is that there is, or can be, and certainly should be, something intrinsically satisfying about *work;* work is a characteristic form of human self-expression, and its reward is not to be found only or primarily in the things it makes available for consumption, but in the nature of the activity itself. The second is that the relationship between a man and what he *owns* is intrinsically significant; there is a substantial bond between a man and his property, a bond which repays philosophical analysis. To speak of such a substantial bond is not to deny that the relationship requires social recognition to exist, or to reveal its true character. But in this tradition of analysis, it is held to be a fruitful approach to understanding work and property to begin by concentrating on this relationship, even when the aim is to uncover what sort of social setting it demands. It is in the further development of this point that the nearest approach to agreement between the two traditions is usually to be discerned.

There is a good deal of further disagreement which can be alluded to now, and developed later. It is, I think, crucially important that the British mainstream was not infected by the need to produce a theodicy. Although Locke's political theory is, on my account of it, *framed* in a theological view of the world, it does not contribute to the specifically Christian theodicy which Locke evidently accepted. The tasks of social theory and theology were kept separate, and this gives an oddly unhistorical air to much British political thought. Social institutions were neither justified as part of the redemptive process envisaged by Hegel and Marx, nor were they condemned for failing to be. The *matter-of-factness* about what *property* was, is, on this view, matched by an unwillingness to see in work much more than what the labourer saw in it. There is in the European tradition a concern for how work and ownership unilaterally create a world more thoroughly human and therefore a world more permeated with (or better able to do without) the divine plan that is hardly visible in British thinking. Blackstone's *Commentaries* are perhaps the most obvious exception to this generalization; but who would suggest that Blackstone is in the same league as Kant or Hegel as a social theorist?[16] The idea of a world redeemed or beyond redemption did not come readily to

[16] William Blackstone, *Commentaries on the Laws of England*, ed. R. W. Kerr, 4 vols. (Murray, London, 1876), vol. II, *Of the Rights of Things*.

Bentham or either of the Mills; and though it came readily to
Locke, no analogue of that specifically Christian redemption and
loss appeared in his politics. In Rousseau, Kant, Hegel and Marx,
things are quite otherwise.

For all of them, the explanation of social institutions lies in their
role in a historical process with an educative and cultural function
– or perhaps we should say, more guardedly, a process whose
educative and cultural impact on man justifies or condemns it.
Their attitudes to history vary in sometimes inexplicable ways:
Rousseau both possesses an acute sense of the unstoppability of the
historical tide and shouts to us to somehow roll it back all the same,
and Kant writes short essays on history and progress which come
oddly from the pen of the man who produced a strikingly timeless
picture of the nature of morality and human knowledge. None the
less, even in Rousseau and Kant the raw materials for a thorough-
going historicism are present, even if they are subsequently
developed by Hegel and Marx in ways their predecessors would
have wondered at.

A second difference lies in the central place that the concept of
alienation occupies within the self-developmental tradition.
Although this is an overworked subject, some account of *why* the
concept has such power to charm cannot be omitted. In the self
developmental account, a crucial problem is that of whether a man
(or men) can recognize their achievements in seeing before them a
world that they have freely created. That the world, though made
by men, confronts them as a strange and hostile place is one
element in the claim that men are alienated; that each man in his
work is confronted by hostile objects is another. The grandest claim in
the theory of alienation is that the meaning of history is that we now
find ourselves in a hostile, though man-created world, and that we can
at last change it and ourselves in such a way that we are at home in
it, surrounded by objects which reflect our own creative powers.[17]

A third difference between the two traditions reflects the way in
which instrumental theories happily embrace legal positivism. The
way in which the analytical side of the theory relates to the theory's
ultimate justificatory or condemnatory aims is very different in the
two traditions. Although utilitarian accounts of the institution of
private property in land (say) usually had a justificatory intention,
there is a sense in which this is independent of the *mode* of analysis.

[17] Karl Marx, *Early Writings* (Penguin, Harmondsworth, 1975), p. 278.

A man who thought that the benefits were bought at too high a price could accept all but the eventual claim that the institution was a good bargain. This is not altogether true of a writer like Hegel or Marx. It is not quite impossible to divorce Hegel's account of property from his approval of it; but the categories in which he offers that account load the argument from the beginning. It is less easy to distinguish *what* Hegel is describing or *what* Marx is condemning from their approval or condemnation than is the case with their utilitarian counterparts.

One conclusion from the comparison and contrast between these different ways of analysing work and property is that both suffer a twentieth-century sea change. The causes are obvious enough: the evolution of legal arrangements which make it possible to possess and transfer all sorts of rights which are part of modern property law, but whose social implications are quite removed from eighteenth or nineteenth-century ideas about what it was to be a man of property, is one. The divorce of management and ownership in modern industry is another. The suspicion that the miseries of work have more to do with technology and managerial techniques rather than with ownership is another again. The way in which socialism in practice falsified the belief that common ownership removed the preconditions of tyranny and exploitation is even more obvious. Just as important, the belief that inequalities of ownership are the major sources of political inequality does not survive the rise of new technologies of war and peace. The state's capacity to unleash amounts of violence unmatchable by private individuals is a fact whose implications reach far beyond our topic, but which certainly reach into it; the way in which this power is managed both politically and bureaucratically provides quite other routes to power than the ownership of the means of production. The decline of the traditions of thought which I shall describe is not wholly and only a decline – we may properly welcome the gain in clarity which twentieth-century industrial sociology, political science and jurisprudence have brought – and it is not complete. If eighteenth-century anxieties about the connection between land-holding and republican virtue have become very remote to us, there are some plausible twentieth-century versions of the same fears; and if I end by asking why both Marx and Mill have been 'let down' by the twentieth century, this is not to suggest that their hopes will be dashed to eternity.

# 1

# Locke, Labour and the Purposes of God

Students of theories of property rightly spend a lot of time in the company of Locke. His *Two Treatises on Government* provide, so he told his nephew, the best account of property that he knew of. They defend the proposition that the sole purpose for which government exists is to defend the property of its subjects; and they give an account of how men can come by that property which has been enormously influential.

The two treatises engage in different tasks; the first harries Sir Robert Filmer, the author of *Patriarcha*[1] and defender of the absolute and arbitrary power of kings. Filmer had defended the moral claims of absolute monarchy by arguing that God had granted to fathers a power over their offspring which was paternal, political and proprietary; children are the subjects and the property of their fathers – save where positive law limits that paternal power. But even where positive law does limit it, the authority of the law-giver is of just the same kind; monarchs have an absolute and arbitrary power over their people, and their people are at once their subjects and their property. This power is God-given. When God gave the earth to Adam, and after the Flood confirmed His donation to the sons of Noah, He made them kings and owners. And Filmer thought that secular history merely confirmed what Genesis taught, because the Roman *paterfamilias* could kill or sell his children without permission from any higher authority. The authority of seventeenth-century monarchs was theirs by inheritance from Adam; more importantly yet, the authority they had was absolute and arbitrary, and being such it was simultaneously the political power to control persons and the property right to control persons and things alike.[2]

Locke's negative arguments against Filmer strike most later readers as a simple, if unnecessarily prolonged, knock-out of a wholly inept target. Even Locke occasionally suggests that the

[1] Robert Filmer, *Patriarcha* (London, 1680).
[2] ibid., pp. 11–12, 16, 38–9.

contest is a pretty one-sided one, and asks whether the friends of absolutism cannot find anything better than *Patriarcha* to support them. His main point is that there is no way of proving that Charles I, for whose benefit the argument had been written, or Charles II, whose supporters in the Exclusion Crisis had appealed to it, was the heir of Adam or of the sons of Noah. For all anyone can tell, it might be he, John Locke, who was the lawful king.

More interestingly, though, Locke defends against Filmer the claim that different kinds of authority exist: ownership is not the same thing as political power; parental authority is neither political authority nor ownership. Although this is very much a claim which Aristotle is famous for making – and which Filmer denied in his *Observations* on the *Politics* – Locke's grounds for making it are Christian rather than Aristotelian. God did not give Adam absolute and arbitrary power over the world or over his children. God is a rational God who gives any of his agents only such power as they need to fulfil the purposes for which he gives them that power. The violence of men's wills is such that to grant them absolute power is sure to corrupt them; what Adam gained from God was the right to use nature and direct his offspring so that they might flourish as God intended. More briefly: Adam never possessed the power Filmer supposes; and it was not the sort of thing he could bequeath; and we have no way of knowing who is now entitled to it.[3]

The positive arguments of the *Second Treatise* have generally been found more intellectually invigorating, for it is there that Locke turns to providing a positive defence of his view that a legitimate government is limited, constitutional, non-arbitrary, and confined to the regulation and securing of men's property. This property he defines as their 'lives, liberties and estates'.[4] Men have a right to this property by nature, not on the mere say-so of an arbitrary ruler. Men know what natural rights they have by consulting their reason; this tells them that they are the workmanship of one almighty maker, sent into the world about his business, made to last during his, not one another's pleasure. It follows from this that nobody is the natural property or subject of anyone else, and that everyone has the duty not to harm another in his life, liberty or goods. The role of government is to enforce these duties, or, to put it the other way round, to secure our natural rights.

[3] *Two Treatises*, II, §1, p. 285.
[4] ibid., II, §123, p. 368.

Since these natural rights and natural duties bind all our subsequent conduct, it follows that we can only set up governments to secure our rights if they do so in a way which does not violate them. That is, the only sort of government which rational men could ever intend to set up is constitutional government. Constitutional government rests on the consent of rational men; arbitrary government has no claim on them at all.[5] Locke sets out a number of recipes for ensuring that governments behave in a constitutional fashion, suggesting, for instance, that it will be a good idea to divide power between legislative and executive bodies; mostly, however, he is concerned to argue that if the head of the executive refuses to summon the legislature to meet, he has declared war on his subjects and they may rightly resist him. This is the defence of the natural right to revolution for which Locke was famous throughout Europe; and what Locke claimed was that revolution was not an interruption of normal politics so much as lawful self-defence. The real rebel in civil society is the man who tries to take absolute power.[6]

The argument thus far has one curious quality: Locke has not used the concept of property except negatively. That is, he has argued that we are *not* our rulers' property; civil subjection is not slavery; and he has argued that we do not hold property only at the pleasure of our rulers. What I have not yet shown Locke doing is explaining what property *is*, nor what justifies the existence of property as commonly understood. Locke tackles these problems in chapter V of his *Second Treatise*, and it is here that he provides his account of how we might naturally come by property by mixing our labour with the raw materials which God has given to mankind in common.[7]

Now, although Locke was very much more concerned to defend limited government against absolutism than to do anything else, giving a coherent account of property rights was something he had to do in order to defeat Filmer's strongest argument. Filmer had challenged his opponents who believed that men were born free, and that the earth naturally belonged to mankind in common, to show how anyone could ever have owned anything. It would seem that nobody could get an exclusive title to *anything* – to the apple I am about to pick, or the mouthful of water I am about to scoop

[5] ibid., II, §90, p. 344.
[6] ibid., II, §§226–32, pp. 433–9.
[7] ibid., II, §27, pp. 305–6.

from the stream – unless he could obtain the consent of the rest of mankind. But how could we get such a consent? Long before we had secured the unanimous agreement of the world's inhabitants to our taking a mouthful of water, we should have perished of thirst.

Filmer's own solution is agreeably simple. God gave the earth to Adam, and people had the property rights Adam had subsequently created. Locke had to show how property rights could originate differently.[8] What Locke argues is that individuals acquire a title to what they need by mixing their labour with the things they acquire. Locke is unexplicit about quite what rights people thereby get; nor does he say anything about their duration or their bequeathability. Nor, for that matter, does he discuss what exactly is to count as labour, save that he seems to take it for granted that I can acquire property through the doings of my servant or my horse. The turf my servant has cut and the grass my horse has bit are 'mine'.[9]

Having claimed that what men take from the common stock becomes theirs upon the taking, Locke sets some limits to what they may do with it, and how much of it they may take. They must leave as much and as good for others, and they must not let anything perish uselessly in their possession. More elaborate processes of acquisition than merely taking an apple to eat or a mouthful of water to drink still follow the same rules. If we cultivate land, and so make it more fruitful than before, the land becomes ours along with its fruits. And if people hit on the invention of money, the process can become much more elaborate: money allows people to pile up property that does not spoil, to employ others, and to acquire so much land that there is, without anyone having his rights violated, no vacant land for the taking.[10]

The reason why inequality and the occupation of all the vacant land do not violate anyone else's rights is that what the appropriator has to do is leave enough and as good for others, not in the sense of leaving as much land for others, but in the sense of leaving others just as able as they were before to get what Locke terms a 'living'. The day-labourer who has no land none the less gets a good bargain from the process whereby money and inequality have advanced together, for he lives, lodges and is clad better than the king of an Indian tribe in the empty wastes of inland

[8]  ibid., II, §§25–6, p. 304.
[9]  ibid., II, §28, p. 307.
[10]  ibid., II, §§48–51, pp. 318–20.

America.[11] This is not to say that progress is unequivocally a good; progress brings with it the *amor sceleratus habendi*, mere greed and cupidity. All the same, God's injunction to 'be fruitful and multiply' is better met than before.

This far, the argument runs smoothly enough; of course, as we have seen, there are lurking difficulties – we do not know whether Locke thinks that the property we get in the apple we pick is merely a right to use it, or a bequeathable freehold, and we do not know quite why Locke supposes that what you get when you pick the apple is the ownership of the apple rather than the tree. None the less, it is not far from Locke's intentions to summarize his case as holding that in the absence of explicit legal convention, men have those rights over external things which they need to have if they are to use them as God commands. Indeed, the same principle holds for our rights over ourselves; we have those rights which we need to exercise to live as God commands, and no others. These we have by nobody's consent, but by God's commandment.

But commentators have notoriously found themselves at odds with one another about this seemingly simple argument. There are two related issues to which we must attend fairly briefly, before chasing Locke further into his account of ownership. These issues are whether Locke is the prophet of a new individualism, at odds with the moral tradition of medieval and early modern Europe; and why Locke should couch his discussion of our rights in terms of *property*. To the modern eye there is something distinctly odd about first of all describing our lives, liberties and estates as 'property', and then insisting that whereas estates may be traded, given away, or perhaps even abandoned, lives and liberties may not.[12] One might think that if one's life is one's property, suicide is no more problematic than throwing out an old pair of shoes. Locke, however, is quite clear that suicide is forbidden.

It has been argued that Locke's discussion of property, as of much else, is modern and revolutionary. In founding property rights on the labour of the first occupier, he seems to emphasize the rights of the individual, to the exclusion of those of society or the rest of mankind.[13] The Christian tradition, recognizing property as

[11]  ibid., II, §41, p. 315.
[12]  ibid., II, §6, pp. 288–9.
[13]  C. B. Macpherson, *The Political Theory of Possessive Individualism* (Clarendon Press, Oxford, 1962), pp. 194–222.

only conditionally legitimate in the manner of other social and political institutions – all of them being the more or less regrettable outcome of man's fallen state – had emphasized the owner's duties to the rest of the world rather than his rights. It was a tradition of obligations, not of rights. Where Christianity had been influenced by the new learning – that is by Aristotle – it had found further inspiration for limitations on the rights of owners. Usury, for instance, was 'unnatural' because money's purpose was to breed useful goods, not more money.[14] The price of goods should reflect their just price rather than the power of buyer and seller in the market-place, and the search for profit was frequently condemned as mean-spirited and anti-social. If it is not easy to find Locke actively *denying* all this, there is something to be said for the negative case; we do not find Locke rehearsing medieval doubts about usury, and when he defends Aristotle's distinction between political power and other sorts of power, it is with none of Aristotle's emphasis on the way trade and everyday work disqualify a man from politics.

The point of effecting this breach with the past, so it has been said, was to free the use of property from the restraints which classical and Christian theory had placed upon it, but also to make the world safe for the capitalist ascendancy – this last aim being what accounts for Locke's talking of rights in terms of property. Classical beliefs were at odds with the modern concern with productivity; it had been generally held that a man ought to have as much as would give him a reasonable living and leave him leisure to do his duty as citizen and soldier, but no more. Property should certainly be used productively; herds ought to increase and orchards yield fruit, but there was no merit in prodigies of production, and nothing to be said for acquiring more resources simply for the sake of having them.[15] This was, in part, Aristotle's political shrewdness; he saw that one of the sources of class conflict and political turmoil – all too common in classical Greece – was the great gap which opened up between the aggressively rich and resentfully poor. Naturally, he was inclined to think that *stasis* could be kept at bay only if the middle rank in society owned the bulk of society's goods. In addition, of course, the same teleogical outlook which lay behind his objection to usury lay behind his objection to endless accumulation: property detached from a

[14] Aristotle, *Politics*, ed. Ernest Barker (Clarendon Press, Oxford, 1948), p. 35 (1258b).
[15] ibid., pp. 29–30 (1257b).

concern for its proper use was 'unnatural'.[16] If, as I have said, it is not easy to find Locke positively attacking this picture, it is at least not the main purpose of the *Treatises* to defend it.

C. B. Macpherson has gone further than this in arguing that the covert point of the *Treatises* is to justify the absolute authority of the capitalist class over the proletariat. Locke lived in the aftermath of the Civil War when some very egalitarian doctrines had been in the air, when the rights of landed proprietors had been disputed – often on those Old Testament grounds which it is part of the aim of Locke's *First Treatise* to eliminate from politics – and when the rights of the landless and propertiless generally were defended by the radicals. Yet, the *Second Treatise* says firmly that men who have no property may be governed despotically; they have no rights and are to be governed arbitrarily and absolutely. Is this not to argue that all political power ought to lie in the hands of those who possess property and employ it rationally according to Locke's new canons of productive rationality?[17]

It goes without saying that Locke was not writing a treatise in defence of the political rights of the average labourer; we might all be born into a state of natural equality, but there is no reason to think that Locke expected any but the better off to take an active role in political life. All the same, it is surely far fetched to suppose that Locke was in any way concerned to take away what rights the poor and landless had. For one thing, the suggestion misconceives the direction from which Locke anticipated trouble; it was not the rebellious proletariat who threatened England, but the Catholic friends of Charles II and his brother the Duke of York. The poor had not been in any condition to threaten the peace since the Civil War, and there is no sign that Locke ever thought they might do so. Indeed, the astonishing thing about Locke is how much he takes it for granted that the poor will not be a source of unrest and disorder. His successors were much more chary of placing the throne at the mercy of the consents of the people than he was, and there is much to be said for the view that Locke was best known throughout the eighteenth century as the somewhat suspect defender of popular liberty, and not as a friend to the propertied interest.[18]

At the opposite extreme, it is sometimes suggested either that

---

[16] ibid., p. 34 (1258a).
[17] Macpherson, *Possessive Individualism*, pp. 223ff.
[18] H. T. Dickinson, *Liberty and Property* (Weidenfeld & Nicolson, London, 1977), pp. 1–10.

Locke's account of politics and property alike is firmly in the Christian mainstream, or even that his views are old-fashioned even by the standards of 1680, and *a fortiori* completely archaic by our standards. That many of Locke's assumptions had a long pedigree is plain enough. It is true that he talks at times as if mankind once lived in a Golden Age when there weas neither politics nor commerce, when men lived simply and healthily, and were sociable and co-operative rather than greedy and at odds with each other.[19] This would make him more of a Stoic or an ordinary devout Christian with a classical education than any sort of modernist; and as for the main thrust of his politics, what is not a defence of the Aristotelian distinction between political power on the one hand and the power of despots, slave-owners, heads of households and so on on the other, is only a reaffirmation of the old distinction between authority over persons and power over things.

To argue that Locke was positively old-fashioned in 1680, one has to make much of his willingness to engage in elaborate biblical warfare with Sir Robert Filmer; it is, of course, true that nobody afterwards engaged in that sort of literal-minded debate about the Bible's implications for English politics – at least nobody of the first rank. Yet, it seems hard on Locke to complain that he was showing himself to be an antique figure when he attacked Filmer, as he often remarked, if the defenders of absolutism had brought forth a more enlightened champion, he would have fought him on whatever ground he had chosen. Rather than try to award points for modernity, however, I want to offer the following picture of what Locke was doing, which captures, I think, what is distinctive in his work, and does something to answer the puzzle as to why he talked of *all* our rights as 'property' – for, after all, when he discusses despotism, Locke's position is not that the man who has lost his property has *therefore* lost all his rights and may be treated despotically, but the odder, if more attractive one, that a man is only completely without property when he has lost all his rights.

Locke did not create his own views about work, property and politics absolutely *ex nihilo;* nobody does. The terms of the debate were quite largely thrust upon him by Filmer. Locke's alarm was probably most keenly aroused by what a Catholic monarch on the English throne might mean for Protestantism and toleration

---

[19] *Two Treatises*, II, §110, pp. 360–1.

throughout Europe – an alliance between Britain and France would have threatened the Low Countries with annihilation. But if he was to fight off the threat posed by Filmer, he had to do it in Filmer's terms. Elsewhere, Locke defended toleration as a good in itself, and on its own terms; here he had to defend limited government in principle – and toleration would be one of the gainers from that defence. Since Filmer had offered to deduce the absolute authority of Charles I from Adam's property in his children – or more accurately from the property of the sons of Noah in *theirs* – he could be met at a variety of points.

If the enterprise was legitimate at all, Filmer's execution could be challenged as inept. The biblical evidence could be undermined and with it the plausibility of the descent to Charles I and II. But the whole enterprise could be made to look silly. The common law assumption that Englishmen had rights – which they not infrequently called their 'propriety'[20] – which were not within the sovereign's gift could be employed against any idea that law is just the sovereign's say-so, while Roman Law and Natural Law conceptions of the modes of 'natural' acquisition could be used to show that property could have originated in something other than the donation of patriarchs armed with absolute and arbitrary power. In the process a blow would be struck for the positive theory that all rights are bounded by the purposes for which those rights are granted in the first place.

But Locke's undertaking had a long-term vitality which is to some extent independent of Locke's own intentions in writing the *Treatises,* and even of the intellectual apparatus which he employed in so doing. Locke's moral theory is a rationalist and theistic theory, which to later ages looks extremely odd and unstable; none the less, it contained utilitarian elements which could easily survive the collapse of some of its theistic elements, and its confidence in the self-evidence of various truths was inherited by people who had less reason than Locke to trust in their self-evidence. Moral law was, in the catch phrase, 'over-determined'. The same rules could turn out to be obvious utilitarian rules of thumb, self-evidently valid, the laws of nature conceived in Aristotelian teleological terms, as well as the commands of God who had built the world for our benefit and with certain moral purposes in mind.

[20] Paschal Larkin, *Property in the Eighteenth Century* (Cork University Press, Cork, 1930), pp. 33–53.

Locke's views about the status of moral principles were on all fours with his views about the laws of physical nature. Just as he thought that the laws governing physical events were synthetic *a priori* principles which constituted God's blueprint for the physical world, so he thought that the moral law was the law of a law-*giver*, and was similarly *a priori* and necessarily valid. And, as in the case of physical law we might get some insight into the blueprint by inductively generalizing from our particular experience, so in the moral order we could discover our obligations by enquiring into the conditions of peace and human happiness.[21]

Locke wavered in his conviction that the laws of morality were plain and simple and obvious to all mankind who would but consult their reason. At one extreme he claimed that when they were not carried away by partiality and blinded by greed, men would acknowledge the same rules of conduct at all times and places; indeed, men *do* show a good deal of constancy – all men acknowledge that a man's property is to be left alone save with his permission, though they may differ a good deal in what they count as the incidents of ownership. At the opposite extreme, he held that there is almost nothing which has been held to be a vice in one place which has not been held to be the height of virtue somewhere else. The difficulty which all this poses for the scholar is obvious there seems no way of squaring Locke's confidence in the accessibility of natural law as expressed in the *Treatises* with his doubts about it as expressed in his earlier and unpublished lectures on the law of nature.

Still, this did not amount to *moral* uncertainty; Locke was confident enough that he knew what the content of the law of nature was, especially since he, as a Christian, could rely on the gospels. His epistemological doubts were not moral doubts, save in so far as they aroused anxiety about the purposes of a God who might conceivably have laid down rules for our conduct which some peoples were systematically unable to discover – the justice of which would be exceedingly problematic. But, if this is true, what of the suggestion that Locke's originality in the *Treatises* lies in his breaking with the Christian tradition of social thought? The answer is that Locke plainly does not break with the *Christian* tradition; but is not for all that a traditional thinker. That is, Locke's indivi-

---

[21] *Two Treatises*, II, §6, p. 289.

dualism is the individualism of Puritan Christianity, neither unchristian nor traditional.[22]

Nevertheless, the place of religion in the *Treatises* and its bearing on Locke's account of property and its origins remains obscure in one respect. If God features so largely in Locke's theory of natural law, why does Locke rely so heavily on appeals to reason rather than the Bible? And if religious toleration and similar matters are Locke's primary anxiety, why do they not feature more obviously in the *Treatises?* The answer seems to be this. Locke has two tasks to fulfil in the *Treatises;* as originally visualized – as a weapon in the Exclusion Crisis – the *Treatises* would have appeared in the reverse order from that in which they finally came out. The first treatise was, as Locke says, only a small part of a much longer work which chased Sir Robert Filmer into every last recess of his theory; and Locke was no doubt as relieved as the rest of us that by the time it was safe to publish the *Treatises,* there was no market for the missing portion.

What is now the *Second Treatise* would have been an introduction to the whole work; and this is a proper role for it, since it sets out the positive grounds for supposing that governments are limited and that their proper task is the protection of our properties, that is, our lives, liberties and estates.[23] Now, this task is performed with an eye to the demolition of Filmer, for it is also argued by Locke that governments are limited because they originated in the consent of men who cannot be supposed to have given themselves into slavery, no matter what inconveniences in the state of nature they thereby hoped to escape. But it also implies that whatever governments are for, it is not to attend to goods other than our worldly welfare – the *bona civilia* of which the *Letter on Toleration* speaks. The defence of toleration and the defence of limited government hang together and the notion that governments exist for the defence of property is a plausible gloss on the notion that they exist to defend 'civil goods' alone. Against Filmer, the point has to be made in terms of subjects having rights which do not depend on the sovereign's say-so; against Stillingfleet, the point has to be made in terms of government's incompetence to achieve our

---

[22] John Dunn, *The Political Thought of John Locke* (Cambridge University Press, Cambridge, 1970), pp. 245ff.
[23] See the editor's introduction, *Two Treatises,* pp. 59–66.

spiritual good, *and* in terms of God's unwillingness to receive a forced submission.[24]

That Locke trades so heavily on the notion of reasonableness in the *Second Treatise,* and only trades biblical reference continuously in the *First Treatise,* is no bar to the above interpretation. For Locke insists that reason tells us what natural law requires only by way of telling us that there is a God who has laid down natural law to govern us. The law we are to discern by reason is the law of a law-giver whose existence and major attributes it is unreasonable to deny. Just as Locke drew the line at tolerating atheists, who had not the same incentive as believers to keep promises and obey the law, so there is no suggestion in the *Second Treatise* that a dyed-in-the-wool atheist is a fit member of civil society or could conduct his life according to the law of nature. Then, naturally, it is Locke's business to show that the Bible confirms what reason tells us – that God, who would grant nobody any more authority than was required for the purpose in hand, had granted Adam and the sons of Noah only limited power over their offspring.

None of this answers two well known awkwardnesses in Locke. The first is the way in which the discussion of property – in the usual sense of external possessions, not the extended sense of lives, liberties and goods – breaks into the *Second Treatise,* the second is the way in which Locke's account of the 'true original' of government (and money and social inequality) mixes genetic and logical considerations. There *is* something odd about the way Locke's account of property in chapter V of the *Second Treatise* is offered. It addresses economic issues which do not again occur in the book – such as the origins of money and the sources of social inequality. It offers hostages to fortune which the limited aim of subverting Filmer does not require Locke to give – for instance, Locke's account of a title to property by labour suggests that labourers have a better title than their masters, and opens the way for a labour theory of value into the bargain.[25] And Locke's comments on the unnaturalness of money and the dangers of greed are at odds with the attempt to justify the change from a non-monetarized economy to one in which money and inequality both abound. Moreover,

---

[24] John Locke, *The Second Treatise on Civil Government and A Letter Concerning Toleration,* ed. J. W. Gough (Blackwell, Oxford, 1946), pp. 123–37.

[25] James Tully, *A Discourse on Property* (Cambridge University Press, Cambridge, 1980), pp. x, 116f.

none of these issues has much bearing on the later defence of the right to revolt, which is the most vital part of the argument. The most plausible explanation I can offer is that Locke knew that the most important argument in Filmer's armoury was the claim that unless someone had been the initial owner of everything, nobody could have come by individual titles; having started on showing how such titles arose independently of either universal consent or donation by a patriarch, Locke was to some extent at the mercy of his own arguments. Since his main aim was to show that we have rights – both personal and proprietary – independently of the say-so of our sovereign, he could afford to be casual about those elements of his case which might give the poor and landless considerable claims against the better off.[26]

Even so, when Locke discusses money he appeals to its origin in consent and thus seems to invoke a consent of just the sort Filmer had said we could not give. And he certainly does so when he discusses the origins of government. How much *did* Locke think that he needed to give a historical account of how governments began? All critics of Locke, and Hume perhaps most famously and decisively, have argued that Locke was looking for genuine contracts where there were none to be had; in any event, they have said, following Filmer in this, even if there had been such contracts, they would tell us nothing, since the only people bound by contracts are those who sign them, and we their successors cannot be bound by their signings.

I think there is something to be said for the view that Locke was not seeking the historical origins of either governments or money when he writes of consent and compact, but that he was quite right to seize on any occasion when governments – or other institutions – were set up by compact of all their members. The reason is this. Locke wanted to prevent the defenders of absolutism from using history against him – from arguing from *is* to *ought* in the brutal fashion of Filmer. They, in essence, met every assertion of 'Man is born free' with 'No, he isn't.' They met every insistence that government is founded on consent, with the retort – 'No, we are born into submission.' Locke had to be able to say that governments were founded on consent, even when in the ordinary sense of the term, there had been very little consenting.

Locke could usefully deny the patriarchalists' history; that is, it

---

[26] See, e.g., *Two Treatises*, I, §§42–3, pp. 188–9.

was useful to be able to find examples where states had *not* just grown out of extended families, and where rulers had become such by being recognized by compact, not by merely extending their patriarchal jurisdiction. So, even if he somewhat stretched the notion of consent in doing so, Locke was quite right to look for all those occasions where governments had been set up upon terms. None the less, Locke saw that in sacred history there was an overlap between being the head of a clan and being a political leader, so he could not afford to agree that *if* governments had grown out of family organization, this told us anything about the sort of authority they could properly wield.

The aim in all this was primarily to sabotage the idea that patriarchal authority had been absolute and that rulers still possessed it. Natural authority, of which the authority of parents is one kind, is like all authority in having its proper limits. The purpose for which the family exists is the care and education of the child; it is, therefore, in Locke's eyes simply wicked to suppose that a power like the Roman *patria potestas,* which was an absolute power existing for the benefit of the father rather than the child, is justifiable by an appeal to God. Adam never had the *patria potestas.*[27] To appeal to consent, then, is to say that authority in political matters exists only to the extent that it commends itself to the rational reflection of the sane adult. Of course, we are all of us born *in the power* of some government or other; whether we are born under its authority is a different matter. This is why the Lockean contract is quite properly a moral fiction; it is a way of explaining what a man has to do in order to put himself under a moral obligation to obey his rulers. Kant, as we shall see, regarded the social contract as an Idea of Reason and as regulative rather then constitutive of civil society – that is, in effect, as a principle which did not explain how just authority *was* created, but as a principle to which any authority which was just had to conform. Unless rational men were continuously willing to re-contract in, then the political authority of that state was ill-founded. Read in this way, Locke's concern with the 'original' of property and government is a concern with the question of what rights a person possesses by being merely human, by being a member of a society, and by being a member of civil society. It is a concern with the question of how we can transfer, or lay down, or merely forfeit our rights, and with

[27] ibid., II, §58 p. 324.

the question of which of them we must transfer or lay down to become members of a political society.

It is time to spell out Locke's argument in detail. The opening of the *Second Treatise* insists that men are born naturally into society. Not everything in social life requires a contractual basis. Our moral duties can be expanded by contractual arrangements; they are not limited to those. Locke insists that we are natural moral equals. Crucially, Locke argues that all must respect the lives, liberties and external possessions of every other person, and that no one has any natural authority to make laws and establish courts of justice. There is one sort of natural authority which we all possess, and this is the power and duty to punish transgressions of the law of nature, God and reason.[28]

We are not merely not the property of other men, we are not our own property, but the property of God. We are His whose workmanship we are, sent into the world on His business, made to endure as long as He should choose.[29] Among other things this makes suicide a sin, as an assault on the property of God. It also raises an interesting question, namely how important it is to Locke that we are God's *workmanship*. It was suggested in the introduction that an interesting feature of the history of thinking about property is the different analysis of work and creativity in the instrumental as opposed to the self-developmental tradition. On the view put forward there, Locke belongs to the instrumental tradition, in that the justification of private property in the *Second Treatise* depends upon the need to reward men for 'taking pains', that is for undertaking the intrinsically disagreeable effort required to make things serve human purposes. Work is certainly important, and working is morally desirable, both as a matter of individual survival and as a matter of social improvement – unless we work we shall starve, and unless we work well, we shall create none of the surplus on which social progress depends. But, there is no suggestion that working is a form of self-expression, no hint that the relation between the creative will and the created thing has any intrinsic significance. Locke argues that the cropping of the grass by 'my horse' establishes 'my property' in that grass, but there is nothing creative about my horse's cropping either. So far as work is done at all here, it is the minimal labour of acquisition and use in a

---

[28]  ibid., II, §§7–9, pp. 289–91.
[29]  ibid., II, §6, p. 289.

not evidently bad cause. In the case of the moral results of our creation by God, there is more than a hint of the view that it is creation that counts, though it is significant that it is only God's work which possesses that sort of moral significance – God alone owns his creatures through and through because God alone really creates anything rather than assembles it. If human work has a non-utilitarian purpose, it lies in its being a form of discipline, and an act of gratitude towards God.[30]

Early on in the *Second Treatise* Locke defines property as that 'whereof we may not be deprived without our consent'.[31] It is worth noting the negative form of this definition. In ordinary parlance, we think of property as something a man can alienate at will, what he has the widest powers of sale and use over. The oddity of Locke's usage – and its appropriateness for his purpose – is clear the moment we link it to his account of property as lives, liberties and estates. For Locke by no means suggests that we can part with our lives and liberties by consent; we can forfeit them but we cannot alienate them or transfer them. We can square the insistence that our lives are our property and the insistence that we are God's property legalistically, by saying that we have no freehold in our life and liberty, only a life tenancy which is inviolable against other men, but not against God, and which we cannot realize in any way that fails to preserve the freeholder's interests.

The aspect of Locke's theory that concerns us is his attempt to account for property rights in the usual sense. This he does by the well-known claim that we own what we 'mix our labour' with. In order to do this, he needs some preliminary machinery, and this concerns us first. The world, Locke declares, was given to mankind in common. This giving did not make all mankind joint owners in the sense that the consent of all is required to legitimate individual appropriation of any part of it. Locke's theory is not one of joint ownership in the usual sense. He recognized that once there was property, and rules about identifying owners and their rights, there need be no difficulty about allowing a *group* of men to be an owner – English law was quite familiar with institutional ownership. But he was anxious to distinguish *that* conventional state of affairs from the natural state in which no one had any exclusive rights – what we

---

[30] ibid., I, §53, p. 197; II, §§31–4, pp. 308–9.
[31] ibid., §193, p. 413.

might call the no-ownership condition.[32] The state of nature has to
be conceived as a state of no-ownership, if Locke is not to need the
impossible consent of all men for each act of appropriation. But
some overtones of the notion of common ownership are useful: to
say the world is nobody's is less suggestive of mankind's legitimate
common interest in its proper use. Locke is insistent that God gave
the world to all mankind, and that the point is that all mankind
may flourish as much as may be. To say merely that no one owns
any of it would fail to say that the non-acquirers have a right to
benefit from the acquirer's use.

The utilitarian aspect of Locke can be brought out by con-
sidering how much is lost if we drop God's donation from the
argument. To call Locke a utilitarian is to claim that what we need
of his account is the Bentham-like observation that if there were no
rules about ownership, men would be free to do what they like with
whatever parts of the external world they could control; that the
general welfare demands rules which limit this freedom, for the
sake of survival in the first place, peace in the second, and
prosperity ultimately. If it is not visible to all that *God intends* that we
should all flourish, the fact is that the world will enable us to do so,
if it is used appropriately, and that it can only be used
appropriately if we have some system of property rights. We do,
obviously, lose something in expelling God from the story. We lose
the argument from gratitude, which holds that hard work is a
minimal expression of gratitude for God's gifts to us. We lose –
though Locke never uses it in the *Treatises* – the suggestion that
divine rewards and punishments back up natural law.

But Locke raises few of those questions which a consistent
utilitarian would raise. He raises so few of them that we may doubt
whether the commentator ought to press Locke for an answer to a
question he did not seriously raise – what it would be like to solve
our moral difficulties in the absence of a religious faith. Locke does
not say much about questions of efficiency; he does not go into
detail about the efficacy of different systems of incentive; he does
not think it part of the province of governments to keep on revising
the positive law concerning property in the interests of economic
growth.[33] His concerns are defensive ones: he wants to prevent one
man from robbing another and, in particular, to prevent sovereigns

[32]  ibid., II, §35, p. 310.
[33]  Tully, *Discourse on Property*, pp. 167–70.

from robbing their subjects, and worse. His attitude to social change is ambivalent, and he has a tendency to hanker after simplicity and the Golden Age, as well as to praise the ingenuity which led to the creation of money and exchange. The *amor sceleratus habendi*, the desire of having more than we need, is for Locke the root of all evil, and the source of the conflicts which governments exist to repress. The suggestion that something like a market economy could exist in the state of nature, which is one of Locke's more striking rhetorical devices, and one which serves an important purpose in the argument against absolute monarchy, does not entail that Locke thought economic growth was unequivocally a desirable thing.[34]

Now, placing men in a condition where no one owns anything, Locke has to get them into a condition where they own external goods as well as their lives and liberties, and where they cannot, save in very unusual conditions, own other men. This move is achieved by the best known of all of Locke's arguments, the claim that in appropriating what we need from the natural world, we mix our labour with it and, in mixing what is *ours* with what is nobody's-in-particular, make it ours as well. The work of a man's body is truly his, and whatsoever he mixes that work with, becomes his. Locke does not rely on the naked statement of this principle. He appeals to the fact that the consumable goods of the world have to be taken into oneself in the most literal sense – they must, before they can do a man any good, be so much his, i.e. a part of him.[35] Again, God's purposes loom in the background: we cannot suppose that God gave mankind the world, but allowed them no legitimate means of using it; it cannot be part of the divine plan that we should starve in the midst of plenty, or survive at the cost of committing a – no doubt pardonable – act of larceny. This assumption again lurks in Locke's throwaway remarks about the lesser animals being created for our use as we are *not* created for anyone else's. Now, the question is: *what* does Locke's argument license? We may begin by noticing that his claim that we have a property in the work of our own bodies is, on the face of it, in tension with the claim that we are God's property. The natural thrust of Locke's initial claim is therefore towards a doctrine of stewardship, not one of absolute individual rights – men possess

[34] *Two Treatises*, II, §111, p. 360.
[35] ibid., II, §26, p. 305.

such rights over things as enable them to fulfil God's intention in creating those things. The ultimate source of property rights is God. Locke *does* have a stewardship doctrine in mind much of the time. But we are doubly stewards: we are *pro tem* custodians and managers of God's property – we have, if you like, leasehold interests for life, or, better, we are put in as managers, but with curious relations with the boss; and in a more nearly Bentham-like way we act as trustees for society as a whole.[36]

Let us move on from the claim that we have a property in our labour. Two obvious questions come to mind: how do we mix our labour, and with what do we mix it? The point is this: suppose I pick the fruit from a tree, and on Locke's account thereby own the fruit; what's to stop me claiming to own the tree too? That is, why haven't I mixed my labour with the tree as well as with the fruit? One might say my intention was only to acquire the fruit – I may say that Locke says no such thing, but the issue becomes important once we reach Kant and Hegel – but that leaves one vulnerable to the man who gets his fruit by shaking the whole tree and saying truthfully that he intends the tree as well as the fruit to be his.[37] And, when we begin to ask this sort of question, we surely find ourselves wondering why mixing our labour makes the thing mine rather than, so to speak, merely losing me my labour. Nozick asks why mixing your labour is not like trying to possess the ocean by contaminating it with a tin of *your* tomato soup which you pour in and mix with it.[38] And everyone has worried about the case of the servant who cuts 'my' turf, where Locke seems to take it for granted that his labour is also my labour and his acquisition the establishing of my property rights, not his. From the point of view of the servant, his labour surely is lost in the possessions of another.

Let us try to unpick the argument. There are, I suggest, three strands here. According to one version of Locke's argument, all we need is some account of when things have left the common stock, and become unavailable for general use. In a society of hunters and gatherers, Locke's reply is intelligible, adequate and in fair accordance with observed practice. No one claims prior property rights over such things as game or berries, and whoever gets them

---

[36] ibid., II, §6, p. 289.
[37] For an entertaining, though ultimately misguided, discussion of such difficulties, see Robert Nozick, *Anarchy, State and Utopia* (Blackwell, Oxford, 1974), pp. 174–82.
[38] ibid., pp. 174–5.

gets the right to them. Societies where some co-operation is needed, have to have, and invariably do have, more elaborate rules, and there is much discussion in both Roman and common law devoted to tricky questions about say, rights to the fish in an unclosed net. Still, rule one, we might say, is that in the most primitive condition, acquiring from nature just is legitimate acquisition, just is getting a property right. Locke runs together first occupation and the first application of labour. It is also worth noticing that there is nothing very special about the labour involved – nothing complicated, intellectually sophisticated, or skilled; no hard work either. All there is, is the work involved in taking and consuming; bending down and taking a drink from the stream is a paradigm case.[39] All we want is a mark to indicate that others are no longer free to acquire it; prior acquisition does the trick. But Locke plainly does want to hint at something more. This provides the second and third aspects of the case. In the second place, then, Locke stresses – though not much in the *Second Treatise* – the fact of men having taken pains about whatever it is. We often find that fishermen tacitly divide the shoal in such a way that those who took the pains to find it get the biggest haul. Locke observes in the essays on the law of nature that men generally recognize some such rule as the establishment of a right in him who has 'taken pains' as the obvious solution to the problem of who owns game. This is a conception of primitive property rights as an equivalent of wages for effort; in the case of the man eating acorns and drinking water, there is little effort, but often there is a lot. Locke's example of Castilian land law, where waste lands belonged to whomever took pains to cultivate them, at least for a given period, tends in the same direction, as does twentieth-century practice of a similar sort.[40] An opal miner maintains a legal claim to the contents of his mine by working the claim continuously; if he fails to start work within six weeks of laying the claim he loses it, and his rights lapse forty days after he ceases work. Here, perhaps, we get some notion of desert; a man deserves to get the fruits of his labour, and he has such property rights by nature as would allow him his deserts.

Within a very short time after Locke's death, holes in the argument were noticed by his critics. For one thing, they noticed the indeterminacy of the duration of the property rights so

[39] *Two Treatises*, II, §26, p. 305.
[40] ibid., II, §36, p. 311.

originated; it is one thing to receive and eat an apple, another to construct and use a cloak. The duration of the exercise of property rights over the apple is so short that all the interesting questions can be dodged – the act of consumption that establishes the right takes the object out of circulation so effectively that no later claims to it are likely to be made. A cloak, however, is a different matter; once made it is likely to last some time.[41] During that time, it may be that someone other than the maker could make better use of it than the maker. Locke's principles ought, on most views, to rule out such a subsequent claim on ground of need, once the first labour-based claim has been made. The necessitous have a claim on the charity of the owner, but not a property right in his possessions. This clear distinction between claims to charity and actual ownership is, however, one of those things which Locke interestingly does not accept. So far as he is concerned, the rich man's superfluities actually *belong* to the starving.[42] So we must not assume too swiftly that Locke would have been embarrassed by the usual distinction between claims of proprietorship and claims of need – he may have intended to subvert the distinction rather than to explain it. The continued existence of the object which one man owns while another has greater need of it, draws attention to the fact that what a man requires in the way of rights is, in the case of cloaks, beds, huts and so on, much more elaborate than what he needs in the case of the objects which Locke first mentions. To say, as I have said, that first acquisition does the trick so far as marking something's exit from the state of no-ownership is all very well, but we need some way of deciding how to tell whether it has stayed out of that state. It would be absurd if, once someone had made something his own and then abandoned it, we could not regard it as having gone back into the common stock. Yet, we should not wish to lose our beds the moment we rose from them or our clothes the moment we took them off. Hence as was said by, among other writers, Blackstone, Rousseau, and Kant, we need some mark of an intention to continue as an owner, for example, continuing rather than continuous use, if we are to talk of property.[43]

This brings us to the third point, the way in which Locke relies on the naturalness of certain boundaries to property rights, the

[41] Blackstone, *Commentaries*, vol. II, pp. 3–4.
[42] *Two Treatises*, I, §42, p. 188.
[43] Hegel, *Philosophy of Right*, §51, p. 45; Blackstone, *Commentaries*, II, pp. 3–4.

argument resting on the utility of those boundaries rather than on their obvious connection with labour. In the case of Locke's first examples of legitimate appropriation, such as acorns gathered in the woods of America, the control required for the use of the things appropriated is all but identical with the control required for their appropriation. In the case of the cloak or the bed, the principle must be analogous; the degree of control needed in order to put these things to their proper use is such that I need some guarantee that no one else will make off with my cloak, or climb into my bed so soon as I cease to be in immediate physical occupation. Creating them gives one the right over them which their use requires. This, however, does not entirely meet the case, for while creation and use would perhaps serve to give me a prior claim over anyone who had no greater need than I, it could hardly do enough to exclude the claims of those with more need. Now, we can quite easily accommodate this point in Locke's simple state of nature, where all appropriation leaves enough and as good for others, but we shall plainly have more difficulty in a civilized condition where it does not.

Before explaining that, I ought to say something about the further step from owning cloaks to owning land. The point made above about the utility of rights of a degree of permanence and continuity becomes crucial if there is to be natural appropriation of land. Locke does not wish to say that a man can appropriate land by, for example, building a fence about it and saying 'It's mine.' Only as much becomes him as he mixes his labour with; and there is no doubt that to mix one's labour with land involves more than picking fruit growing on a tree, rooted in some piece of land. A man must make the right kind of difference to each. Locke's discussion in the *Second Treatise* and elsewhere envisages the case of clearing a piece of waste. It is the work of rendering nature fruitful and abundant that allows one to claim the land so cleared and improved – and Locke has a number of things to say about the man who does this, the chief being that we do not lose land from the common stock when this happens, but gain what the improved land produces.[44] But here, too, Locke is not concerned to show that a man acquires a negotiable freehold interest in the land; what Locke's argument generates is a service tenure. A man may hold the land on condition that it is productively employed, and should

[44] *Two Treatises*, II, §37, p. 312.

lose it if it is not. No doubt public policy would allow him the right to assign his tenancy to someone else, and perhaps would suggest that, *ceteris paribus*, we ought to allow his heirs first refusal of the tenancy; but none of this amounts to giving a man rights of ownership which hold against the claims of public interest, or against the demands of the needy. We must not beg the question of how anxious Locke was to generate such rights in any case. The more limited rights we have outlined would be enough to defeat the claims of royal absolutism; we can generate by natural law alone a system of property rights, if not freehold landed private property in its modern form, and this leaves no room for those rights to be overridden by a monarch's mere say-so.[45]

Locke goes on to produce a somewhat odd but interesting account of what happens to primeval ownership. Locke sets his problem by raising the question of how inequality of possessions can have arisen (legitimately). At this point, we ought to attend to Locke's two initial saving clauses on the limits of appropriation. These are that we may only take so much as leaves others as much and as good for themselves, and that nothing may be allowed to perish uselessly in our possession. These we may call the sufficiency rule and the no-spoliation rule. The first thing to notice, as Locke did notice, is how easily met these requirements are in the state of nature. When we are so few that we scarcely encounter one another, there is rather little damage we can do to the environment. My drinking from the brook is not likely to take so much water that anyone else is going to find it becomes scarce; of course, where nature is sufficiently niggardly, we shall be driven into organized society because of the need to prevent war breaking out, as Locke believed. There is, in this simple condition, no evident reason why a man should attempt to enclose ground, or do any of the things which we would usually associate with the notion of engaging in first appropriation; he could gather what he needed from the environment, and would have no incentive to do more.[46]

As for spoliation, we can see here a nice example of the role of God or a teleological conception of nature. Locke mentions that it would be foolish as well as wicked to let anything perish uselessly, and one can easily see why.[47] A man who gathers apples and lets

[45] ibid., II, §35, p. 310.
[46] ibid., II, §48, p. 319.
[47] ibid., II, §47, p. 318.

them rot has wasted his efforts, his behaviour is therefore *foolish*. But, why is it wicked? Suppose a man enjoys watching apples decay, or playing bowls with them; his behaviour is not in any obvious way foolish, but is it wicked? The answer seems to hinge on what strain in Locke's conception of natural law we emphasize. If we press the utilitarian case, the misuse of apples is a misuse in so far as it yields less happiness than any other use, so if the gatherer does not impair anyone else's chances, and so long as he does enjoy the use he makes, then his behaviour is not wicked. But, as all critics have agreed, the one thing utilitarian theories need, but cannot supply of themselves, is an account of which ways of enjoying we should prefer. This lack is supplied by divine command and natural teleology alike. The former tells us that God grants the world to be used in certain ways only, the latter that things have certain natural and proper uses, such that it would be perverse to use them otherwise. On either view, misuse has a wider range than inefficient use; we can display ingratitude to God, or a corrupt understanding, and thus be wicked as well as foolish.[48]

In moving from this egalitarian condition in which simple needs prompt us to act only within the bounds of the law of nature, Locke introduces us to money. It is the invention of money which allows inequalities to arise, and to be perpetuated; it is money which allows a society to arise, and to be perpetuated; it is money which allows a society to use up all vacant land, and to have none left vacant to be appropriated by the first legitimate user.[49] Locke's account of ownership will explain property rights in what we immediately gather and consume and how I come to own the garments I sew together out of skins or whatever. It explains how we give the largest slice of meat from the carcass to the man who actually killed the deer in a collective and co-operative chase. In all such cases we rely on the idea that people are rewarded for effort, and are rewarded out of the difference made to nature's bounty by their efforts. This clearly is why merely fencing a piece of ground will not suffice to create ownership of it; Locke's notion of mixing our labour is linked with our ability to bring land into cultivation,

---

[48] It is this that Nozick, *Anarchy, State and Utopia*, pp. 175–6, cannot say in his secular natural rights theory; but Locke, too, clouds the issue by talking of us invading our neighbour's share by allowing things to spoil (II, §37, p. 313), which we can hardly be doing if there really is plenty of whatever it is still available.
[49] *Two Treatises*, II, §45, p. 317.

and thereby make it very much more fertile than it was in the wild.

The question is how money makes this process easier; the answer is not hard to reconstruct. Suppose, says Locke, that a man likes gold, silver, even cowrie shells. These have only a 'fancy' value, in that they are not physically consumable, they will not by being eaten sustain his life. None the less, he who gathers them makes them *his*.[50] Moreover, these are goods which are subject to fewer restrictions than other, more useful goods. They cannot spoil, and a man who accumulates any amount of them cannot exceed his natural right in so doing. Whether money can be held uselessly is not explained in the *Second Treatise;* the silence which often daunts the interpreter of Locke is audible here too. We get no clue whether Locke would have been taken, and would have wanted to be taken, as implying that money ought to be held only to finance trade, agriculture, employment in manufacturing and was not being used properly if it was merely hoarded. Locke had no wish to praise the love of money; he subscribed in a perfectly orthodox way to St Paul's dictum that the love of money was the root of all evil, as to the Stoic view that the Golden Age was subverted by gold and the lust for gold.[51] Still, the initial argument is simple. A man who acquires gold, silver or the like, can, if he finds another man willing to enter into exchange, exchange his valuable but useless property for its equivalent in naturally useful goods. Locke sees this quasi-money facilitating a process of exchange which *could* be carried out by direct barter, but could not go to the same lengths. It is not difficult to see how this underpins commonsense beliefs about the division of labour. The man with a handy nut tree can gather nuts and exchange them for more perishable foods as he requires them; the man with a handy apple tree will have to exchange his fruit for more durable goods. The acceptability of some common medium of exchange will make the process much simpler; money simplifies the process of adjusting the supply of apples to that of nuts, thence to shoes and the like.

Money has two crucial characteristics – general acceptability and non-perishability. Locke does not devote any effort in the *Second Treatise* to showing what will determine the money price of goods, but the assumption must be that so long as Locke thinks in terms of employing gold as money, the rate of exchange between

[50]  ibid., II, §46, p. 318.
[51]  ibid., II, §111, p. 360.

goods and gold will reflect the effort required to produce the goods in question as compared with the effort required to mine and refine the gold. Locke's references to money having only a 'fancy' value bear more than one meaning. Sometimes it is that the natural foundation of money is fancy in the sense of mere liking – for, after all, we cannot eat gold or shells. At other times, 'fancy' seems to mean 'conventional'; money has value because we are all willing to take it in exchange for really useful goods. In this sense, a paper currency has fancy value, though it is dubious that it could have fancy value in the first sense. A third sense, which does not emerge until later, is apparently equivalent to a denial that gold and silver have any value at all.[52]

Given money, the following process can take place. A man who works a plot of land may sell its produce, and thereby acquire money; he may employ the money to hire labourers, who work upon his land and thus produce for him rather than themselves. If there is empty land, he can employ them on that, and thereby acquire the land by mixing with it labour that has now become 'his'.[53] In so far as the process causes problems for Locke's theory, it does so at the point where our own acquisition would cause problems. That is, if the turf my servant cuts becomes my turf, because I have acquired the right to the product of his labour, the question whether the land he works on becomes my land, is very much the same as, what has to be different for my cutting turf to give me a right to the land itself. The implication certainly seems to be that if I employ him to improve the land, I acquire as good a right to the land as I would by my own efforts. The existence of wage labour and the mechanisms of exchange means that more and more land can be taken into cultivation, hence all the waste used up. Now, a man born into a society where money is known, may find himself either in the position of a landowner or a landless labourer. Some will have much land and some a little, and some none at all. The question Locke faces is whether this is justifiable.[54]

It is not easy to know how enthusiastic Locke is for the economic advance in terms of which he sets out to justify this inegalitarian state of affairs. In spite of commentators who see Locke as the

---

[52] ibid., II, 184, p. 409, where Locke allows the conqueror to take any amount of his enemies' treasure on the grounds that this does them no real injury.

[53] ibid., II, §36, p. 311.

[54] cf. Nozick, *Anarchy, State and Utopia*, pp. 178ff.

defender of capitalist agriculture, and the ideologist of enclosures and the like, Locke's references to the disadvantages of civilization make him anything but an unequivocal defender of economic progress. He has two arguments to show that the new state of affairs is justified, one from consent, and one of a kind familiar from the work of John Rawls. The argument from consent is simply that since money exists only because we agree to employ it, we have agreed to its consequences, too, and inequality is one of them. It is not a plausible argument. It is, no doubt, even more true of a paper currency, such as our own, that its existence depends upon its general acceptance. But, no single one of us has consented to its operation. If I go into a shop and plead my need rather than my ability to pay, I shall not get any further by pointing out that I never agreed to the system by which the currency was established.[55]

It is not obvious why Locke is so insistent on the foundation of money in consent, when he is so insistent that the initial title to property does not require that consent. It is, however, worth noticing that at any rate in genetic terms Locke is quite right to distinguish the two cases. The objection to founding property on consent is that if I had to get everyone else's consent before I could lawfully acquire the means of life, I should starve first. The case is not the same once there is individual property; if I can get someone's consent to use his property, then I do have rights over it. Similarly, once we have property, consent to money can be got individual by individual; if I proffer gold to a man who owns some piece of property, he can accept it or not as he chooses. Hence, money cannot become an institution among property owners unless they all agree to it.[56]

But to the landless labourer this is mere mockery. If he had land enough to subsist on, he could opt out perhaps, but if he is born into the world without access to the land which would keep him alive, he has no choice but to sell his labour to whomever will employ him. This is the point which all Marxists urge against Locke, and one which his pre-Marxian critics were not slow to notice.[57] The more effective argument does not rest upon consent; it simply points out the benefits going to the worst off under a system

---

[55] cf. J. P. Plamenatz's discussion of consent in Locke: *Man and Society* (Longman, London, 1963), vol. I, pp. 228ff.

[56] *Two Treatises*, II, §46, p. 318.

[57] David Hume, 'Of the Original Contract', *Essays* (Clarendon Press, Oxford, 1963), p. 462.

where there is greater inequality than in the state of nature. This is sometimes linked to consent both in the modern version of the argument and in Locke's, by way of the claim that a member of the state of nature society would volunteer to join the more advanced society, even he was sure to be one of the least advantaged members of that society.[58]

At this point, we come to two questions Locke never asked, but perhaps should have done. The first is whether the appeal to the benefits of the least advantaged is as effectively made out as it might be. The second is whether the landless labourer has had his natural right to property rendered nugatory. When Locke defends the inequalities of a more advanced economy by appealing to the pay-offs to the worst off, he does so by arguing that the Devonshire day labourer has a higher standard of living than does the Indian chief in the wastes of middle America. There are two things Locke fails to argue. In the first place, Locke does not suggest that there might be some differences in the tastes of Indian chief and Devonshire day labourer which would affect the comparison of one way of life with the other. He takes it for granted that they can be compared, and the day labourer's ranked more highly. This is just what subsequent writers would deny, either arguing as Rousseau did, that the Indian, whether chief or not, had a happier and better existence than anyone in a more civilized society, or, as more thorough-going relativists did, that the comparison was meaningless, since there were no common standards to judge each existence.[59] Moreover, Locke leaves out of account the social status of the figures he compares. He contrasts the day labourer and the Indian chief; but, anyone who thinks that goods satisfy men for complicated reasons, such as what they show about the social standing of the consumer, will think that this complicates the comparison and makes Locke's own view less plausible. It may be true that the labourer's cottage keeps out the rain better than the Indian's wigwam; but the grandest tepee in the tribe may well give its owner a degree of pleasure that the poorest cottage in the village cannot. All the commonplaces of everyday observation point up the same thing – the elderly motor-scooter is slower and less efficient than the newest saloon, but the Javanese youth ten years ago got

[58] John Rawls, *A Theory of Justice* (Clarendon Press, Oxford, 1971), pp. 11–17, 60ff.
[59] Plamenatz, *Man and Society*, vol. II, pp. 409ff.

more pleasure from the first than his younger brother will get from the latter in ten years' time.

Locke plainly assumes that we can, so to speak, hold human nature constant, beg the question of what purposes goods properly serve, and thus assume that the welfare of each of us is in no essential way affected by what happens to other men. Perhaps it is unfair to suggest that he begs the question of the proper purpose of one sort of goods and another; there is in the *Second Treatise* an uneasy combination of claims – that we live better than we should have done in the absence of money, and that we have come to desire more than we need, have come to want things out of mere possessiveness and greed, and *amor sceleratus habendi*. To argue that the day labourer really is better off than the Indian chief, even, say against the evidence that the labourer regards his cottage with less enthusiasm than the Indian regards his tepee, we have to 'correct' his wants – the rational labourer wants shelter not a status symbol, and if he is better sheltered, he is better off.[60] There is some circumstantial evidence from his *Letters on Education* that Locke would not have flinched from such a 'correction'; at least, parents are advised to take no notice if children clamour for meat, but none the less to see that good healthy food is supplied. In these difficulties, if such they be, Locke is at one with writers like John Rawls who must similarly find some way of ruling out the effects of irrational comparison on the wants they examine when estimating the gains from inequality.[61]

The second thing Locke makes no attempt to argue is that the worst off man does *as well as possible* under a particular system of property rights. Readers of Locke who are familiar with Rawls' work would expect Locke to argue that the day labourer does better under the system being defended than would the worst off member under any other system of property rights. That is, we are not merely trying to defend the inegalitarian system by comparison with the universal and equal poverty of the moneyless society, we are trying to show that some system of inequalities will do more for its least favoured members than any other system available. Locke does not. They get a good bargain, not the best possible. Some commentators on Locke, for instance Professor Macpherson, have

---

[60] But Karl Marx refuses to adjust their wants in this way; the peasant's cottage *is* a hovel when a palace is built next door.

[61] Rawls, *A Theory of Justice*, pp. 530–41.

credited him with some very elaborate arguments to the effect that the worst off in his own society, the landless day labourers of the argument, deserved to be poor, because they were less than fully rational creatures, a fact demonstrated by their failure to acquire property. God, who gave the world to the industrious and rational, not to the quarrelsome and envious, would have approved the distribution of wealth and income obtaining in late seventeenth-century England. If Locke had argued from desert or merit, he would, in essence, have been arguing like Plato and Aristotle rather than Rawls. That is, he would have been employing justice as desert, rather than justice as fairness, and, so far from feeling obliged to show that the least favoured in his England got as much as it was possible for the least favoured to get under any system of property rights, he would have felt obliged to show that what each person got reflected his merits.[62] Locke never tried to show any such thing. It is true enough that Locke's attitude to the labouring poor is not, in general, one which commends itself to twentieth-century defenders of the welfare state; but the least plausible explanation of his motives is that he saw the labouring poor as a threat to the accumulating capitalist, and therefore took pains to show they deserved no better than they got.[63]

No history of ideologies need claim that thinkers were aware of, and committed to, all the social implications of their doctrines. If Locke was more concerned, say, to distinguish earthly, secular political society from the communion of the elect, than to demonstrate anything about the rationality of unlimited capitalist appropriation, he may still have stuck a blow for emergent capitalism. He may have done so, for example, by assisting his readers to separate the limited concerns of human justice from the concerns of divine justice, by encouraging them to distinguish between the strict obligations imposed by justice, and the less strict obligations imposed by charity or benevolence. A man might feel that his employers were stern, uncharitable characters, but not feel that they were acting unjustly, and this would perhaps make the world so much the safer for employers. Still, it seems to me truer that the impact of Locke is two edged, and I shall end this chapter by emphasizing first those strains in Locke's argument which are

[62] Macpherson, *Possessive Individualism*, pp. 222–4.
[63] Dunn, *Political Thought of Locke*, pp. 219ff.

not explicitly defused by Locke, and which tend to discredit obvious features of a non-socialist economy, and second, those elements which would allow Locke to appear as a theorist of nascent capitalism, even though Weber is a better guide than Marx to anyone wanting to explore them.

The two hostages to egalitarianism which Locke leaves in the *Second Treatise* are the suggestion that the point of having private property is to reward effort, and the apparent implication that everyone ought to begin life with an equal chance to acquire property. It may be worth repeating that it is very likely that Locke's own concerns were at odds with this. The *Second Treatise* may well have been meant to do no more than answer the awkward genetic question of how property could have arisen without universal consent to individual acquisition. None the less, what is left by Locke is an argument with awkward implications. If the title to property is labour, naive common sense will be sure to wonder why the natural title of the worker is so much weaker than the legal title of the owner at any given time.[64] Even naive common sense may be willing to agree that what labour entitles one to is the fruits of that labour, rather than to the physical thing on which effort has been expanded – to value added, so to speak. But that is no comfort to the landowner, who does not lose his title to his labourers, perhaps, but certainly loses his title to the land. Nobody created the land, so nobody can get a natural title to more than the improvements that their efforts make to it. The so-called original agents of production may pass into the temporary custody of some men, but they cannot be *owned*. I have already explained why it is not easy to tell how much of such an argument Locke would.have accepted. If it is a mistake to attribute to Locke a conception of absolute ownership (in the misleading sense employed by Macpherson), it is not unlikely that Locke would have agreed that the natural title to things naturally useful was, so to speak, conditional on making good use of them, but that the exigencies of society demanded something more fixed by way of legal titles.

This, indeed, is not implausible. We might agree that the task of rewarding men according to desert, or effort, or even according to value added, is so hopelessly difficult that the best we can do is to invent freehold, enforce contracts, and allow men to have what they contract for. But behind all this there is a difficulty which we have

[64] Menger, *Right to the Whole Product*, pp. 1–8.

seen but not solved. Common sense would distinguish between the right to life and the right to own property, which Locke runs together as our property. A society which secured its members against want would satisfy the first, but need not satisfy the second. Locke's readers, I think, would frequently have failed to see or acknowledge his claim that what we have a right to is 'a living', that is, that we may not be prevented from owning property, but need not be given land so long as we are given a living. Rousseau, as we shall see, takes up Locke's discussion, and in the course of arguing about the justification of property, claims that society ought to ensure that anyone who wishes to work can thereby earn a living.[65] But this requirement could be met by provision of work by the government. No doubt, *some* constraints on the system of property would be necessitated by this – taxes would have to be levied, or there would have to be publicly owned farms, mines, factories or whatever – but it is far from implying that anyone or everyone has a right to have some property in the usual sense. Macpherson, who sees Locke as a capitalist apologist concerned to justify differential access to the means of life, thinks of the provision of equal access to the means of working for a living as the democratized, twentieth-century theory of property.[66] The claim I would want to make is that Locke's concern with property in the lawyer's sense is secondary to his concern with the broader rights that a civil society can help to protect. Once Locke had argued to his own satisfaction that property was not held as a gift from the supposed heirs of Adam, nor with the consent of all mankind, he was unconcerned to argue for any particular sort of property rights, as opposed to any particular attitude to one's possessions. So far as the latter goes, we have seen that he treated the ownership of property as a trust, an opportunity to work as God intended. But there is no suggestion that small-holders are more politically virtuous than large landowners, no claim that only certain sorts of property are really property.[67]

If what natural right entitles us to is a living, and not, say, three acres and a cow, Locke is absolved of the need to either show that everyone in seventeenth-century England had an equal chance of acquiring a piece of land, or else to condemn that society because

---

[65] Jean-Jacques Rousseau, *Social Contract and Discourses* (Dent, London, 1973), p. 138.
[66] C. B. Macpherson (ed.), *Property* (Blackwell, Oxford, 1978), p. 201.
[67] Unless we read a great deal into *Two Treatises*, II, §111, p. 360.

there was not such an equal opportunity. So long as there is work for all who seek it, and a decent standard of living for those in work, there needs to be no recognition of individual ownership of the means of production as a natural right which all men were entitled to have recognized by being given a patch of land or whatever. Locke, even on Professor Macpherson's view, held the mercantilist belief that the government should drive trade, that is, ensure full employment. Locke's harshness towards the unemployed needs no far-fetched explanation in terms of a belief in the irrationality of the labouring poor, only the usual misconception about the ease with which a willing worker could obtain employment at a living wage. Hence, it is very probable that Locke would have remained unconcerned by the fact that one's chances of inheriting or acquiring property were far from equal at birth.

Lastly, then, in what sense could Locke's account of work and property be a capitalist account? There is a number of rather different ways, and in them the role of Locke's religious attachment varies a good deal.[68] First, one might say, Locke's attitude to property as a trust, and his emphasis on re-earning it by diligent work on it, is precisely the sort of Protestant conscientiousness which Weber relied on as a partial explanation of the rise of capitalism.[69] This has nothing whatever to do with defending the rationality of unlimited capitalist appropriation – an ideal framed in those terms would have looked like the justification of greed. Rather, as Weber stressed, the side effects of an other-worldly attitude make the capitalist exploitation of advances in science, access to new materials and so on, that much the easier. Again, those habits of rationally accounting for time spent with which the Protestant conscience was replete could carry over into the world of business. The question of causal priority – whether men became Protestants first and capitalists second or the other way about – is not one to be settled here. All we need claim is that in so far as Locke can be represented as one of the inspirational forces behind developing English capitalism, it must be in this very indirect fashion.

The second impact one might claim for Locke is that in detaching the title to property from allegiance to a sovereign, he

[68] Dunn, *Political Thought of Locke*, pp. 245ff.
[69] Max Weber, 'The Protestant Sects and the Spirit of Capitalism', in H. H. Gerth and C. W. Mills (eds.), *From Max Weber* (Routledge & Kegan Paul, London, 1948), pp. 321–2.

depoliticized property and turned it into an economic rather than a political category. It would be absurd to suggest that Locke made *much* difference here; late eighteenth-century writers were still arguing over the connection between political virtue and the ownership of land, and as late as 1867 Bagehot was plaintively suggesting that, rather than abandon the idea that suffrage represents property rather than persons, reform of the franchise should proceed by admitting secure personal property to the same rights as real property.[70] None the less, an essential element in the growth of a capitalist economy is the willingness of the law to allow men to devise new economic transactions, and to allow them to use their property more or less as they choose. In a Lockean world, property is not primarily a tie to a superior of inferior, it is an asset. Obviously Locke would have made no impact if men had not already begun to see their property in that light, and the evident peculiarities of land ownership perhaps meant that a Lockean view could never triumph in a society of great landowners intent on founding dynasties, and eager to prevent their successors dissipating what they had built up.[71] Locke did not overtly condemn perpetual entails; but the world which accepted Locke was one to which the idea of ancestors trammelling their remote descendants had come to be increasingly alien.

A third way, whose impact is quite uncertain, but which endures to the present, is the frame of mind which sees an elaborate economic life as something 'natural', uncoercive, and sustainable by men of good will even in the absence of government. Locke's state of nature, in which there is property, money, inequality of fortune and ownership, and yet no government, is just the kind of fantasy which Marx deplored.[72] It suggested that a system of commodity exchange was what any group of human beings left alone and not corrupted by government would automatically create. Locke, of course, did not simply *assume* that individual private property was possible in the absence of government, he endeavoured to show *how* it could arise and what its boundaries were. From a Marxian point of view, so much the worse, for the

[70] W. Bagehot, 'Parliamentary Reform', in *Collected Works*, vol. VI (*The Economist*, London, 1974), pp. 187–235, esp. pp. 209–10.

[71] Dickinson, *Liberty and Property*, pp. 13ff.

[72] Karl Marx, *Capital*, vol. I (Penguin, Harmondsworth, 1976), ch. 26, 'Of the So-called Primitive Accumulation'.

effect of Locke's argument was to play down the extent to which economic arrangements were dependent upon a balance of political forces, or the result of political decision. Although Locke does happily grant that different regimes may and will establish different systems of positive law to regulate property, the suggestion that individual ownership and free exchange of commodities is the natural condition is not really defused by this.

Moreover, although Locke certainly allows that we may set up for the regulation of property whatever rules seem most likely to promote the general good, the honorific connotations of an absence of coercion stick to the relations of the state of nature economy. Government is the realm of force, society the realm of consent, exchange of benefits and voluntary agreement. It is the essence of government that someone or some body of persons should be able to coerce the recalcitrant. In the natural state, even with the Lockean fantasy of private punishment, people only do what they agree to, so that, for example, there can be no question of a forced redistribution of property legitimately obtained.[73] All this means that Locke seems to provide the picture of an exchange economy which Marx thought of as one of the most important ideological props of nineteenth-century capitalism, suggesting as it did that it was exempt from explanation as a phenomenon of a particular time and place, and that government interference was no more nor less than interference with the workings of a naturally benign mechanism.[74] To see Locke as no more than an apologist for capitalism is ludicrous; to suggest that wilder minds in other ages would see him as such, and side with him or against him for that reason is not.

---

[73] *Two Treatises*, II, §34, p. 309.
[74] Macpherson, *Possessive Individualism*, pp. 216ff.

# 2

# Rousseau and Progress

Rousseau is best known for his account of the nature of sovereignty and government in the *Social Contract*. His defence of the idea that a state should be responsive to the demands of a General Will which is infallible and – under certain conditions – eternal or at any rate timeless, has attracted innumerable commentators. For our purposes, however, that side of Rousseau's work is not central. Rousseau did not, as Locke did, base politics on the defence of property;[1] he never wrote an extended account of just what right over external things a man ought to possess when he owned something, and he never wrote very much about the connection between work and ownership. None the less, it is to Rousseau that one has to look for two themes, the first ancient, the second modern.

The ancient theme is the conviction that only certain sorts of property are consistent with the maintenance of free republican institutions; this view, which owes a good deal to Machiavelli's *Discourses*,[2] and which has a Roman and Greek pedigree of considerable length, is essentially hostile to all sorts of property other than fixed agricultural property, and in particular the fixed agricultural property of the small independent farmer. The Roman republic, which is – sometimes – the model of political perfection, rested on the social base of small independent farmers who were politically virtuous and militarily courageous. Large property leads to corruption as the rich man tries to buy his fellow citizens; moveable property leads to corruption as it allows men to take their wealth wherever they choose, and it allows them to escape the censorship of their fellow citizens; the rise of money and commerce leads to corruption as it exacerbates these tendencies by creating a dependent urban mob who will follow the bidding of their corrupters.

---

[1] He did once call property a right even more sacred than liberty itself: *Social Contract*, p. 138.

[2] Niccolo Machiavelli, *The Discourses* (Penguin, Harmondsworth, 1970), pp. 102–4.

Rousseau's idealization of Rome is not complete; he never swerves from the conviction that slavery is intolerable, for example, and he is not moved by Roman military success so much as by the courage and endurance of the ordinary Roman soldier.[3] But in general it is true that Rousseau's thoughts about the relationship between property and politics are coloured quite decisively by this classical republican nostalgia. It has implications for Rousseau's view of work, too, of course. Most of the occupations associated with the rise of commercial society are dismissed as either servile or mere huckstering, just as most of the products of that society are dismissed as frivolities for which we have no real need. The simplicity of life for which Rousseau praises the Romans entails a like simplicity in the occupations they recognized.

The modern theme is less easy to sketch quickly. The simplest way to characterize it is to say that Rousseau is one of the first writers to place human self-consciousness so firmly at the centre of his work. I have said before that one thing which utilitarian or instrumental theories require, but cannot supply from their own resources, is an account of what sort of happiness suits us, and an account of what we get out of doing our duty beyond our limited share of the social benefits that doing our duty creates.[4] Rousseau in effect takes seriously the thought that our 'selves' are not given to us by God, nor fixed by nature, but are constructed by society. And this construction is challengeable; we can complain – on his view we can hardly help complaining – that society inculcates in us desires which society is organized to frustrate, and moral ideals which society is designed to render it impossible to realize. Rousseau is one of the first theorists of the divided self, and a particularly powerful theorist because he has so little conviction that any recipe is available for reconstituting the self as an undivided unity.[5]

Work and property might in principle be elements in a prescription for restoring this psychological unity. A man who works at a worthwhile task, where he can exercise some skill in making useful and enduring objects, will be happier than a man who either slaves away to make a rich man richer or who wastes his time selling knick-knacks to society ladies. A man who owns a plot

[3] *Social Contract*, p. 148.
[4] cf. Hegel, *Philosophy of Right*, §149, p. 107.
[5] Marshall Berman, *The Politics of Authenticity* (Atheneum, New York, 1970), pp. 75ff.

of land sufficient to support him and his family if he exerts himself, is independent of the favour of the world, and his life has a point and a purpose to it which most urban existences lack. So much we can readily glean from Rousseau. The more interesting feature of his work, however, is his conviction that we have got into such a state of emotional and cultural disorder – we have become so 'alienated' – that we are incapable of following this recipe.[6] For this reason Rousseau's most interesting speculations about the history of human society and its impact on our souls are almost invariably pessimistic and critical, telling us of our plight and telling us too how little hope we have of improving it. Nowhere is this more true than in his *Discourse on the Origin of Inequality*, an essay which provides much of the raw material of this chapter.

To a modern reader, the move from Locke to Rousseau is a move into the contemporary world. The reason is that Rousseau, however clumsily, has a feeling for history which Locke very conspicuously lacks. Rousseau, for all his emphasis on the dictates of reason, and on the need to establish political society on natural principles, is a writer who takes history seriously. For him, there is more to be explained than how society based on natural law became political society; his *Discourse on the Origin of Inequality* begins with a state of nature peopled by creatures who are human only potentially, and who only under the impact of society become the men and women whom we see in civilized societies.[7] This is not to deny what indeed I shall later stress, that Rousseau was alarmed by change, wanted to 'stop history' in various ways, and wanted to see societies in which the kinds of property rights which were recognized, and the kind of work which men did, would lead to none of the alarming changes caused by economic activity, economic and social inequality, and an attachment to our possessions rather than to the pursuit of virtue or simple pleasure.[8]

It is the work of a scholarly lifetime, not one chapter in a book on one limited topic, to set Rousseau's ideas in order. It is a commonplace that his work is full of internal contradictions, and that he offers altogether too many images of the causes of human misery and their possible cures. What follows picks out themes which recur with great frequency in the two centuries after

[6] *Social Contract*, p. 198.
[7] ibid., p. 47.
[8] ibid., p. 108.

Rousseau, themes which provide much of the raw material for Hegel and Marx, as well as for all sorts of individualists and liberals. I shall not undertake to show that any of the various Rousseaus depicted by other commentators is more *the* Rousseau than any other. I shall only say a little about Rousseau's account of what property rights *are,* then show his ambivalence about them in the *Discourse on the Origin of Inequality* in particular. This discussion will also provide an opportunity to suggest something of Rousseau's lack of interest in the productiveness of work, and his ambivalence towards the impact of work on our desires and abilities.

Rousseau's innovation in the *Discourse on the Origin of Inequality* was to insist that what man had been like in his truly *natural* state was far different from anything previously supposed by philosophers.[9] He had supposed that men were born rational, moral, competitive, articulate and almost certainly into nuclear families. Rousseau denied every one of these assumptions. These qualities, which men *now* certainly possessed, were not gifts of nature but society. Man had been quite otherwise when he first came into the world: he had been solitary – he would have copulated with any willing female who came his way and gone on his way again, ignorant of any connection between sex and procreation; mothers could quite well have looked after their infants on their own, and in the absence of a natural basis for the family, families would not have existed. Equally, isolated creatures like these would have had no speech; in the absence of speech they would have had none of the capacities we now think essential to rationality.

Nor would there have been very much scope for competition; there would have been next to no occasion for any sort of conflict at all – these solitary creatures would have encountered each other rarely, would have hardly recognized each other as members of the same species, would anyway have had very limited wants, and so could hardly encroach on each other's welfare. In addition, Rousseau thought mankind had been equipped with two basic instincts, what he called *amour de soi* and *pitié;* these were not 'self-love' and 'pity' in the usual sense, for those are highly developed emotions.[10] Self-love in the natural condition was no more than an impulse to preserve oneself and enjoy harmless pleasures; pity was no more than an instinctive shying away from what harmed

[9] ibid., p. 45.
[10] ibid., pp. 57ff.

creatures of one's own kind. The result, of course, is that there is no natural cause of conflict – which is Rousseau's answer to both Hobbes and Locke.[11]

What Rousseau's drastic rewriting of the notion of natural man achieved was two things. The first to raise the stakes of social theory in a quite dramatic way. If everything we ordinarily regard as distinctively human is actually the result of men living in society, social change can make much more difference than either Locke or Hobbes had ever thought. There was no need to put up with the miseries of existing society on the ground that they were the price we paid for the security we needed in face of our innate aggressiveness and competitiveness. If Rousseau was right, there was no such innate aggressiveness and competitiveness to be paid for. This makes utopian speculation much less utopian than is usually thought.[12] The second crucial thing it achieved was to widen the gap between what went on in any particular society and what was 'natural' to man. By the time we get to Hegel, Mill and Marx, this distinction between what is spatio-temporally local and what is built into the necessities of any society at all is firmly understood. What Rousseau needed the distinction for was to show how optional were the social and political arrangements of his own time and place. But once one puts the two points together, we get the beginnings of a thorough-going sociological perspective on social and political theory in which the role of society in creating the creatures who then have the task of recreating society is continually stressed.[13]

I have claimed that a major preoccupation in Rousseau is a concern with self-expression, and that this allows such concepts as that of alienation to find a plausible place in Rousseau's social theory. Rousseau was committed to the view, which is later made explicit in Hegel, that an individual needs to see his position in the world reflecting his own image of his self, not as something imposed on him, and at the same time that he must be able to approve of the character which is thus reflected in the world. If he cannot identify the self he desires to be with the wants he now finds himself with, he is alienated. The notion of alienation which Rousseau works with is expressed by his claim that man has become *hors de lui-même* – man

[11] ibid., pp. 68ff.
[12] Berman, *Politics of Authenticity, passim.*
[13] *Social Contract*, pp. 57ff.

has come to live outside himself.[14] What this mostly means is that
our wants and ideals are determined not by our own choice, but by
social pressure, and that our satisfactions such as they are, depend
not upon our own feelings, but upon how society assesses our
success and failure. Men have created society, and their creation
now dominates them. Ownership and its impact on how we see
ourselves and each other features in Rousseau's investigation of the
way man has become *hors de lui-même*. The history of society is the
history of our creative powers turning against us; we invent
economic and social institutions, and find that they control us as
effectively as merely material forces and objects would. For this
reason, Rousseau's view of evolution is of a process in which gains
are invariably matched by losses; whether they are outweighed by
the losses is a difficult question, since the gains and losses which
enter into the account are rarely commensurable, and Rousseau's
own judgement is fickle. Moreover, none of Rousseau's suggested
'solutions' to the difficulties he diagnoses can be taken entirely
seriously; their role is rather to emphasize Rousseau's dislike of
features of his own society than to suggest that these features can
readily be eliminated.[15]

Rousseau has little to say about the definition of property. He is
primarily concerned to deny that property is natural, concerned to
deny that there is any natural right to property, anxious to insist on
the difference between mere possession and genuine property. The
distinction is a distinction between fact and law; a man possesses
whatever he can actually keep hold of, or exclude others from,
whereas having property is having a title. Again, a man's
possessing something says nothing about the attitude of other men
to what he possesses. Other men may assume that if he has, say,
already gathered a pile of acorns he will try to hang on to them –
assuming in him the sort of natural possessiveness which, as
Herbert Spencer later pointed out, is to be found even among
dogs.[16] In the state of nature as Rousseau describes it, we only take
from nature what we want for some useful purpose; presumably the
man who has gathered acorns to eat will wish to retain them in
order to eat them, and will resent anyone else removing them. In

[14] ibid., p. 64.
[15] ibid., p. 112.
[16] Herbert Spencer, *Social Statics* (1st edn, Chapman, London, 1851), pp. 132–3.
[17] *Social Contract*, p. 73.

which case we may well decide that if we want acorns we had better go and gather our own, rather than risk a fight. At the beginning of the *Discourse on the Origin of Inequality*, Rousseau claims that the really primitive forebears of the human race would have acted so.[18] Even if the creature was dispossessed, he would not contest the issue but simply retire and make good his loss. There is little more that can profitably be said about Rousseau's distinction between possession and property as an analytical distinction; it is a sound distinction, but Rousseau was not consistently interested in elaborating it. We need only notice two things.

The first is that Rousseau is very emphatic about the distinction – which is merely one facet of his insistence on the radical difference between moral and legal relationships, relations of right and obligation on the one hand, and relationships of mere natural power on the other.[18] Thus, he rejects what he describes as Grotius' attempt to derive political power from the 'right of the stronger'; authority is what we *ought* to obey, and strength is no more than what we have to obey. The distinction between possessing and owning is the distinction between having power over a thing and having the right to exercise power over a thing.

Secondly, we must notice that Rousseau is concerned to say how very different any natural 'rights' are from real, fully fledged rights. Thus, where Locke merged first possession and property in the state of nature, Rousseau did not. Rousseau's point was that to talk of property is to talk of a relatively developed stage of human society, and outside such a context men have nothing it makes sense to call property. And one important result is how unlike Locke Rousseau is when he insists that property rights cannot antedate the political constitution.[19]

Rousseau was above all concerned to show how great a difference it made to men when they lived in a society which had an authoritative legal system which could define and enforce property rights. It is, however, important to recall that Rousseau's concerns are with moral issues rather than sociological ones; unlike his Scottish contemporaries such as Adam Ferguson, he is not particularly concerned with an exact historical sociology of ownership, not concerned with the precise operation of economic

[18] ibid., p. 168.
[19] ibid., p. 178.

and social causes.[20] For the purpose of drawing political morals, he could work with some fairly simple oppositions. Sometimes, these are very extreme, as when we are asked to contrast the orang-utan-like creature which was the truly natural man with the fully dressed Parisian of his own day. At other times, the contrasts involve a less dramatic opposition, say that between hunting and gathering societies on the one hand and agricultural ones on the other. What there is not very much sign of is a disinterested and academic concern with economic history.[21]

Rousseau's political and moral concerns mean that we cannot look for detailed answers to the questions which we might put to someone today who held somewhat similar views. Moreover, quite what would have caught his contemporaries' eye is sometimes hard to capture. So, for instance, one consequence of Rousseau's attack on the whole idea of original sin which catches our eye is that he does not think that primitive man is lazy. Since man had not sinned, he had not been condemned to earn his living in the sweat of his brow; the apparent idleness of the primitive is therefore no vice.[22] Moreover, Rousseau does not think that the pre-lapsarian condition of the innocently idle need ever have been disturbed; what others would see as the establishment of civilization is seen by Rousseau as the creation of disturbance and the destruction of tranquillity. This is the consequence of Rousseau's position which most interests us here, and we would be eager to press him further on exactly how much or how little disturbance of primitive tranquillity he would want. But his contemporaries may have been interested in his unorthodox views about original sin to the exclusion of most else.[23]

In the *Discourse on the Origin of Inequality*, then, Rousseau begins human history with a state of nature peopled by asocial, un-propertied, speechless, amoral creatures who have more in common with the orang-utan than with the inhabitants of eighteenth-century Paris. All the same, natural man is a unique species with one very remarkable property. This is his capacity to

[20] cf. *The Discourse on the Origin of Inequality* with, say, Adam Ferguson, *An Essay on the History of Civil Society* (Edinburgh University Press, Edinburgh, 1966).
[21] *Social Contract*, pp. 74–5.
[22] ibid., pp. 107–8.
[23] At all events, *Emile* was burned by the public hangman in 1762, which is some evidence of public interest in Rousseau's religious unorthodoxy; Rousseau received thousands of letters of support, however. His cause was more dangerous than unpopular.

learn and to pass on his knowledge to his offspring. It is this capacity which gives mankind a history. All other animals learn all they know in a few months, and the species is unchanged after millenia, so that they cannot have a history in the proper sense at all. None the less, in the beginning man is an animal with neither speech nor reason, and with no consciousness of himself or his species. There has been some dispute about the extent to which Rousseau regarded his sketch of natural man as an empirically accurate account of our ancestors. Rousseau says 'écartons donc les faits' in describing the state of nature, and some commentators have therefore thought he was entirely uninterested in the historical authenticity of his hypothesized natural order. Others, however, have noticed his interest in Lord Monboddo's work on the origins of language, and his readiness to accept Monboddo's view of the orang-utan as the 'missing link'.[24]

The truth, perhaps, is this: Rousseau's account of natural man chiefly seeks to establish some key differences between natural and civilized man – the one solitary, the other sociable, the one lacking all consciousness of self, the other crippled by the excesses of self regard, the one moved by immediate impulse, the other by virtue or vice – and the rhetorical effect of these oppositions needs no more than a purely hypothetical state of nature. So long as a coherent and internally consistent account of how pre-civilized man *might* live could be given, the features of civilized life which Rousseau wanted to highlight, in order to condemn them – or more rarely to praise them – would be adequately illuminated. Any socialist or anarchist who offers to show us something of how society would function were property eliminated and work rationally organised is doing as much. One might in the same frame of mind view the *Discourse on the Origin of Inequality* in the light of Durkheim's essay on Rousseau as a sort of moral fable.[25] The self-contained orderliness of the animal existence is contrasted with the chaos of modern society in order to enforce the claim that only in a society where norms have the same necessity as the laws of physical nature can men find again the orderliness they once had and have lost.

Still, even if the hypothetical state of nature would have served Rousseau's purpose, the rhetoric would have been even more

[24] Arthur O. Lovejoy, *Essays in the History of Ideas* (Putnam, New York, 1960), pp. 38–61.
[25] Emile Durkheim, *Montesquieu and Rousseau: Fore-runners of Sociology* (University of Michigan Press, Ann Arbor, 1960), pp. 65ff.

effective if he could have pointed to a pre-historical condition in which men had really lived as he had guessed they might. And, since it seems that Rousseau had a practical reason for denying the historical accuracy of his story – that is, he had to say nothing which looked like a direct challenge to the account of creation given in Genesis if his essay was to escape the public hangman[26] – it is at least plausible that Rousseau expected his readers to take his disclaimer less than seriously.

For our purposes, not very much hangs on the point; we might suggest that the more historical Rousseau's account, the more it opens the way for a recognizably modern approach to a sociology of economic life, and the more it brings history out of the realm of religious myth; but against this we should have to set not only Rousseau's casualness about the quality of his historical and anthropological sources, nor merely his attachment to stark, non-evolutionary oppositions, but the refusal of Kant and Hegel after him to take up these hints, if such they were, and the attachment of writers over the next two centuries to just the same exaggerated and ahistorical antitheses.

Merely animal, natural man relates to the world as all animals do. He has no sense of time, and therefore cannot envisage a not-yet-existent state of affairs; but all work and all creativity presuppose the ability to imagine that which we have not yet created. The idea of doing new things with what is about him simply cannot occur to him. Like any other animal, he consumes what he needs when he needs it, but any analogy between instinctual behaviour in, say storing food, and the developed activity of saving or investing is of the thinnest. There is here a perfect natural balance between need and effort. As an animal, man is drawn to what will feed him and quench his thirst. He has no motives for wasting his time in acquiring what is of no use to him, and he is not attracted to what will harm him or do him no good.[27]

In such a condition, property is literally unthinkable. We have seen that for Rousseau, the great difference between merely having and 'owning' lies in the move from the mere fact of control to the moral realm of having rights. The intention of Rousseau's *Discourse on the Origin of Inequality* is thus to demonstrate that moral

[26] *Social Contract*, p. 45.
[27] ibid., pp. 48–9.

relationships are not natural but social; they arise only when men find themselves pressing on the means of subsistence, through population growth, and only when they have for the same reason found themselves so much in each other's company that they have acquired the linguistic and conceptual resources to make moral claims on each other, and recognize moral obligations.[28] Rousseau thought morality was generated by the impact of reason on natural desires, and he wanted to show the social setting that was needed to provoke that impact.

Thus, the all-but-animal, natural man is equipped with an instinct for self-preservation and an aversion to the suffering of his fellows; these are mere impulses, with no moral connotations. They become moral principles when they are based on principle. Thus, the aversion to the suffering of others, natural sympathy or *pitié*, becomes the principled avoidance of harm to others, and the principle can govern a man's conduct where the natural sentiment alone might not. There is not a great deal of overt moral philosophy in the *Discourse on the Origin of Inequality*. It is not very fruitful to press Rousseau on the question of how we move from impulse to morality, if the aim is to extract from him an articulate account like Kant's, or, in twentieth-century terms, R. M. Hare's.[29] All we need to notice is that the arrival of moral principles coincides, as it conceptually must, with the arrival of an ability to compare one man's welfare with another's, and one man's success or failure with that of another. While Rousseau is not concerned to establish precise causal connections between each element of the new situation, the ability to make comparisons, the ability to think about the future, and the desire for just treatment by others, all hang together and jointly provide the explanation for the *malaises* of civilization. For under civilized conditions, we learn to estimate our successes and our failures according to how they compare with those of other people. Our original self-sufficiency is irrevocably lost. Moreover, now that we have a sense of time, as well as consciousness of our own existence, we can begin to feel anxiety for the future, to fear death, to wish to insure ourselves against misfortune. This gives us some reason to hope to guarantee our future possession of whatever it is we need and currently possess; from this comes the desire for something which is recognizable as

[28] ibid., pp. 78ff.
[29] e.g., R. M. Hare, *Moral Thinking* (Clarendon Press, Oxford, 1981).

property in the full sense. Such a new state of mind also does
something to explain how work becomes possible; for here, too, it is
the consciousness of an uncertain future to be provided for which
both makes sense of the idea of disciplined work and gives us some
incentive to engage in it.[30]

It is a moot point whether Rousseau much cared about the
details of the transition from man's primitive independence in the
extremest sense to his membership in savage hunting and gathering
societies, and thence to membership of settled agricultural communities. It is not implausible to suppose that he mostly had three
stages in mind: a pre-human, minimally human, and all too human
stage, but would very willingly have made more elaborate and
detailed distinctions as he needed them – so that once we have
agriculture firmly established, he was ready to distinguish between,
say, the peasants and fishermen of Corsica, the sharecropping
peasantry of rural France, and the tenant farmer of eighteenth-
century England, and so more and more cautiously on.[31] In the
*Discourse on the Origin of Inequality*, he needs no such finesse. Here we
have one main claim – that iron and corn ruined man and that the
invention of property was the root of all our later misfortunes.[32]
That is, once the iron plough and the discovery of corn made
agriculture a possibility, societies could live very much better as
settled agricultural communities than as pastoral tribes, let alone
hunters and gatherers. But agriculture demanded fixed ownership
of land; fixed ownership of land demanded political arrangements
capable of defining and securing that ownership. Before we look at
Rousseau's reasons for supposing that we should have remained
content with the life of the Carib Indians, it is worth recalling one
important point.

Although Rousseau's hatred of much of contemporary civilization was the hatred of a disappointed man, the disappointment was
not merely personal. It was the disappointment of a thinker who
saw that just those features of human life which made man higher
than the animals also made him more vulnerable than they,
vulnerable both to suffering and to corruption. Work and property

[30] *Social Contract*, p. 77.
[31] As he does in, say, his project for a constitution for Corsica, or in discussing the peasants
of the Haut Valais and the Bas Valais; cf. Judith N. Shklar, *Men and Citizens* (Cambridge
University Press, Cambridge, 1969), pp. 23–4, and *passim*.
[32] *Social Contract*, p. 83.

have their place in Rousseau's sense of this vulnerable elevation. A man *might* find in a decent trade a secure livelihood, a stable place in a stable society, the opportunity to do something useful, or improving, for his fellows. The work might be healthy, and engage his interest and intelligence without exhausting him. But, it is more likely in modern society that the work a man does will be boring and unskilled drudgery, or servile and corrupting, and probably useless. Similarly, in a stable society property might 'mean' the piece of land which was passed down from father to son for generation after generation, which would yield an austere but sufficient living, and allow its owner to act as a free and independent citizen who knew he need kow-tow to nobody for a living. But, it would more probably mean the wealth of the vulgar rich, employed to dazzle and impress the mass of the population, or the resources monopolized by a few men and used to force the propertiless to work for them; it might mean the capital which the go-ahead entrepreneur employed in novel ways and so used to create more wealth, more intricate commercial and social relationships, and hence a new political regime too. Property of its very nature involves a degree of inequality, inasmuch as laws about property defend the haves against the have-nots; such laws need not, but they very likely will, promote inequality of status, envy, snobbery and class consciousness. These inequalities are the ones which Rousseau's *Discourse* and other works are concerned with, indeed obsessed with.[33]

One needs to bear in mind Rousseau's disappointment: the institutions of private property and the organization of work can serve a valuable purpose in attaching men to society, to their families, and to one another individually – but they usually have not done so. What gives his writing on the limited themes which we are concerned with their peculiar tone is the psychological insight which makes Rousseau's moral theory so compelling. Once men become capable of moral virtue, two crucial changes in their psychology occur. In the first place, they become vulnerable to guilt; they can reproach themselves for failing to live up to their own standards, and, of course, guilt is closely allied to shame, the feeling of failure to live up to what are at any rate believed to be the standards of others in whose eyes one wants to be respected. In the second place, they can resent inequalities which they believe to be

[33] ibid., p. 81.

unjust. It is not misfortune which maddens us, but injustice.[34] And Rousseau perceived that the two phenomena of guilt and resentment were closely linked. By temperament and intellectual allegiance Rousseau felt the difficulty of maintaining a calm self-respect and resisting the temptation to abase oneself in order to curry favour with friends, patrons and critics at one moment, and to humiliate one's supposed accusers at the next.

In the *Discourse on the Origin of Inequality*, Rousseau's concern is with inequality in all its forms, and in the end with the impact of competition and envy on the individual psyche.[35] Here we can pick out some obvious, central themes. If men were self-contained, harmonious creatures when they were solitary animals in the forests, what do they gain by leaving that state? Rousseau does not suggest that primitive existence is comfortable, only that it is stable, and free from the internal contradictions of civilized life, where we are forced into reliance on each other and suffer the consequences.[36] If we are thrust by increase of population into some sort of society, let it be the least complex possible; what can be said for the Caribs is that they have no great inequality of conditions, and there is no drudgery. Their social life is one of singing and dancing under the trees; even this gives rise to some envy, some anxiety, some vanity, but there are no resources for more elaborate forms of inequality. The same, largely negative, defence of small, stable communities, free of commerce and preserved from the evils of money making, is offered when Rousseau praises Sparta. What Rousseau admired about Sparta was that the same constitutional arrangements sufficed for eight hundred years. The price of this, as classical republican theorists always pointed out, was austerity, inwardness, and a certain cultural crudeness.[37]

Yet, if the *Discourse on the Origin of Inequality* tells us that the man who invented property was the originator of all our ills, it does so in some very ambiguous ways. One crucial difficulty is knowing what the political results of the existence of fixed property are. Did Rousseau think that political societies, protecting each man's possession with every man's strength, provided a service for

[34] It is also the constant preoccupation of Berman, *Politics of Authenticity*.
[35] *Social Contract*, p. 108.
[36] ibid., p. 82.
[37] ibid., p. 10.

everyone, or only for the rich?[38] It is evident that Rousseau had grave doubts about the psychological effect of ownership; once we have possessions we can be hurt in our property as well as our bodies; we became vulnerable to wounds we could never have felt before. The boundaries of the self expand to include the self's possessions, and then the self can be injured by theft, and even the mere fear of it.[39] But if Rousseau sometimes sees those vulnerable possessions as the superfluities of the rich, and as the means whereby they enslave the poor, he also sometimes thinks that everyone does have or could have at least enough to desire the advantages of political society.[40] This yields two very different pictures of the actual social contract which established the first state. Sometimes it seems to have been a contract in which the rich persuaded the poor the lend them their strength in order to assist them in their object of oppressing the poor whose aid they sought; at other times, Rousseau says that such a contract is so manifestly contrary to reason that nobody can ever have entered political society on those terms.[41] Ancient states, therefore, must have been relatively unexploitative and must have developed into something less attractive. On either view, the clear implication is that states exist to protect property, and that where this protection is not upon fair terms, the state is illegitimate.

One way of reconciling the tension between these two pictures of how states started is to suggest that Rousseau *did* believe that states had begun in a conspiracy of the rich to exploit the poor, and was interested in contrasting this historical condition with the recipe for a legitimate state in which everyone had something, nobody had too much, and the force of all protected the possessions of each on equitable terms.[42] The only difficulty in maintaining this otherwise plausible distinction is that it cuts across Rousseau's view of history. In general, Rousseau praises states such as Sparta and Rome; but Sparta and Rome were built upon agriculture, and in the *Discourse on the Origin of Inequality* agriculture is blamed for ruining mankind. If Rousseau's apparent belief in the inevitability of ruin, once private property in land is established, can be set aside as

---

[38] cf. ibid., p. 89 and p. 148 with ibid., p. 92.
[39] ibid., p. 91.
[40] ibid., p. 92.
[41] ibid., p. 92.
[42] ibid., p. 134.

nothing more than a rhetorical flourish, or can be drastically dis-
counted in the face of his praise of agriculture in *Emile*, then the
contrast between the state as it is, and as it might be and ought to
be, can be sustained. We need then not be too troubled by the fact
that our images of the stable community are sometimes drawn from
the Spartans, who depended on agriculture for their subsistence, and
that the happy Caribs are left to remind us that if only there was no
landed property at all, there would be no state either.[43]

It is in *Emile* that Rousseau sets out to explain what the value of
good work is – that is, what constitutes satisfying work for an
individual, what benefits it yields him and his fellows. Although the
most sustained discussion of property rights, taxation and the like
occurs in the *Discourse on Political Economy*, it is in *Emile* also that
Rousseau's most famous argument for the sanctity of property is to
be found. The child Emile is induced by his tutor to plant some
beans; these are torn up by the enraged gardener Robert who
points out that the plot is *his*.[44] The ground of Robert's title is
interesting in that it appears to commit Rousseau to a mixture of
'first occupancy', labour and family inheritance as the crucial
elements in any understanding of property. Emile is forced to
understand that Robert had prior possession, and therefore that he,
Emile, had no right to try to grow his beans on the land; and
Robert's view of the sacrosanct character of his property seems to
depend both on the fact that his father had had it before him, and
on the fact that he himself had both settled and worked it. Whether
Robert's decision to give Emile a plot for nothing although the
whole garden was his, bears any elaborate economic interpretation
is dubious. Throughout his later discussion of Emile's prospects of
employment when he has learned a skill, Rousseau affects an
optimism about the ease with which a willing worker will find a job
which is not paralleled in the *Political Economy;*[45] it may equally be
true that one should not look to interpret Emile's discovery of the
ethics of ownership more strenuously than its pedagogic context
suggests.

In the *Discourse on the Origin of Inequality* Rousseau had appeared
to care nothing for work and to have thought that property was a
disastrous invention. In *Emile* he seems instead to wish to advocate

[43] ibid., p. 76.
[44] J.-J. Rousseau, *Emile* (Dent, London, 1974), pp. 62–3.
[45] ibid., p. 160.

the work of the artisan and craftsman as good in itself, and to defend the rights of proprietors as all but sacred. There is a way of partially reconciling the two essays: property as the means of oppression is nothing but an evil, while property as the means by which a man keeps in touch with the soil of his country and the labours of his forebears is entirely good. Work is mere drudgery if it is sweated labour for some rich man; the application of a useful skill is another matter. Even then there are problems, especially with skilled work because, among other things, Rousseau vacillates between treating the division of labour as a process of turning men into machines by making them into adept, but narrow performers of a cramped and limited range of tasks, and treating it as a symbol of, and an important element in the kind of dependence of each man on the whole community to which we should aspire.[46] This latter suggestion may itself induce more anxiety about just what Rousseau's commitments were, since he swings in *Emile*, as he does elsewhere, from wanting each man to remain wholly independent, if necessary at the price of isolation from his fellows, to wanting each man to become so dependent on his fellows that he is nothing without the concurrence of everyone else.[47]

Rousseau, under the guise of Emile's tutor, foresees that Emile may have to wander the world — as he himself had done, of course. Keeping Emile alive is therefore an important consideration, and Rousseau duly devotes some thought to how he can keep the wolf from the door. Rousseau's argument in favour of Emile's learning a craft is both local and general. It is local in the sense that much of Rousseau's argument is devoted to criticizing snobbish standards which make the idle rentier look down on the man who earns his living with his hands. A recurring theme in Rousseau's work is that snobbery is one of the most damaging things about a wealthy, civilized society. Here it is linked very straightforwardly to several radical commonplaces. A man who can work, but does not, makes it necessary for somebody else to work harder, and is therefore a burden on society. To teach Emile to despise idleness is the first goal of teaching him a trade.

Rousseau has a very clear idea of which occupations will encourage hard work and independence and which will not. The

[46] Clayre, *Work and Play*, pp. 7–14.
[47] John Charvet, *The Social Problem in the Philosophy of Rousseau* (Cambridge University Press, Cambridge, 1974), p. 144.

argument steadily progresses towards the declaration that the best
of all occupations for Emile is that of the carpenter. Musicians and
authors are dismissed early in the argument, and for reasons which
are solidly within the republican tradition; they depend for their
livelihood on the favours of the wealthy and the well-connected,
they have to ingratiate themselves with these to get a living, and
this is to sacrifice their standing as independent citizens. There is a
familiar psychological twist to this in Rousseau's account too. The
artisan who did not care for his employer or his customer could
pack up his tools and materials and leave; musicians and authors
were unable to take their feet from under their patrons' tables.[48]

Locke's advocacy of manual labour for children of the propertied
classes is, unfairly, dismissed as trying to teach a little more or less
fancy work to children, with no useful goal in mind. Emile may
have to *use* his skills. Rousseau thinks it unnecessary to teach Emile
the skills of the agricultural worker; in a decent household these
will have already have come naturally to him – all of which argues
an enthusiasm for agriculture as the first and most useful of all the
arts, which is hard to reconcile with the denunciation of it in the
*Discourse on the Origin of Inequality*.[48] Rousseau's egalitarianism does
not show up well in his prejudices about the natural division of
labour between the sexes. Men ought not to serve in shops, make
jewellery, embroider and so on, since to do so is effeminate. On the
other hand, in spite of his belief that a trade ought to tire the body
rather than the mind, Rousseau has no 'macho' enthusiasm for
brute, hard labour – Emile is not to be Cyclops at the forge.

The *Political Economy* is, for the most part, a treatise on taxation,
and its interest to most readers lies in the fact that in it Rousseau
spells out the theory of the General Will in a particularly clear and
persuasive fashion, several years before the *Social Contract* was
published. Its interest for us lies in the way it spells out some of
Rousseau's views on property and its legitimacy. For, it is an
obvious problem for Rousseau (as it remained, indeed, in the
several declarations of the Rights of Man)[49] to give sufficient
weight to the sacredness of an individual's right to his property

---

[48] *Emile*, p. 160.
[49] e.g. article XVII of the Declaration of the Rights of Man of 1789: 'The right to property
being inviolable and sacred, no one ought to be deprived of it, except in cases of evident
public necessity, legally ascertained, and on condition of a previous just indemnity.' This, of
course, raises all sorts of contentious questions.

while giving the same weight to his insistence that 'our' property belongs in the last resort to the sovereign community rather than to us individually. One might think, from reading the *Social Contract* and from the echoes of its language in the later declarations of the Rights of Man, that ownership is a strictly individual right, limited only by the necessity to raise money by taxation, and perhaps by the state's right to take extraordinary measures in time of war or other emergencies.

The *Political Economy* makes it plain that Rousseau's unit of calculation was more often the family than the individual; indeed, in the *Political Economy* there is a direct claim that the best regulation of property is that which secures that it does not come into or leave the family.[50] The stability of society, which is Rousseau's great goal, requires that there should be little or no social mobility; he seems to have taken it for granted that there would not and could not be complete equality of conditions, and to have thought both that the gap between the better and worse off could under those conditions remain small, and that it would be less destructive of self-respect if it also remained stable. In this he really did give Durkheim grounds for supposing that his concept of anomie had been prediscovered by Rousseau.[51]

The *Political Economy* is, of course, alien to the twentieth-century eye in the way it takes a concern with sumptuary legislation seriously. Rousseau's attitude to taxation in general is not unusual even in the nineteenth century, where J. S. Mill follows his father and Bentham in distinguishing between a man's requirements and his superfluities; Mill proposed only to tax the latter, and that at a flat rate. But Rousseau's concern that no members of society should flaunt their wealth in the faces of the poor, as well as a debt to theorists of classical republican virtue and their influence, lies behind his suggestion that taxes should be imposed on such things as coaches. These were things whose use the state might properly forbid altogether, and which therefore they could certainly tax. The image of the austere, indeed poverty-stricken republic of Sparta is always before Rousseau's eyes; modern cities are parasitic, a drain on resources, not places of industry and legitimate commerce, but the home of luxury and waste, snobbery and servility. Only isolated agrarian society can aspire to political stability and psychological

---

[50] *Social Contract*, p. 139.
[51] Durkheim, *Montesquieu and Rousseau*, pp. 70–1, 84–8.

health. The other strange feature of Rousseau's views is his
conviction that the system of forced labour, the *corvée* which caused
such resentment before 1789 and was instantly abolished by the
Revolution, was less inimical to freedom than were taxes in money.
It is, however, easy enough to see why Rousseau would have
thought so. His contemporaries' notion of freedom would have led
them to think that a tax on income or wealth was less of an
interference with their right to choose how to spend their time and
less of a case of placing them under someone's *orders* than was an
obligation to do compulsory labour.[52] Rousseau's notion of
freedom, tied as it was to Roman and Spartan ideas about civic
duty, led him to think that making everyone *do* something for their
country was one of the things which preserved their freedom;
letting people discharge their duties by buying other people's
efforts weakened their commitment.

The difficulty of reconciling Rousseau's insistence on the sanctity
of individual rights with his insistence on the whole community's
right to control the exercise of those rights is only one consequence
of the general indeterminacy of his theory of individual and social
human nature. Rousseau's view of the relationship between raw
nature and human artifice is one of the great unresolvable
mysteries in his anthropology and political theory. On the one
hand, he seems to turn his back on the accomplishments of human
effort. Everything is in good order when it comes from the hand of
the creator, and is ruined by human intervention, yet, Rousseau is
clear that we are not to return to live among the bears, but must
educate ourselves and reconstruct society in order to make
something new of nature's raw material.[53] Rousseau's insistence on
the goodness and completeness of what comes from the hand of
nature rather than man is so emphatic that one feels a good deal of
sympathy for all those critics who thought Rousseau was praising
the noble savage and advocating that we should turn our backs on
everything to do with work and ownership. For, Rousseau deprives
himself of the most obvious props of the Lockean account, without
availing himself of the substitutes set out by Kant. That is, when he
says that things come from God in their full perfection, he does not
argue that they come predestined for some particular purpose, does
not even appear to assume it unquestioningly as Locke does.

[52] *Social Contract*, p. 152.
[53] ibid., pp. 112–13.

This is why there is no great pressure to represent work as the process of turning God's gifts to the purposes for which He gave them to us. Rousseau takes it for granted that some relationships are natural, and that matters are managed perversely if we do not work within them. The young should not command the old, nor the foolish the wise, and so on. But Rousseau does not wax lyrical about the replacement of waste land by smiling fields and orchards, and he does not see mankind as destined to make the world the place its creator intended it to be. In a paradoxical way, Rousseau's refusal to admit that sin was original in mankind also makes him less ready to praise the work of men's hands. To Locke and many orthodox Christians, hard work was a discipline and a way of paying one's debts to God. Since Rousseau never saw men encumbered with these debts in the first place, he had less to say about the obligation to pay them off. Nor did he inherit from Calvinist Geneva anything much of the view that hard work and application are not *means* to Grace, since there are none, but are perhaps *signs* of Election.[54] He is not a theorist of the Protestant ethic, however loosely we characterize that elusive animal. In a decent society, work is a debt to society, and one we should all pay without snobbish inhibitions. But there is no suggestion that men find very much fulfilment in work, and no suggestion that it can provide an area in which one's daily work can turn into creative activity.

Similarly, although Rousseau commits himself to the view that property is perhaps even more basic than the state, and also to the view that what we inherit has to be re-earned by its new owner through his own efforts, he does not have much to say about *how* occupancy and labour give us a title, nor about the sort of relationships which men may have with their property. It is entirely proper to reply that there is no reason why Rousseau should have felt obliged to provide any such account; once he had shown that inequality in the economic sphere ruled out genuine political equality, he had done as much as the disillusioned Jacobins ever did, and perhaps as much as Marx in his first critique of Hegel's political philosophy.

But the baffled reader is likely to feel that Rousseau is *interestingly* unlike, say, Adam Ferguson, in that he gives himself the same room to discuss historical and social variations in what men recognize as

[54] Weber, 'Religious Rejections of the World and their Directions', in *From Max Weber*, p. 332.

property, what they do and do not value about work and so on, and
yet makes very little use of it. Striking dichotomies are imposed on
an evolutionary framework. Human history results according to
Rousseau in mankind stamping the world with the image of men's
abilities and ambitions; but this record is a record of missed
opportunities. There is none of Hegel's suggestion that we shall
become reconciled to it in understanding it more fully, and none of
Marx's optimism that (a different) understanding will show us how
to recapture control of the process and turn it into a record of
human liberation from toil and disorganization. Rousseau provides
much of the vocabulary and many of the insights of Hegel and
Marx; he sees the results of human history in fundamentally the
same light, but he never attains anything like their conviction that
he knows what the whole process means.[55]

In part, this seems to be a matter of their making different
judgements of the process. In simple terms, both Hegel and Marx
think they are recording progress even if progress is more often
impelled by our vices than our virtues. Rousseau, by contrast, is
always reminding us that every silver lining has a cloud to it. In
part, it is a matter of Rousseau's obsession with the past, lost unity
of republican Rome and Sparta, which makes him less ready to
scrutinize different social, economic and political arrangements
with the relatively detached eye of the historian or sociologist.

The other crucial point that perhaps accounts for this is
Rousseau's concern for the individual psyche. He is continuously
pained by the injuries to a man's pride, self-esteem, vanity and
whatever other aspects of transformed *amour de soi*. Where Marx
and Hegel move away from the miseries of the individual to the
wider social framework, and devote little attention to the ways in
which individuals, as opposed to social groups or classes, adjust to
their surroundings, Rousseau is mainly interested in how the
individual devises and implements a self-protective strategy in a
hostile world. Moreover, where Marx sees economic oppression as
the key, Rousseau sees men as wounded in so many ways that his
characteristic fears are not concentrated very directly on the way
men are exploited at work rather than everywhere else. Again,
since Rousseau's thinking about the political oppressiveness of a
regime of the propertied harks back to classical models, he is not
concerned, as later writers were, to expand on the relationship

[55] *Social Contract*, pp. 106–13.

between oppression at work, and oppression in the political sphere. A classical account of 'corruption' and a decidedly non-classical account of the anguish of the socially insecure is what is we are left with.[56]

Finally, there is the question: *cui bono?* Rousseau explicitly defends the virtues of the middle classes, and denounces both the arrogance of wealth and the feebleness of poverty in the *Political Economy*. It has been shown, too, that the writing of the *Social Contract* was occasioned by the struggles of the *petite bourgeoisie* of Geneva to regain the political influence which had slipped out of their hands and into those of a well-to-do hereditary oligarchy.[57] But, it would not be accurate to describe Rousseau as the defender of the *petit bourgeois,* however tempting the similarities between his social unease and that of the twentieth-century lower-middle classes. For one thing, Rousseau also admires the fishermen and farmers of Corsica, and the shepherds of the Haut Valais (but not those of the Bas Valais); in the *Political Economy* he praises a traditional peasantry as a *petite bourgeoisie* or at any rate a stable middle rank in a fashion which perhaps looks forward to the supporters of Pierre Poujade, but which also cuts awkwardly across eighteenth- and nineteenth-century insistence on the differences between real and movable property, between agriculture and commerce, rural and urban attachments and thus between Rousseau's farmers and modern shopkeepers.

If Rousseau *is* to be seen in such terms, it is as the defender of 'the small man' of many twentieth-century right-wing movements, and even this is surely to run grave risks of anachronism. When Aristotle praises the middle ranks of society in Athens of the fourth-century BC, we do not feel much temptation to think he is defending any sort of bourgeoisie. Should we really look to Rousseau for anything more than two rhetorical positions – the Aristotelian emphasis on the virtues of the 'middle ranks', and something like a Stoic picture of innocent cultivators? Even if Rousseau had been a great deal more whole-hearted in his praise of sobriety, calculation, hard work, frugality and so on, and had done less to suggest that the play of the Caribs was more natural to and more likely to bring happiness to mankind, it is dubious that he

---

[56] Shklar, *Men and Citizens*, pp. 1–12.
[57] Peter Gay, *Voltaire's Politics* (Random House, New York, 1965), p. 199.

would have had much time for the virtues of a commercial or industrial bourgeoisie.[58] Rousseau largely looked backward, even though his psychological insights were 'modern'. Where he did not, and demanded political rights for humanity, he did not emphasize their standing as bourgeois, but their common humanity.

[58] *Emile*, pp. 161ff.

# 3

# Kant and Possession

In recent years Kant's political philosophy has once again attracted the scrutiny of scholars in the English-speaking world. For the most part this is because of his views on international relations. But even for our more narrow concern with the role of property rights in political theory, Kant is a central figure. In the hands of Kant the ideas of both Locke and Rousseau – especially the latter, of course – underwent the most striking transformation. For in Kant's work the connections between property and personality are for the first time fully explored – if only in their legal aspects; again, Rousseau's rather desperate view of the results of history is explicitly taken up in Kant's *Universal History,* and shown to be incorporable into a rational justification of the whole historical process. The defence of bourgeois values is made explicit, and the attack on feudal principles in private law and political right as explicit. That the state is founded on, and exists to serve, private property is argued as energetically as it ever was in Locke, but the moral foundations for property are derived from very different Roman Law principles, in which the roles of labour and occupation are reversed.[1]

The political consequences which Kant draws are also in some ways like Locke's – the state is concerned to prevent each man exercising his freedom in such a way as to impede the free actions of others; it employs coercion to defeat coercion and nothing more – but where it would take a great deal of argument to show that Locke intended to confine political activity to the propertied, Kant is very clear about it.[2] Again, Kant derives the legitimacy of government from a social contract, but removes the contract from history more effectively even than Rousseau had done. But on many issues Kant was much less of a liberal than either Locke or

---

[1] I. Kant., *Philosophy of Law,* tr. W. Hastie (Clark, Edinburgh, 1887), p. 82.
[2] Hans Reiss (ed.), *Kant's Political Writings,* pp. 78, 139–40.

Rousseau – in his treatment of revolution and the legal obligations of the sovereign most notably so.[3]

The starting point of any explanation of Kant's impact on political and legal thinking must be the extent to which he associated personality with possessing a legal persona and this with being the owner of property. In essence, Kant seems to take it for granted that what a lawful state in which justice reigns can do is to regulate the dealings of independent possessors of property. They will need the state's aid in defining and securing their property, and in enforcing contracts, but they may not ask it for more.[4] In particular, they would commit a great wrong against one another if they were to seek the aid of government in imposing any particular view of the good life on other individuals. A man is entirely responsible for his own moral virtue, and to nobody other than himself. He *has* a duty to make the most of himself, a duty of humanity in his own person, but not an obligation to anyone else.[5]

Perhaps the most important thing to insist on in explaining Kant's political theory is the place of law. What Kant was concerned to do was explain how law could be legitimate, and this for him was a question of explaining how an organization – the state – could have the right to enforce the perfect external duties which legal obligations amounted to. Legal obligations are perfect external duties, in that they are obligations to particular people to do particular things – for example, to pay exactly five pounds to Jones in particular from whom I have just bought a shirt – but not to do them in any particular frame of mind. It is worth insisting on this, both because it reminds us of the place of politics within Kant's general moral philosophy, which separates action and motive in the most stringent way, and because it does something to explain how Kant manages to reconcile himself to extreme economic inequality, while insisting that the essence of a legal system is equality before the law for all comers. That the political life is not a man's only life could readily be inferred from the above, but it is worth noticing too that Kant's insistence on the limited role of the state comes from a moral scrupulousness different in kind from anything a utilitarian might argue, and which even in its

[3] ibid., p. 145n.
[4] Kant, *Philosophy of Law*, pp. 22–4.
[5] I. Kant, *The Metaphysical Principles of Virtue*, tr. James Ellington (Bobbs-Merrill, Indianapolis, 1964), pp. 43–6.

uninstrumental features is different from Locke's arguments for toleration.[6]

Earthly life is not the search for happiness but the pursuit of virtue; we are here not to be happy, but to make ourselves deserving of happiness.[7] The criteria of virtue are essentially inward, tied to goodness of heart and will, and not, other than negatively, to outward performance. Thus, it is not that the state is a clumsy or ineffective instrument in achieving the ultimate ends of life, rather that it is not operating in that realm at all. We can, of course, rewrite this in a less formal mode, as writers such as T. H. Green did in due course. Emphasizing how much of what we value in morality stems from the fact that we *know* that what is done is done voluntarily, we make it seem very improbable that in the case of an adult at least we can secure what we value by legal compulsion.[8]

An ethics in which the good will is of supreme importance plainly rules out the legal enforcement of moral principles; even one in which it is not will result in the same prohibition so long as the voluntariness of moral acts and attitudes has any very considerable value. Kant, it may be recalled, claimed that even a society of devils could maintain a just polity; so long as men have private interests which they can agree to secure by a system of impersonal, coercive laws, they can maintain the justice of a political society.[9] In such a state, we deal with each other at arms' length. Kant did not deny that warmer, face-to-face relationships were eminently desirable; he only held that it was no part of the legal and political system's role to enforce them, even though the fact that we value such relationships is much of the explanation of why the legal system should protect them.

The paradox in all this, if there is one, lies in Kant's emphasis on the nature of the external, public self in terms which both seem to promise a great deal from the public sphere, and yet to push most of what we value in life back into essentially private concerns. That is, there seem to be two kinds of community in Kant, one strictly legal in which our relationships to each other are contractual, and

[6] cf. *A Letter Concerning Toleration*, pp. 123–37 and *Kant's Political Writings*, pp. 73–4.

[7] *Kant's Political Writings*, p. 64.

[8] H. L. A. Hart, *Law, Liberty and Morality* (Oxford University Press, London, 1963), pp. 57–8.

[9] *Kant's Political Writings*, pp. 73ff.

generally at least instrumental, the other the flesh and blood community of common purposes and mutual regard. Kant so obviously opens the way to the desire of Hegel and Marx that the latter should be the only community, and yet proceeds on such wholly rationalist and legalistic lines, that it is not easy to see quite how he sustained this split vision of human nature. Yet that is plainly what he does.[10]

One explanation of why Kant does so can plausibly be looked for in another somewhat awkward aspect of his work, his philosophy of history. Both on biographical and logical grounds it is unfanciful to see the 'sketch of a universal history' as a reply to Rousseau's *Second Discourse*. Kant wanted to admit that Rousseau's complaints against the results of progress are largely justified, and yet rescue the whole process from the condemnation which Rousseau had levelled at it. In doing so, he broached one of those dilemmas which has haunted historical theories ever since – is history, justified as a process of education and development, an endless educative process, or does it reach some goal after which the notion of further progress would not make very much sense? On Kant's account, there is at least one determinate goal, and this is the creation of a perfectly just and legal state.[11] To many of Kant's commentators, this is of most interest in so far as it leads into the argument of *Perpetual Peace* – that a just state requires the establishment of an international order in which peace and justice between states is a prerequisite of peace and justice within states. Here, however, two rather different things are of more importance.

In the first place, it is worth noticing that Kant's perfectly just community is not a state in which much politics seems to happen. Kant is concerned with the conditions of the legitimacy of laws, and their proper administration, not with the management of the ship in uncertain waters. In that sense, Kant very firmly belongs to the school which holds that the end of historical processes lies a timeless, or repetitive, condition in which further basic changes are not to be looked for. Yet, his insistence on the fact that no straight thing will be made out of humanity's crooked timber does not suggest that everything will run smoothly in a just state, and Kant is wholly content to register the fact.[12] Neither Rousseau's desire

---

[10] Howard Williams, *Kant's Political Philosophy* (Blackwell, Oxford, 1983), pp. 52ff.
[11] *Kant's Political Writings*, pp. 45ff., 50.
[12] ibid., p. 46.

for a timeless harmony, nor Durkheim's gloss on that in terms of his own sociology, fits the cheerful tone of Kant's observation that man is destined for disorder. The other, crucial point is Kant's insistence that what makes for historical progress is humanity's vices and humanity's difficulties, and that this is the hidden educative intention of nature. Man's unsocial sociability is the driving force, and again Kant is content that it is so.[13]

What Kant argues makes peculiarly good sense when set against what Rousseau had said before him. Kant praises the niggardliness of nature which forces men to develop all their talents to provide themselves with what they desire. This is not to side with Smith and Hume; they saw the fact of scarcity as the explanation of economic laws, and of the need for property and government, but not as a fact possessing this kind of moral significance. Nor is it to side with Rousseau;[14] he did not see scarcity as a fact at all, but, as Hegel and Marx did later, as a consequence of our unnatural desires. Natural man wanted what nature offered, and nature offered what he wanted. But Kant, who was willing enough to agree with Rousseau's account of *why* there was scarcity, did not emphasize the resulting dissatisfaction, but the ingenuity, effort, persistence and intelligence it called out. If nature had not been such a niggardly mother, her offspring would always have remained children. Nor is Kant inclined to follow Rousseau in despairing of competition, vanity and envy. These are all aspects of the unsocial sociability of mankind, according to which we need one another simultaneously as collaborators and as competitors. Emulation is one of the great propelling forces of history, though no virtue in itself.

At this point, however, it is necessary to remember another side of Kant's project. He is not quite accurately represented as praising change, progressiveness, and economic advance. For one thing, he is very ready to admit that the horrors of human history are quite enough to justify a good deal of Rousseau's unhappiness.[15] And when justifying the ways of history to man, he is only very indirectly concerned to justify them to any given individual. Kant's description of the way economic advance teaches mankind the nature of human abilities and talents may look like an anticipation of Marx's

[13] ibid., p. 44.
[14] cf. ibid., p. 45 and *Social Contract*, p. 112.
[15] *Kant's Political Writings*, p. 42.

claim that work will eventually be an all-round activity of the *allseitiger Mensch*. But Kant himself points out quite bleakly that it is the race rather than the individual which benefits.[16] That is, as a steelworker I may *represent* humanity's ability to work metals of all kinds; I may *represent* the intelligence of the metallurgist, and the enriched lives of the consumers of all the products into which the skills of foundries, forges and whatever have gone. Yet because of the division of labour I in particular may well possess one small skill, and because of the balance of economic power I may have a low income and a cramped life altogether. Kant's purpose is to justify nature and history to Man rather than men.

Moreover, the notion on which the whole justification hinges, that of a historical teleology, is not very securely established even within Kant's own philosophy. There can be, he argues, no empirical proof of teleology, no proof that history has *a* purpose, let alone this. [17] The empirical world reveals nothing but cause and effect sequences in time, and tells us nothing about any final causes which may govern the process as a whole. A teleological conception of history is a regulative rather than a constitutive idea: we are to see history as a progressive realization of human potentialities, and its goal as the formation of a perfectly just civil society in a federation of such states. But there is, as always in Kant's world, a vertiginous sense of having to make a leap of faith; perhaps we can *make* history the progressive enterprise which Kant depicts, but this is necessarily very different from knowing that this is what history is *meant* to be. One can sympathize with Marx's determination to have nothing to do with any sort of teleology in historical explanation, and with Hegel's efforts at constructing an internal framework to carry the teleology along. Kant has resources to meet such doubts, but these are less arguments in defence of a teleological theory of history, than appeals to men who see the past as Kant depicts it to give that past a new sense by seeing more clearly what their present situation and aspirations are.[18]

The crucial elements in Kant's political philosophy hinge partly on his conception of law, but they somewhat more obviously stem from Rousseau's conception of sovereignty and citizenship. Kant's jurisprudence is very closely tied to his political theory, not merely

[16] ibid., pp. 42–3.
[17] ibid., pp. 51–5.
[18] ibid., p. 51.

in the sense that his account of 'Public Law' contains Kant's most extended discussion of political rights and political participation, in a treatise on the *Elements of Justice* which is otherwise devoted to explaining, above all, the nature of external justice, and in particular the nature of possession and ownership. It is equally a matter of the legalism with which Kant treats political relationships, especially in such contexts as that of revolution, and the right of the ruler to legal immunity.[19] This is one way in which Kantian politics are not particularly 'political' at all; the emphasis rests, not on how leaders can gain support, or how their followers can keep them under control, but upon the structure of formalized legal relationships. Almost the only *political* action which is mentioned is revolution and the establishment or re-establishment of civil society.

The foundation of law lies in the fact that men have interests which they need to protect.[20] Yet Kant does not think that the empirical existence of desires means that law can only be empirically understood. Man as a willing creature is *homo noumenon,* even though the interests he has are those of a man as *homo phenomenon.* The legislative self is that of *homo noumenon,* and the principles of law are the deliverances of reason; in effect, they are the rational rules by which we may regulate interests which we empirically happen to have, and the formalism of the Kantian theory reflects this. In laying out the consequences, Kant has to employ such notions as natural right and the General Will in novel and more philosophically reputable ways than his predecessors had found for them.[21]

It is fruitful to see Kant asking, 'What fundamental principles must underlie any system of law, if it is to be legitimate?', and to see that this is analogous to the question about knowledge which the *Critique of Pure Reason* answers.[22] Thus we find Kant *both* asserting as vigorously as any legal positivist that men only have property in external things when a legal order gives them that property and provides remedies for its loss, *and* asserting that we have to assume a 'natural right' to appropriate unowned things and make them our

[19] ibid., p. 145n.
[20] I. Kant, *The Metaphysical Elements of Justice,* tr. John Ladd (Bobbs-Merrill, Indianapolis, 1965), pp. 33–4.
[21] ibid., pp. 46–7.
[22] ibid., pp. 3–8 (Kant's own preface to the work).

property in a state of nature. The state of nature, again, is for
juridical purposes a logical fiction. Men may, in some respects, still
be *in fact* in a state of nature with respect to subjects of other civil
societies, but Kant only wants to say that, in so far as the property
rights of a present owner are warranted by his acquiring them by
lawful means from previous owners, it must follow that somebody
would have originated these property rights, had he become first
occupier in the state of nature.[23] We have to hang the moral
acceptability of the positive law of any actual legal system on the
principles which would be the only natural principles of right to
govern men in the absence of a formerly constituted legal and
judicial system.

Kant was anxious, as his twentieth-century successors have
been, to retain enough of the notion of a natural law and a natural
right to envisage positive law as preserving and protecting men's
*rights* against one another, without being forced to imagine a
historical state of nature governed by the legislation of God or
Nature. In doing so, he requires something more elaborate than the
very minimal theory of natural right provided by Hart,[24] but not
much more elaborate, and certainly something defended in very
much the same spirit of enquiring into the moral presuppositions of
our capacity to bind ourselves by promise or contract.

Arguing that private law consists of the coercive laws which
secure each man in his possessions, Kant sees all those rights
against other men which we have in virtue of promises or contracts
on their part as 'things' we 'possess'. The intrinsic implausibility of
moving from such ordinary phases as 'I have his promise to do it' to
numbering his promise among my possessions does not really
concern us. For Kant moves on from recognizing that 'meum et
tuum' in general is the subject of justice in its widest sense, to
dealing with the narrower possessory relationship involved in
owning a *thing* as property. In his discussion of marriage and the
family, as well as in his analysis of real property, Kant relies
heavily on the concept of possession, and primarily the concept of
'rational' possession, though he readily finds room for actual
physical control too.[25]

Ownership of things is derived from the concept of possession by

[23]  ibid., pp. 56–60, 65.
[24]  H. L. A. Hart, 'Are there any natural rights?', *Philosophical Review*, 64 (1955), pp. 175–91.
[25]  *Metaphysical Elements of Justice*, p. 57.

way of the observation that a man who claims to own something intends that claim to hold good even if he is not presently in physical control of it; so the kind of possession proper to an owner is not sensible but rational possession.[26] This view of rational possession as central leads to some important consequences.

In the first place, Kant, unlike Locke and Rousseau, does not start from the appropriation and consumption of immediately useful things, and move on to raise the awkward problem of how to derive real property from such a source. He reverses the argument, so that the *intent to occupy* a piece of land or any other object exclusively of all others, and to bring it under one's will, is the basis of ownership. What grows on the land and is immediately usable adheres by ownership to the owner of the land in the same fashion that accidents inhere in substances.[27] This is why Kant refers to the *original* rather than the *primitive* common ownership of a territory as the foundation of property. Kant's point is that for ownership to exist, a community must recognize the owner's intention to control the destiny of a piece of ground – whether societies once recognized common ownership, or family ownership, or anything of the sort is of no concern. Indeed, the fact that private ownership of land is rather recent in many societies make it all the more necessary for Kant to insist on an *original* rather than a *primitive* community; our individual holdings are licensed by a community which has constituted itself one legal community. A society in which there was no private property in land would, for Kant, be defective, because it was primitive; its communal ownership patterns cannot be part of the sufficient or necessary conditions for creating private property. The *original* community of property in contrast amounts to a society's right to assign its members rights to particular pieces of property.[28]

In the second place, the primacy of *ownership* of some sort is an aspect of the relative downgrading of *use*. The Kantian scheme certainly requires that the world should be used by mankind. But once again the thrust of the argument is not towards individual owners acquiring rights by use, as in Locke, but towards showing how mankind as a community can dispose of rights over external things. Kant's method is to argue by an informal *reductio*. Nature

[26] ibid., pp. 56–7.
[27] *Philosophy of Law*, p. 87.
[28] *Metaphysical Elements of Justice*, p. 57.

would not be usable by mankind unless there was some lawful partition of the soil. So it is a presupposition of systems of property that the world is to be made use of. An individual's title does not however stem from his use of property; to have a right is to have the right to exclude others, and to *have* such a right it is only necessary to belong to a community and to take up that right, in the sense of manifesting the intention to restrict the freedom of others, by insisting on that right.[29]

In the third place, this emphasis on the will, and the analysis of possession in terms of an intention to possess, do much to make sense of at least some of the standard modes of acquisition in Roman Law. What it does to illuminate the underlying aim of a system of property rights is much more difficult to determine. That is, just as we may analyse punishment as the inflicting of something disagreeable on a criminal, and so make a retributive element *constitutive* of punishment, leaving open what is the general justifying aim of punishment, so here the role of intention in having an individual right is stressed as part of the analysis of what *constitutes* property, leaving further problems about the justifying aim of the whole system of according people property rights.[30]

It is evident that *some* utilitarian elements enter into that justifying aim. The observations about man's right to use nature, mentioned above, are plainly such. But there are others less readily characterized. For example, Kant holds that the state must possess some kind of reserve authority to alter the principles on which property is held. It is not an act *ultra vires* for a state to deprive religious houses of the right to hold and acquire property. Kant assumes that a society may at one time be committed to a goal which will be served by allowing monastic houses to acquire large holdings of land and other property, but which at another time will be better served by forbidding such acquisitions. And it certainly seems that a society's goals may alter in such a way that the appropriate rules governing ownership ought also to change. If no one believes that masses said for the dead do them or the living much good, a bequest made in order to have masses said for the benefactor's soul may be nullified. This evidently allows Kant to argue that property rights are inviolable *vis-à-vis* any other private

---

[29] ibid., pp. 64–5.

[30] cf. H. L. A. Hart, 'Prolegomena to a Theory of Punishment', in *Punishment and Responsibility* (Clarendon Press, Oxford, 1968), pp. 1–27, esp. pp. 3–13.

citizen but not *vis-à-vis* a legitimate state, and that although such rights are in principle transmittable from one generation to another, there is, without injustice, room for the state to intervene in the name of those principles and goals for whose sake such rights exist in the first place.[31]

In this, Kant is in tune with the spirit of the Declaration of the Rights of Man of 1793, in which property is held to be absolutely immune from interference, save by the state and on grounds of 'public necessity'. As to the extent to which those overriding public goals are utilitarian, it is tolerably clear that they are less concerned with happiness than with freedom, less concerned to make the best instrumental use of natural resources for high standards of living and the like, than to enable as many people as possible to lead responsible, independent existences as free agents.[32] And this sits very easily with the general intention of the *Universal History*. The tension in both places between the collectivist, or species-oriented argument and the individualist account of freedom may be resolved in the suggestion that individuals who confront one another in contractual relationships are best understood as free agents endeavouring to construct the just society which history has in mind for us.

But all this leads Kant into some odd corners. One of the oddest is an analysis of marriage and the family in which the attempt to assimilate personal relationships to possessory ones is carried to an extreme. Roman and other lawyers distinguish between *jus in rem* and *jus ad personam* or between *real* and *personal* rights. Ownership is a right *in rem*, not so much because what one owns must be a *thing*, where its thing-like quality is morally or metaphysically interesting, but because one's right to what one owns is good against all the world, whereas a personal right is good only against some particular person.[33] A contract with Jones only gives me rights against Jones, and not against anyone else, whereas if Jones delivers to me a piece of land, my right to it is good not only against Jones, but against anyone else who may try to deprive me of it. In all legal systems the transfer of ownership of real property has tended to require some actual or symbolic act of taking physical

---

[31] *Kant's Political Writings*, pp. 147–50.
[32] ibid., p. 78.
[33] Nicholas, *Introduction to Roman Law*, pp. 99ff.
[34] *Philosophy of Law*, pp. 114–17.

possession, either in virtue of a physical entry upon the property or some gesture such as accepting a handful of earth.

Kant, for reasons which puzzle all commentators, decided to treat marriage as a (mutual) possessory relationship rather than as a purely personal contractual relationship; but since he set great store by the principle that only *things* and animals (as beings without wills) could be so to speak vacant and ready to acquire a purpose from the will of an owner, there could be no owning of wives and children.[34] There could, however, be a possessory right over them, in so far as they were regarded in a thing-like way as corporeal beings. Accordingly, he devised the category of 'real personal right' which no subsequent legal scholar has ever cared for in the least, to denote the right to have a person – wife, child or servant – under your control and to have them physically brought back under your control if she or they should run away.

The botched quality of this category has been a source of intellectual outrage ever since. But moral outrage rather than intellectual outrage is what greeted Kant's claim that marriage was an arrangement whereby husband and wife mutually leased each other their sexual organs. It is not impossible to see what may have driven Kant to the view – if marriage had to be explained in possessory terms, it was necessary to find something distinctive to be the object of possession. And, equally, it would follow that some act of delivery was required to complete mutual possession, and consummation fitted the bill excellently. What one is to make of it is another matter. There are two obvious views.[35]

One is that Kant is blindly attempting to cramp the realities of East Prussia into a rational and contractual framework which is at odds with them. The individualism of Kant's theory with its modified Roman Law framework simply clashed with a society in which a wife was more or less a chattel of the husband. Such an interpretation of Kant is not to be despised; it seems to gain confirmation from Kant's very feudal-seeming views on the family, where he gives the head of the family real personal rights over both the children and the family's servants, especially when with servants, too, there is a tension between Kant's insistence that the contract of service of a servant had to be of a limited length, and his evident assumption that servants were indentured labourers to be kept under the physical control of their masters. It is a tension

[35] cf. Williams, *Kant's Political Philosophy*, pp. 114–21, 221–41.

between a view appropriate to a universe of employers and employees on the one hand, and a view of the world of masters and servants in the patriarchal family on the other. A Marxian analysis suggests that the incoherent concept of real personal right is simply a reflection in Kant's theory of the incoherent social arrangements of a society which was liberating its conceptions of ownership from the feudal context.[36]

The alternative view would see Kant as entirely and radically committed to the modern world; the insistence on the legal framework of marriage being limited to the enforcement of conjugal rights is one way of saying that love was unregulated by law, and a matter of entirely private judgement and taste. And, even in putting forward his rather bleak view of the legal side of marriage, Kant insists on the reciprocal rights of wives against husbands as much as those of husbands against wives. Still, there must be something odd and unsatisfactory about a discussion of marriage that ends as Kant's does by assimilating extra-marital sexuality to cannibalism.[37]

The political consequences of Kant's legalistic view of the state are baffling in something of the same way, inasmuch as Kant certainly deserved his reputation as Germany's theorist of the French Revolution; yet he went to all lengths to deny the right to revolt, and put forward a defence of passive obedience which would have been old fashioned in England a hundred years before. One can just about see how Kant got into this position. The state existed to defend positive legal rights; to claim a 'right' to revolt seemed to be to claim the right to overthrow the entire basis of rights. In a way, Kant is choosing one horn of a dilemma visible in Locke's account of the right to revolt – for Locke was either saying we had a legal right to revolt, which would be odd, since it was one which no government could conceivably be willing to enforce, or else that we were sometimes morally justified in going outside the letter of the law to re-establish the constitution.[38] Kant had too much of a horror of promise-breaking to accept the second view, and too clear a sense of the connection between legal rights and their enforcement to accept the first. If governments broke their own rules, the subject might engage in passive disobedience, but there was no

---

[36] ibid., pp. 221–8.
[37] *Philosophy of Law*, p. 239.
[38] e.g. *Two Treatises*, II, §§222, 227, pp. 431f., 434.

popular right to revolt. Similarly, since the sovereign was the
source of law, he could not be subject to it too; thus the people
could not do what the English had done and put their King on trial
for his life. He was not personally liable for the crimes of his
government. What Kant did admit as a possibility – and it seems to
be one which serves the purpose of licensing the French in cutting
off the head of Louis XVI – was that a sovereign might have
abdicated and then tried to re-establish himself. At this point, he
would not be the sovereign of his people, but an enemy like any
other.[39]

As I have said before, Kant's emphasis on *legality* means that he
has not very much to say about what one might call the prudential
aspects of constitutional arrangements, about which Locke with his
suggestions for a separation of powers, and Rousseau with his
defence of elective aristocracy and his praise of Roman repub-
licanism, both have a good deal to say. For our purposes all that
need be noted is the rigidity with which Kant confines citizenship
to the owners of property, and the absoluteness of the barrier he
erects between the propertied and non-propertied. Wage earners
*must not* have the vote.[40] In essentials, Kant's case rested on
Rousseau's notion of independence. To have given oneself to all in
the social contract is no infringement of independence, because we
are not dominated by the particular wills of all, rather we are
governed in accordance with general rules which are not so much
chosen as discovered. Dependence is the condition of having to
obey some particular other person.

The property owner, even if he is only a small shopkeeper, is
master of his own goods and able to deal with whomever he
chooses. The wage earner is a man who has had to put himself
under the command of another in order to stay alive. Kant's
examples. of the distinction vary between the perceptive and the
preposterous. Perceptively, he sees the important social consequences stemming from the difference between the European
independent blacksmith, say, who owns his forge, his raw materials
and the finished product, which he then sells, and the Indian
blacksmith who is taken into a princely household and given his
materials and so forth, which are never owned by him.[41] The

[39] *Kant's Political Writings*, pp. 145–6, 82–4.
[40] ibid., p. 78.
[41] ibid., pp. 139–40.

former is the basis for an expanding bourgeoisie, the second is not. The former is, and will see himself as, a rational capitalist in a small way of business, the latter is not, and cannot.

The argument becomes unpersuasive when Kant tries to distinguish between the standing of the barber when he merely comes to shave a customer, and the barber in his role as wig-maker, who may indeed sell me a wig made from hair which he has cut from my head, but who is for the purpose of the suffrage a property owner. To sell a wig is to sell a *thing*, not one's self.[42] Kant's further distinction between the mere private tutor who, again, has no property, and the professor who, it seems, has a sort of property, looks quite incoherent. What Kant has done is something which has been familiar in the twentieth century, namely to move from the claim that a man with property (in the usual sense) has a certain security and independence to the claim that a man with a certain security and independence has property (in an unusual sense).[43] But, in both cases what we have is the familiar spectacle of a dichotomous division of people into dependent/independent superimposed on the discussion of property.

Even so, it is odd that there is no recognition of degrees of security of employment and the like; a landless day labourer, whose security of tenure lasted no longer than sunset, is a very different creature from the worker whose *de facto* security is more or less absolute during good conduct. One might reasonably feel more dubious about enfranchising the former than the latter. Kant may, however, have simply intended to re-echo Rousseau. A public employee such as a professor has given himself to all, rather than to anyone in particular. It is not so much the exchange of *owned things* on a contractual basis to which moral significance attaches, as the extent to which one has to take arbitrary orders. Even then, one might compare Kant's idealized professor with his own experience of Frederick William's censorship of his views on religion.[44]

If, by way of conclusion, one asks *who* would be the ideal citizen of Kant's state, and *what* he would devote his property to, we for once have an unequivocal answer. Kant really was, and knew he was, the defender of the bourgeoisie and *petite bourgeoisie*. In some senses, he was, as Locke was not, the theorist of possessive

---

[42] ibid., p. 78n.
[43] cf. Macpherson (ed.), *Property*, pp. 201–7.
[44] *Kant's Political Writings*, p. 2.

individualism.[45] Independent persons, linked through their possessions, constituted a society which needed and could maintain the
role of law under a republican government. This is not to say that
Kant was the defender of 'unlimited acquisitiveness', or that he saw
particularly far into the workings of a market economy. His ideals
were bourgeois and commercial, not whole-heartedly capitalist, let
alone industrial. What he admired was independence, self-reliance,
and stability, not the amassing of great sums of money or hiring
great armies of workers. And this yields some predictable, but
interesting consequences.

Since, in his eyes, it was essential to have *some* property to be a
citizen, but all men *qua* citizens were equal, Kant demanded a
property franchise, but repudiated any suggestion that men with
more property should have more votes or more influence than men
with less.[46] There is an equality of men *qua* citizens, so long as they
are all qualified *as* citizens, and, as one would expect from Kant,
this is an all or nothing matter. The capacity to give an
independent vote on legislation qualifies one as a citizen, and since
we are reaching for a general will, undisturbed by private interests,
it would be wrong to bias the result by weighing votes according to
wealth or anything else. A striking difference between Kant and the
usual utilitarian view on all this emerges as one would anticipate:
any utilitarian would be bound to fear that enfranchising the non-
propertied would result in one kind of political disorder or another,
as they tried to push through egalitarian legislation, but Kant is
more inclined to argue that the non-propertied simply have *no right*
to vote on taxation and matters affecting the property of others.
Where the utilitarian would see the check of one man's extrava-
gance by another's thrift as a way of squaring the private and the
public interest, Kant makes this reciprocal vulnerability both a
qualification for entry into a system of rights and one of its major
subject matters. None the less, and here too in distinction from
utilitarian benevolence, Kant insists that those he calls *passive
citizens* really are citizens, really have all the *rights* to fair treatment,
equality before the law and the rest which the republican

---

[45] cf. Macpherson, *Possessive Individualism, passim* and Dunn's criticisms, *Political Thought of
Locke*, pp. 204ff.
[46] *Kant's Political Writings*, p. 78.

constitution maintains. Active citizens are morally obliged to vote as they would if passive citizens could vote as well.[47]

The question of what sort of political equality we are left with is difficult to answer. Plainly, Kant has a notion of dependence and independence which ensures that women, for example, will never gain the franchise – though, on Kant's own premises, a woman who was unmarried and owned property in her own name should be perfectly well qualified. The dependence of the labourer on his employer was only one of the varied ways of depending on the will of another and women in general depend on the will of men. But a philosophy of law is bound to have more to say about the machinery of ownership and contract than about more personal dependence and independence. Between husbands and wives there is formal equality, but personal inequality. Between the propertied and non-propertied there is *formal* inequality, an inequality of legal status which is simply transferred into inequality of political standing.[48]

Yet Kant does display a concern that there should be as great a spread of property as possible; in essence, a society which is divided into a few wealthy men and a great mass of unpropertied non-citizens has failed to live up to the political imperative which requires all men so far as possible to enter into civil society, and into lawful relations with one another. Minimal compliance is, no doubt, secured when passive citizens are treated in accordance with the rule of law; but a full compliance would require that we create as many active citizens as possible, and this in turn requires that everyone should be able to acquire property in order to qualify.[49]

What Kant has in mind is that feudal restrictions should not hamper the rise of the bourgeois, rather than that the wage labourer should be able to set up in business on his own account. Like his English and French counterparts of the same date, what Kant is eager to see is that the restrictions imposed by entails, or by limitations on an owner's freedom of testamentary disposition, should all be done away with. To say this is not to accuse Kant of bad faith or to suggest that he was hell bent on excluding wage labourers from political life. It is merely to say that he lived in Königsburg in the eighteenth-century, not Manchester in the

[47] ibid., p. 79.
[48] ibid., p. 78.
[49] ibid., p. 77.

nineteenth. Industrial activity, such as it was, was the province of small groups of artisans, not of an industrial proletariat, and the republican vision of independent artisans and small freeholding farmers was a radical enough contrast with pious absolute monarchy on one hand and the semi-serfdom of *Junkertum* on the other.

# 4

# The Utilitarians: Security and Equality

It is a commonplace among their critics on the left that the English
— in fact rather frequently Scottish — utilitarians were deeply
committed to capitalism, and therefore to unfettered private
property rights, along with freedom of contract, a free market in 'all
commodities including land and labour, and finally the cheapest
possible government machinery to secure them.[1] It is not the aim of
this chapter to deny these claims outright. It is its aim to unsettle
the idea that utility and private property were ever, let alone
always, entirely happy allies. The moral I want to draw has two
branches.

The first is that utilitarianism has rightly had at least an uneasy
conscience about the distribution of income. Although utilitarianism is inhospitable to the concept of desert, the fact that utilitarian
accounts of property rights so often invoke arguments about the
incentive to labour makes it embarrassingly hard to overlook the
way in which those who work hardest generally receive least.[2] In
something of the same vein, the fact that for most people most
goods yield diminishing marginal utility implies that an equal
distribution of goods mazimizes overall utility. If there is redistribution, the loss of utility suffered by the rich man who loses
one unit of income or wealth is smaller than the gain enjoyed by the
poor man to whom that unit is transferred. These distributive
anxieties were certainly fought off by Bentham and James Mill, but
not entirely convincingly; and, being fought off on utilitarian
grounds, they remained ready to be resurrected on utilitarian
grounds, since it is characteristic of utilitarian arguments that they
are reversible in the face of altered factual suppositions.[3]

The second moral will gain in force only when Hegel's anti-
utilitarianism is discussed, but it is that utilitarians do not take
either ownership or possession very seriously as, so to speak,

[1] Karl Marx, *Capital*, vol. I (Penguin, Harmondsworth, 1976), p. 280.
[2] J. S. Mill, *Principles*, II, xvi, 1, p. 383.
[3] e.g., Mill, *Principles*, II, ii, 6, pp. 228ff.

concepts with a moral life of their own. In essence, the utilitarian looks at two things, one the welfare of everyone, the other the pattern of secure expectations which will induce people to work productively and effectively. It is certainly true that utilitarians have always taken very seriously the question of whether a given system of conventional rights and powers over things — i.e. property rights — will have good effects on the general welfare. They have been perhaps too quick to believe in the damaging effects of uncertainty and insecurity on the general welfare, in advance of much in the way of evidence, and perhaps even in contradiction to some of their own premises, and have therefore been quick to defend property. But in none of this have they suggested that ownership implies any special relationship between the will and the world, or between mind and matter; nor are notions such as alienation readily translatable into the lexicon of utilitarian moral and political theory.

That utilitarianism is as readily available to the critic of private property as it is to its defender is evident from Godwin's discussion of property rights in book VIII of his *Political Justice*.[4] Because Godwin initially accepts an absolutely unrestricted form of utilitarianism, even though the argument is couched in terms of rights, he can only conclude that things 'belong' in those hands where they will do most good. The claim that a field belongs to me cannot mean that regardless of the general utility, *I* am entitled to decide what is done with or to the field, who enters on it, what is grown there, and so on. The claim can only mean that I am the steward of the field on behalf of mankind generally. If I am eating something and a hungrier man appears, who cannot be sustained otherwise, then 'my' food is really 'his'; if a more effective or more public spirited farmer appears, then 'my' field is really 'his' as well.[5]

Godwin employs the language of rights because he is a rigorist as well as a utilitarian; I have an absolute duty always and at all times to do what I can for the general welfare, and conversely I have an absolute right to what I need for the purpose. It is this that sustains such unlikely and unlovable doctrines as that of the impropriety of gratitude; if my 'gift' is well bestowed, it will go where it does most

[4] William Godwin, *An Inquiry Concerning Political Justice* (Toronto University Press, Toronto, 1969), II, pp. 420–67.
[5] ibid., II, p. 432.

good, from which it follows that I had a duty to give it and the recipient a right to have it, and hence that gratitude is out of place.[6] If I chose badly, I had no right to act as I did, and the recipient had no right to receive what he did, in which case gratitude is even more out of place — it is like thanking a thief for a present of stolen goods. One argument in favour of the more usual view of property rights by contrast is that in making room for us to give people things that we are entitled but not obliged to give them, property rights can increase the amount of friendliness and mutual good will in the world.[7]

It is evident that Godwin's view amounts to the denial of anything one can call property rights at all; anyone who thinks Godwinian utilitarianism a plausible version of utilitarianism has to accept that utilitarianism is not in principle favourable to property rights. A recent critic of utilitarianism, Robert Nozick, relies very heavily on the view that each of us is in some sense his own man, so much the proprietor of himself as to defeat the claim that we have any general duty to promote any other person's welfare; Godwin's position amounts to the denial of this initial or basic proprietorship.[8]

If there is any proprietor in that sense in his system, it is humanity generally; but even with mankind at large Godwin more commonly employs the language of stewardship. Each of us is steward of himself and what he happens to have; we must act on behalf of mankind generally. That direct applications of the principle of utility have the effect of wiping out what we ordinarily count, or appear to count, as property rights suggests that Hume was correct to argue that when a utilitarian develops an account of justice and property which justifies rights, it must be by way of an argument which shows that the general welfare will be promoted by the creation of artificial rights which, paradoxically, permit people to act on considerations other than a concern with the general welfare.[9]

The major problem which any doctrine as extreme as Godwin's faces is that of the co-ordination of everyone's intentions. Recent

[6] ibid., I, pp. 128–9.

[7] John Charvet, *A Critique of Freedom and Equality* (Cambridge University Press, Cambridge, 1981), pp. 165–71.

[8] *Political Justice*, I, pp. 158ff., II, pp. 433–4.

[9] David Hume, *A Treatise on Human Nature* (Clarendon Press, Oxford, 1888), III, ii, pp. 477ff.

economic theories of property rights have been very concerned to justify private property in terms of management and resources: we — mankind generally — want somebody to be able to co-ordinate the productive activities of numbers of people, and one way of ensuring that somebody can do this is by allocating to people property rights in resources and efforts; the question of what sort of rights these should be under particular conditions is, of course, the technically interesting part of the economists' arguments.[10] But what all such theories show up quite simply is what is missing in Godwin's account.

Godwin certainly saw that something was needed, but his enthusiasm for resting everything on the individual conscience prevented him from giving careful thought to the question of what sort of device for co-ordinating our actions we might invent if we did not care for existing property rights. In the event he rather feebly falls back on insisting that since coercion is the great evil, we must not settle the question of how resources are to be employed by anything that smacks of brute force.[11] This means that if I am eating my dinner and you cannot persuade me that your hunger gives you more claim to it, then I may carry on undisturbed; and, equally, if you cannot persuade me that the quality of your husbandry trumps my present occupancy of the field I am ploughing, you must leave me in possession. This, however, seems to leave the first comer more securely in possession than he is in theories — such as Herbert Spencer's say — which are generally much more friendly to outright individual proprietorship, but which propose an equal right to acquire property too.[12]

All this may suggest that Godwin is simply too eccentric a thinker to show anything very serious about utilitarianism and ownership. But this would go too far; Godwin was not an isolated utilitarian critic of private property. Robert Owen, an admirer of Godwin, is a better known one, and J. S. Mill is a much better organized one, but a good deal of the argument recurs in many different writers. Fundamentally, utilitarianism is inimical to proprietorship in the simple sense that on any occasion when somebody employs resources in a way that does not benefit everyone, the reply 'it was *his* to do what he liked with' is not

---

[10] Donald Regan, *Utility and Co-operation* (Clarendon Press, Oxford, 1981), ch. I.
[11] *Political Justice*, II, p. 434.
[12] Spencer, *Social Statics*, pp. 112ff.

conclusive.[13] In Godwin's work, the unwillingness to accept what we would ordinarily call rights, i.e. options one can take up at will, is extreme; but in Mill, much later, there is a sustained effort to detach personal liberties such as the right to say what you think from property rights, precisely so that 'he has a right to speak his mind' will be conclusive and 'it's *his*' will not be.[14] Individual property rights *must*, to be rights at all, trump most claims most of the time, and even the claims of government some of the time; but they are not good against the considerations which warrant establishing them in the first place. Bentham's account of those considerations and what they entail is about as brief and, up to a point, as persuasive as anything in the tradition.

It is supporting evidence for the claim that utilitarianism is not attached to ownership as such that Bentham tackles property rights in particular and at length only in his *Theory of Legislation* — a slightly suspect work which was assembled from Bentham's manuscripts by his French editor Dumont.[15] The discussion, however, is exemplary in the way it makes systematic use of the apparatus of utilitarianism. It is, therefore, no surprise that Bentham's account includes such observations as that the notion of an interest is wider and more general than the notion of property, so that understanding what we want to protect by institutionalizing property rights requires us first to disentangle the interests with which we are concerned.[16]

It is also no surprise that Bentham's account of the goals to be promoted by the legal system is couched in terms of promoting security, equality, subsistence and abundance. One might wonder at the inclusion of both abundance *and* subsistence, but Bentham is forearmed. It is not that abundance comprehends subsistence, so that the attainment of general abundance would entail the attainment of subsistence for everyone too. In Bentham's mind, the prospect of abundance is held out only to a small portion of the population.[17] The chance of affluence for unskilled manual workers lay very long way in the future; so far as Bentham was concerned, labourers could expect a modest comfort, perhaps to save a little,

[13] Alan Ryan, 'Utility and Ownership', in R. G. Frey (ed.), *Utility and Rights* (Blackwell, Oxford, 1984), pp. 261ff.
[14] *Utilitarianism etc.*, pp. 150–5.
[15] Jeremy Bentham, *Theory of Legislation* (Trubner, London, 1887).
[16] ibid., pp. 93–5.
[17] ibid., pp. 113–14.

but not to achieve anything properly described as abundance. Bentham's intention is twofold. The first point he makes is that there is nothing to be gained from limiting the wealth of the wealthy. But it is characteristic of Bentham that he defends the abundance of the wealthy because it provides a resource for the whole community in time of trouble. All societies face bad harvests or other natural hazards; primitive societies must often have been entirely wiped out by starvation for lack of a layer of fat to fall back on.[18] Unlike Rousseau and other eighteenth-century critics of luxury, Bentham sharply insists that developed societies have insulated themselves against natural calamity in a way that no rational man could complain of. The second point is one that Bentham makes much more elaborately, and is indeed the point on which the utilitarian account of property rights must hang. To do no more than mention it here, it is the claim that the abundance of the wealthy, and resulting inequality is the inevitable result of the security of property; without property, there would be no general guarantee of subsistence, without security there would be no property. Without abundance for some, there would be less certainty of subsistence for all.[19]

Bentham is curiously reluctant to go far into the definition of property. He makes several points, however, which are of some importance. One which is particularly well taken is his denial that the absoluteness of our rights over an object illuminates its status as property. Anticipating later writers, he points out that if I might do absolutely what I liked with my property, it would follow that if I chose to strike someone on the head with my walking stick, I could resist anyone who stopped me by pointing out that it was my stick and that I could therefore do as I chose with it. As a later writer says in this vein, the fact that my knife is mine means that I can put it where I like, but not in your chest.[20]

There are several ways in which the point can be made. One familiar one, which we find in Kant and Spencer, is to argue that each man's freedom of action is limited by the same freeom of all other men, and by extension that what I may do with an object is limited to what is consistent with the similar rights of everyone

[18]  ibid., p. 101–2.
[19]  ibid., p. 102.
[20]  ibid., p. 124n.

else.[21] Bentham, of course, will have no truck with this sort of semi-contractual view; it is part and parcel of the view of liberty enshrined in the Declaration of the Rights of Man where it is claimed that liberty is the right to do what we choose without harming others. Bentham insists that the liberty to do evil is as much liberty as liberty to do good.[22]

Law works by curtailing liberty, so even where the point of a law is to preserve freedom, it does do by curtailing freedom. What liberty men should have is a question in censorial jurisprudence to be dealt with on utilitarian grounds; what interests in objects should be so protected by law that they become property rights is similarly a question to be settled by censorial jurisprudence. There is no prospect of settling the question by asking what property 'really' is along the lines of asking what 'real' liberty amounts to. To own something is to have the most extensive rights in it that the law offers; what these are in any given system is a matter of fact, what they ought to be is a moral matter.[23]

This is part and parcel of the general antipathy to theories of natural rights which Bentham's work displays. If there were such a thing as natural right, it would be impossible ever to establish governments, since nothing but genuine consent and a transfer of rights by each individual could create legitimate authority — and such consent cannot be had. Similarly, natural property rights would imply governmental bankruptcy, since governments could not legitimately tax their subjects, and would have to rely on contributions they each and individually agreed to make. Bentham dismissed all this as the anarchical fallacy, and it is a tribute to his percipience that modern libertarians are so often natural rights anarchists.[24] Property is entirely the product of the law; 'no property no law' is a logical truth, not a contingent observation about the chances of hanging on to one's property in the absence of enforcement.

What the legislator has to work with is the facts of human and

---

[21] See Declaration of the Rights of Man and of Citizens, article IV.

[22] *Theory of Legislation*, p. 94.

[23] This is the basis of the distinction between 'expository' and 'censorial' jurisprudence on which Bentham was so insistent: J. Bentham, *An Introduction to the Principles of Morals and Legislation* (Athlone Press, London, 1970), pp. 293–5.

[24] e.g. Murray Rothbard, *For a New Liberty* (Collier Macmillan, New York, 1978), for a defence of the absolute minimum of state authority; Nozick, *Anarchy, State and Utopia*, takes a similar line.

non-human nature. There is, for example, no need for the legislator to require men to attend to their own subsistence; their natural desire to stay alive, and the world's recalcitrance unless they devote some effort to extracting their subsistence from it, combine to press men to work for subsistence. What the legislator does have to do is ensure that men can enjoy the results of their efforts. They will otherwise find the natural incentive not operating, since the cause and effect relationship between work and subsistence and non-work and non-subsistence would be broken.[25]

This suggests the general line of Bentham's case. He rests almost everything on expectation. Property is mostly about expectation; and Bentham all but defines it as a basis for expectation. There are two sorts of expectations, those which exist prior to law or naturally, and those which are the creation of the law. The fact that law creates expectation is a source of happiness, and also a potential source of unhappiness. Expectation is itself enjoyable, and by creating expectation the law creates happiness directly. Thus, by assuring me that I shall be able to live in my own house when I choose, the law gives me the pleasure of anticipation now, even if I shall not actually live there for some time.[26]

The same thing applies to inheritance: before I inherit I have the pleasure of looking forward to my inheritance, and my parents have the pleasure of looking forward to my future enjoyment of their property. This possibility of pleasure is bought at a price, however, for if the pleasures of anticipation are sweet, the pains of disappointed expectation are particularly severe. There are many things which we should not much miss if we never had them, which we should very much miss if we had had them and had lost them. The disappointment of expectation is thus one of the things we should guard against in legislation; innovations by the legislator will almost inevitably disturb some expectations, and skill is required to minimize these disappointments. One of the things on which almost all utilitarians, other than utopians like Godwin, agree is that there is an asymmetry between gains and losses; losses do not simply leave us where we were before, but make us much worse off.[27]

Not all expectations are created by law, and those that are need a

---

[25] *Theory of Legislation*, pp. 110–14.
[26] ibid., p. 113.
[27] ibid., p. 111, pp. 148ff.

natural foundation. It is natural for a child to expect to enjoy the property of his parents. He has lived with the owners and surrounded by their possessions, and gets into the habit of seeing his own future bound up with them. The parents, too, project their present concern for the child into the future, and if nothing disturbs them expect him to enjoy their goods in due course. So the law has raw material in the form of expectations to work on.

In general, Bentham's position is to require the legislator to reinforce natural expectations. There is a presumption in favour of confirming a present possessor in his possession if there is no better legal title in contention; once a man has something in his possession, he will hope to continue in possession and to enjoy whatever it is. The law has to work against his natural inclinations if it sets out to deprive him, so there has to be some overriding good to set against his disappointment. Hence in the absence of any contending title he should be confirmed in possession. The man who finds a diamond in a field, say, will feel inclined to hang on to it since he can readily hide it until he has a chance to pass it off as having come his way by a proper transfer; he will feel attached to it in a personal fashion because he found it or dug it up or whatever. Accordingly, there is a strong case for making it his unless some better title already exists.[28]

It is clear enough from this how Bentham's position accommodates in other terms much of what preoccupied Locke or Kant. There is nothing 'special' about the embodiment of the labour of one's body and the work of one's hands in external objects. First occupancy, first possession by working, taking or whatever, can all found a title by reference to the general objects of law and the nature of property. There is no emphasis on our wills, no emphasis on our standing as uniquely free moral agents. A common-sense understanding of ordinary human needs and wants, and a common-sense acceptance of everyday ambitions underpin the theory. Institutions do not express human capacities, and they are not to be understood by reference to the hidden purposes of history. A positivist view of law allows the theorist to stand back and enquire how well or badly the legal recognition of various interests in things of value will promote the several elements of the utilitarian goal.[29]

[28] ibid., p. 159.
[29] ibid., pp. 1ff.

In contrast to Locke again, the account is wholly secular. There is no sense of the world being God's gift, no sense of man owing God a duty of care, development and rational use of the world. It takes no very great attachment to Lockean Christianity to make one wonder whether Bentham does not read back into human nature many of the aspirations which Locke tried to represent as our minimal debt to our maker. However that may be, what is striking in Bentham is not that he writes in what, two hundred years later, looks like a simple and commonsensical fashion, but that he so completely breaks out of the theological and natural-law framework of his predecessors.

The main interest of Bentham's arguments lies in his worries about the conflict between the goals of security and equality.[30] The premises are familiar to us, but original in Bentham. There seems at first sight no particular reason for Bentham to concern himself with *equality*. That is, there is no particular reason for Bentham to regard equality as a value. The slogan 'each to count for one and nobody for more than one' is not in itself an egalitarian slogan, since the meaning it bears is only that since it is pleasures and pains which we are counting, the unit of account, so to speak, is the unit of pleasure and pain, not the social standing of the person whose pleasure and pain it is.[31] What, of course, one might expect Bentham to be in favour of is something like the welfare state – and it is not uncommon for people who are really advocates of a welfare state to be thought to be egalitarians. But they certainly need be nothing of the sort; and in general, the obvious loyalty of utilitarianism is to welfare rather than equality – the crux being that no utilitarian would think it was worth accepting a lower level of welfare for the sake of greater equality; few egalitarians would prefer an equality of misery to general prosperity combined with a moderate degree of inequality, but most egalitarians would think some sacrifice of welfare for the sake of equality a permissible exchange. Bentham was well placed to argue that people who cannot manage to look after themselves should be looked after by the state – and he did argue just this, claiming that governments are like insurance companies, in so far as they properly require us

[30] ibid., pp. 100–23.
[31] This is not to say that their social standing will not affect the amount of pleasure and pain they feel upon a given stimulus; see Bentham, *Introduction to Principles of Morals and Legislation*, pp. 51–72.

to put in our premiums in the shape of taxes in order to insure ourselves against the risk of destitution.[32]

Bentham's arguments are both sensible and humane. He admits that some people may think that destitution in old age is both the just reward for earlier improvidence and a valuable deterrent example to set before rash young people, but he will have none of this. In the first place most people will not be able to save enough, and many will simply meet with misfortune that no amount of providence would avert. And the deterrent impact on the young of the misery that the poor suffer in old age will be minimal; the young will not identify themselves with the elderly and will not feel the deterrent, while it is in any event unjust to threaten such long-delayed retribution. Minimal welfare state provisions thus flow quite naturally from Bentham's premises.[33]

But these are not in themselves arguments for equality. There are, however, some conflicts between these considerations and one interpretation of security. An interpretation which identified security with an absolute immunity even to taxation thought of as premiums for an insurance policy would conflict with such taxes. But there are two things to be said about this, both of which Bentham does say. The first is that on any such interpretation security is in conflict with itself, a conclusion to which Bentham perfectly happily subscribes, believing as he emphatically did that liberty could only be protected by curtailing liberty.[34]

To secure our property we must evidently have governments, policemen and soldiers, who cannot be supported except by taxes on the productive property of everyone else. To preserve our immunity to attacks and thefts by private individuals, we must surrender our immunity at least to the exent of paying taxes for law and order and defence. The second point takes up this argument by reminding us that reliability and predictability are the crucial virtues of government action. We can, if we know in advance what sort of taxes we are liable to, plan our lives with as much certainty as in any other conditions. If, say, the tax is a tax on property rather than income, the value of the property will reflect its liability to tax; it will be less valuable to a buyer or a seller than it would be without the liability, but nobody's expectations are frustrated by

[32] *Theory of Legislation*, pp. 127–33.
[33] ibid., p. 132.
[34] ibid., pp. 124–5.

the tax's existence. Sudden or arbitrary levies would, of course, have this damaging and disturbing effect. Thus, while there are very good reasons for taxing property to provide for the un-employed or the ill or whatever, it is also important that these taxes should fall predictably and calculably.[35]

One way in which this argument for what one could call the minimal welfare state begins to turn into an argument from equality is by way of the consideration that the needs of those in distress are so much greater, that is, more urgent and more exacting, than the needs of the better off, that anything transferred from the better off to the hard pressed will do more good to the recipients than the loss of it will do harm to the better off — assuming, all along, that the method of transfer does not itself affect the computation.[36] Bentham subscribes to the more elaborate doctrine which lies behind this commonsensical point, which has long been known as the theory of diminishing marginal utility; this gives his views on equality a general interest, of course, but here we need pick up only a few points about them. The main point, to which we will shortly come, is the speed with which he defuses the egalitarian implications of the theory of diminishing marginal utility.[37] But by way of preface two other points may be made. One is that Bentham is ready to include among the contributions of equality to the general welfare even such dubious pleasure as the pleasure of the poor in the sufferings of the rich. An equalizing measure may give pleasure to the worse off just because they are glad to see the previously well off lose out, and Bentham does not do what many of the developers — or refurbishers — of utilitarian-ism subsequently do by denying even a prima-facie claim to satisfaction to such misanthropic desires.[38]

There are excellent reasons for not satisfying malicious wishes, and there are excellent reasons for trying to get people to repress such wishes in the first place. None the less, in any actual social order there will be some room for the pleasures of gratified envy, and those pleasures are one argument for equalizing measures. The other point worth noting is that Bentham's egalitarianism is not an

[35] ibid., p. 132n.
[36] ibid., pp. 104–5.
[37] ibid., pp. 120–2, but cf. p. 123.
[38] Jan Narveson, *Morality and Utility* (Johns Hopkins University Press, Baltimore, 1976), pp. 161ff.

egalitarianism of rights: he mocks all such doctrines as beneath contempt — do they mean that the highwayman and his victim have an equal right to the victim's wallet? Do they mean children and parents should have the same say in running the family? And if not, what rational meaning can they bear that is not better elicited by utilitarian considerations?[39] It is, for all that, an egalitarianism which has some of the same social implications as the rights-based egalitarianism he rejects.

Bentham insists that the rich man's porter feels as acutely as the rich man himself; the equality of mankind in Bentham's version of it might plausibly be called the doctrine of the identity of the human nervous system. Human nature is uniform and the capacity for pleasure and pain is no respecter of social distinctions.[40] What this means, then, is that when we calculate the benefits of a law or a policy, we must count *all* its consequences; it does not matter in whom a quantum of pleasure or pain inheres, only what that quantum amounts to. We should not ask whether the porter has an equal right to his pleasure or a right to equal pain. What he *has* a right to is a question of what the law says he has a right to; but what the legislator who employs the utilitarian calculus to guide him in creating rights must do is count any given quantity of pleasure to the porter with the same seriousness as he counts the same quantity of pleasure to his employer. That the porter will have less pleasure in total than his employer is taken for granted by Bentham for the porter will have fewer of the world's goods, though he also takes for granted the obvious ways in which one's expectations and habits of comparison will drastically affect one's happiness. He is not blind to the fact that the meal which costs the nobleman a porter's monthly wage will not give to the nobleman his employee's monthly quota of pleasure at the table.[41] The crucial point is that the justification of the way the system of property rights allocated happiness lies in the total amount of happiness it produces, and that in making the calculation the happiness of every person must be counted with no attention to *whose* happiness it is.

This, though, brings us to the crux. If the theory of diminishing marginal utility is true, the only distribution of goods with any serious claim on the legislator's attention must be an equal

[39] *Theory of Legislation*, p. 99.
[40] Or not very much anyway — ibid., pp. 33–48.
[41] ibid., p. 104.

distribution. If transfers from those with more to those with less yield more happiness to those who receive than they take away from those who lose, it follows that for a given stock of goods an equal distribution is uniquely right, because it is uniquely efficient.[42] Now, it is instantly obvious that any such conclusion is vulnerable from an indefinite number of directions. The moment we introduce differences of taste, or differences in our ability to derive pleasure from what we have, the tidiness of the argument collapses, and we are obliged to find a narrower version of the principle or some more technical definition of a good to save ourselves. (We might say that only something which does obey the law of diminishing marginal utility is a 'good' for an economist's purposes, and so on.)

Bentham, however, is not interested in the by-ways of welfare economics or the theory of rational choice. Here, at least, he is offering advice only to the legislator; hence, he allows himself some (acceptable) qualifications. The legislator makes laws for most people under most circumstances; and by implication, though not explicitly, we are to think of an economy in which goods are all readily bought and sold, so an acceptable rule of thumb is that for most people money income yields diminishing utility at the margin. This means that, whatever the technical interest of twentieth-century discussions of 'utility monsters' − that is, persons who are supposed to derive either no utility from what they possess or consume, or who derive extraordinary and undiminishing amounts of pleasure, and, therefore, induce counter-intuitive consequences for analyses of optimum distributions − they do not touch Bentham's case.[43] At least, they do not touch the case he offers. Of course, if we can show that for some goods − education, say, or the fine arts − all of us are utility monsters to some extent, we can begin to argue for so many exceptions to Bentham's general case that we may make the whole utilitarian scheme look thin or silly.

But Bentham readily accepts a version of the theory of diminishing marginal utility which he thinks strong enough to yield a presumption in favour of equal possessions. This is perhaps less surprising in view of what follows, because the point of making a strong case for equality is to show how that case is overwhelmed by arguments from security. It does not matter to Bentham if the case

---

[42] *Theory of Legislation*, p. 104.
[43] ibid., p. 103.

for equality is weaker than he supposes. Still, it would be wrong to press this thought too hard, for Bentham does in fact find some room for governments to pursue egalitarian policies in providing for security. If an owner dies intestate and with no near heirs, for example, the estate should go to the crown for redistribution; in the absence of near heirs no expectations have been aroused, and a man who could not be bothered to make a will can hardly have had expectations whose frustration would cause generalized alarm.[44]

But broadly speaking Bentham's argument is simply that constant redistributive efforts to achieve equality would so frustrate expectations that even those who get least out of the existing system and might anticipate doing well out of greater equality would suffer over the long run. The argument is one which has recurred in the twentieth century. In one way or another a version of the argument is to be found in such diverse writers as von Hayek, Rawls and Nozick.[45] And writers who begin with not even a prima-facie argument in favour of equality find themselves arguing along the same lines. Even the natural rights theorist whose first line of defence against the egalitarian is to claim that what the egalitarian tries to lay hands on for himself or others is simply *not his* to lay hands on at all, generally tries to back this up with utilitarian arguments about why the egalitarian — or his 'clients' — should accept the rights of current owners as morally compelling.

The argument is that anyone inventing a hypothetical legal order to promote the welfare of an anonymous individual who, by hypothesis, will be relatively badly off would do well to invent an order where property rights are securely entrenched.[46] For there the worst off will do better than in any other system. Of course, some actual named individual might do better out of any amount of unheaval — Al Capone would do well out of civil war and general mayhem — but under the constraint of having to choose on behalf of a random rather than a specially picked individual, the argument is plausible.

The argument offered by Bentham is not an argument in favour of anything so narrow as capitalism. There is an implicit argument

[44] ibid., pp. 122, 177ff.
[45] Nozick, *Anarchy, State and Utopia*, chs 7 & 8; Rawls, *Theory of Justice*, pt 1; F. A. von Hayek, *The Mirage of Social Justice* (Routledge & Kegan Paul, London, 1976).
[46] Rawls, *Theory of Justice*, pp. 266–76; and see too *Theory of Legislation*, pp. 118–19 for a panegyric on security.

perhaps — Bentham relies on arguments from incentive which simply presume that individuals can sell their own labour and that property owners can employ whomever they want at whatever wages they can agree. But this would be of extreme casualness if it were meant as a defence of capitalism.[47] Of course, Bentham wrote energetically and defiantly in defence of usury and adopted an uncompromisingly hostile view of government regulation of economic activity. It is widely accepted that Halévy's claim — that Bentham's utilitarianism is no respecter of individuality, but in his hands is, in England anyway, an instrument of individualist *laissez-faire* — hits the mark.[48] All the same, Bentham's defence is not a defence of capitalism, but a defence of everyone being allowed to pursue his own good in his own way. Bentham shows no anxiety to legitimize *profits* as a form of income, and it seems clear that any articulate defence of capitalism must either provide such a defence or a way of blunting the supposed need for one. In Marxist terms, one can see Bentham defending merchants' profits and interest, but not the profit that Marx insisted arose in the process of production and was only realized in exchange.[49]

Bentham's argument is simple, vulnerable to erosion, and attractive to anyone who does not want to defend all-or-nothing capitalism or all-or-nothing socialism. In essence, the claim is that since there are no natural titles of ownership, they may be created in any way the legislator chooses; rationally he should so choose that utility is maximized; *ceteris paribus*, utility *is* maximized when almost anything can be bought and sold at prices agreed by willing buyers and willing sellers, and the system of property rights should therefore facilitate such a commerce. This argument is standard in recent accounts of the economic theory of property rights.[50]

Once it is launched, we have a series of cruces at which arguments may occur: for example, we may for overriding moral reasons not wish to create property titles in human beings even though we may want to allow each person a property right in his own efforts and thus allow him to sell his services to another; we

---

[47] Apart from much else, consider how much time he spends in discussing the game laws — ibid., pp. 165ff.

[48] E. Halévy, *The Growth of Philosophical Radicalism* (Faber & Faber, London, 1955), pp. 102ff.

[49] Marx, *Capital*, vol. I, introducution, pp. 32–3.

[50] Harold Demsetz, 'Towards a Theory of Property Rights', *American Economics Review*, 57 (1976), pp. 347–59.

may wish to take the physical human being out of the realm of property by distinguishing very clearly between assaults and damage to property or by refusing to accept as enforceable contracts such things as my agreeing to sell you my left arm whenever you would like to buy it.

Again, we may think that even in those areas where the existence of a market is morally acceptable, we will find many cases where the assumption that contracting partners each know what they are doing simply fails — cases where one party is excessively unworldly, cases where they may be too volatile in their wants, cases where they are ignorant of alternatives which are better by their own standards and which are readily available to them; in some of these we may interfere to improve the market, in others interfere to abolish it.[51]

Again, bargains are not made without cost, and sometimes there will be a bargain unmade because there is no way of splitting the cost of making it between the beneficiaries; or there may be economies of scale in making the transactions in question, but unless someone expedites these transactions in a professional fashion they will either not be made or will be made expensively. Here, too, governments may intervene in a variety of ways, either by bearing the costs and recouping them through taxation, or by inventing legal forms which encourage entrepreneurs to set up in the same sort of business.[52]

It cannot be said that Bentham goes far along such a path. Nor can it be said that he should have done. What he was very largely concerned to do was to show how the law of property, which was in his day amazingly complex and expensive to operate, could be brought into order. Nobody reading an account of the complexity of eighteenth-century conveyancing could doubt that Bentham was doing enough in demanding that governments formulate a legal code which would tell everyone whether what he supposed was his property was really such, without fear of excessive and long drawn out litigation. Although Bentham's defence of security was primarily directed against the egalitarian pressures of the doctrine of diminishing marginal utility, the ultimate point of the whole discussion is to show how security can be provided by the law, and

---

[51] Mill, *Principles of Political Economy*, V, xi, pp. 936–71.
[52] ibid., V, xi, II, pp. 954ff.

how the insecurity of a badly designed legal system is a real insecurity and to be deplored as such.

Given that the benefits of property require the sacrifice of the claims of equality to those of security, we should anticipate that Bentham would adopt a generally conservative view about introducing change in the system, and so he does. We have already seen that he allows the state to step in in cases of intestacy only because there are no expectations to be disappointed, and we find him applying the same principle more generally.

Where an evil is to be remedied, the present beneficiaries should not — unless they got the benefit by criminal means — be the losers.[53] An example which will illustrate the general moral to which so much of my discussion has been directed is that of slavery. Unlike Kant, and unlike anyone of a natural rights persuasion, Bentham cannot and does not argue that persons simply cannot be property. He does not even suggest that there is something odd and anomalous about slavery in that a slave is treated as a mere thing — i.e. utterly non-responsible, *qua* owned object — and yet is criminally liable on his own behalf — i.e. responsible as a person.[54]

Anything in which the law creates a title can be owned, and that is that. None the less, when he discusses slavery Bentham hardly stops to bandy utilitarian considerations at all. He resorts to something more like the arguments we find today in Hare or Rawls. He declines to take seriously the arguments of the defenders of slavery on the grounds that they would not risk changing places with the slave no matter what. This is, of course, much nearer a pure argument from justice than an argument from utility, since it amounts to saying that we have no right to impose on others institutional burdens which we would not risk imposing on ourselves.[55]

But if there are slaves already, and their owners have bought them in good faith in a lawful market, it is not upon their owners that the loss of emancipation should fall. This turns out not to be an argument about the *distribution* of the burdens of emancipation,

[53] *Theory of Legislation*, pp. 207–8.

[54] cf. Hegel, *Philosophy of Right*, §57, pp. 47–8.

[55] *Theory of Legislation*, pp. 202–4; but it would not do to exaggerate the point — Bentham is mostly eager to denounce those who suggest that slaves might not dislike their condition, and the fact that nobody would swap places with a slave is for him proof positive that the slave's state is a miserable one.

however much it may look to be heading that way. (One might in passing note that it is quite a good argument about that, so long as we do not flinch at the idea of an innocent slave-owner or an innocent sinecure holder, and that the British experience of emancipation, where the slave-owners in the West Indies were bought out rather than simply expropriated, suggests that it was quite widely attractive.) Bentham's argument is solidly utilitarian: the pangs of loss are very severe; the contaminating effects of fear of expropriation are very damaging; accordingly, we should wait until present beneficiaries depart the scene before we wholly abolish the benefit.

He backs up such considerations by a piece of common sense which has subsequently acquired the grander title of 'the theory of relative deprivation', which observes that discontent and envy are mostly produced by comparisons we make with those who are only very little better off than we. The poor man does not feel deprived when he sees the nobleman's castle, but when he sees his neighbour's additional kitchen chair or whatever; whether there is anything special about freedom which suggests that similar arguments do *not* apply to slavery, he does not say, but it looks as if he does not think so.[56] Other writers, of course, have been eager to claim that being a slave is quite unlike being free but poor. Considerations about the painlessness of poverty for those who have been inured to it and who do not much compare their lot except with others in much the same state are held to be merely irrelevant or even insulting to those whose whole standing as human beings is so desperately damaged by their status as slaves.

Anyone who subscribes to such a view will perhaps be more moved by the thought that the slave owners are no wickeder than their non-slave-owning fellow citizens and should not suffer all the loss involved in the abolition of slavery; but he is equally likely to think that the slave-owner has bought something on a par with the right to abuse and maltreat another, and therefore cannot shelter behind comparative considerations any more than a murderer can shelter behind the equal wickedness of other murderers and non-murderers. The lesser injustice is a very small price to pay for remedying a larger evil. At all events, what we can see is that the utilitarian calculus cannot without supplementary resources simply rule out slave ownership as morally wholly impermissible.

[56]  ibid., pp. 201–9, but cf. p. 206.

By the same token, Bentham does not devote very much attention to many of the familiar anxieties and interests of political theorists of property. The labourer's labour is not sacred; there is no suggestion that the ownership of immovable property plays a special role in fitting men for political life, whether by way of creating the armed peasant militias of Machiavelli's republican daydreams or by way of anchoring major economic interests to their estate as in standard Tory thinking.[57] In a way, Bentham was quick, or too quick, to credit everyone with his own cool, sceptical rationality; he could certainly identify corruption, venality and superstition, but he did so by reference to the rational pursuit of everyone's happiness, not by reference to the military virtues and austere civic spirit of the Romans or the Spartans. To all this, we must attach one important qualification: Bentham was as well aware as anyone that people were inclined to proportion their allegiance to the extent to which governments secured their 'legitimate' interests, but he was not committed to the view that some sorts of interest were specially potent.

None the less, he recognized that one important feature of property is the extent to which we see something of ourselves in it. The things we have made, the houses in which we have lived, the fields we have farmed, all have in them some part of ourselves says Bentham, and it is this which justifies tenderness towards the fears of owners for the security of their property. The point towards which it is worth at any rate gesturing here, though, is that this personal attachment is neither built into Bentham's account of the concept of property nor taken as a starting point in the explication and justification of private property.[58]

This is much the same point which we have already had occasion to make in connection with Bentham's emphasis on enjoyment and pleasure as opposed to freedom and the will. What it leaves out will become clearer in our subsequent account of Hegel. But recognition of it now may be enough to suggest the breadth and depth of the gulf which separates Bentham and utilitarian positivism from their continental critics. The idea of analysing the legal arrangements which uphold property rights and examining their consequences for social and economic life in terms of a collective human

[57] Machiavelli, *The Discourses*, pp. 102–4; Edmund Burke, *Reflections on the Revolution in France* (Penguin, Harmondsworth, 1974), p. 140.
[58] *Theory of Legislation*, pp. 96–7, but cf. p. 115.

project of self expression, or looking for a hidden rationality in the course of history, is wholly foreign to Bentham, and indeed to any utilitarian who has not been to some extent infected by the romantic influences which made J. S. Mill's views so much richer and so much less tidy than those of his mentors.

This, of course, is not to say that Bentham had no feeling for the importance of history — he certainly knew that time and place made a difference. None the less, there is a sense in which history for him has only two epochs. In one of them men are rational, well informed and benevolent; the other epoch embraces all ages in which they are not. The enlightened legislator sees his task as getting his subjects from the second stage to the first as painlessly as possible, and once in the first epoch as providing efficient and economical rules for their conduct of their own business. One need not be a Marxist to find it rather a thin and mechanical view of the matter. Indeed, there is much to be said for the view that Marx himself strays rather close to Bentham's urge to simplify matters, and that a conservative like Hegel, or like the English Idealists much later, is the most persuasive critic of this simplicity.[59]

On the social, political and, if the anachronism is not absurdly grating, what we may call the industrial relations and job satisfaction consequences of all this, we can be fairly brisk. It is in James Mill's *Essay on Government* that we get the pure political doctrine associated with the concern for equality and security. In a world where human and natural resources alike are inadequate to human wants, that is, where scarcity is and always will be, the order of the day, the chief task of social organization, is to guarantee to each man as large a portion as possible of the product of his labour.[60]

This seems to be intended as a simple argument from incentive, though Mill may also have inclined more than Bentham towards the view that a man's own labour is more or less sacrosanct as his property. At all events, the dilemma of all government emerges very promptly: the need for government arises because men are tempted to acquire what they want by taking it from those who have got it already; they need to be deterred from so doing, but anyone with enough power to deter them may succumb to the same

[59] Charles Taylor, *Hegel and Modern Society* (Cambridge University Press, Cambridge, 1979), pp. 140 onwards for a criticism of the thinness of Marxism and Enlightenment thinking.
[60] Mill, *Essay on Government*, p. 49.

temptation. Power enough to deter prospective thieves is power enough to make theft attractive to its possessors; more than one village has placed itself under the protection of a warlord only to find his depredations worse than those of the bandits he was hired to fight.[61]

By a variety of moves which need not detain us here, Mill concludes that the only way to make sure that the temptations of power are not too much for the government to resist is to make the government accountable to the people at large. The whole people can hardly have a settled interest in oppressing itself. Its vote will therefore reflect the general interest and not some sinister interest, and democracy will therefore promote security. As a rhetorical move, this was more impressive than is apparent to a twentieth-century reader who is accustomed to using ideas from the theory of games in thinking about politics and who can spot the fallacy of composition a mile off.

For although in a sense this is an argument about cost-benefit calculation, it is also an argument which denies the existence of an old dilemma. The old dilemma suggested that governments could choose popular liberty and democracy or they could choose stability, security and the protection of property, but they could not choose both. The price of security and stability was a monopoly of political power by the propertied and preferably by those with substantial landed property.[62] Mill denied this outright. To deny it, he had to beg the question against the peculiar virtues of *landed* proprietorship, and to make two assumptions that were not usually made very explicit. The first was that the distribution of objects of value (which covers anything ownable without distinguishing between income and wealth) could and should be made to approximate a lozenge pattern, rather than a steeply rising pyramid — or to put it another way, that there should be an overwhelming majority of the population somewhere around the mean income. That this is a requirement for stable government goes back to Aristotle and on to Seymour Martin Lipset; it amounts to requiring that there should not be a mass of very badly off inhabitants who have almost no stake in the system, and who could look to benefit from almost any conceivable redistribution — at any

[61] ibid., p. 50.
[62] Dickinson, *Liberty and Property*, ch. 1.

rate in the short run which, it has generally been held, is about as far as their anticipation extended.[63]

Equally, the absence of people who had inordinate wealth would both diminish the envy of the poor and reduce the chances of a mischief-making oligarchy getting power.[64] Conversely, the most damaging of all possibilities would be what one might call a wasp-waisted distribution where wealth was bi-modally distributed, and no middle class could hold the ring between rich and poor. Anyone identifying James Mill as the uninhibited apologist for capitalism that he has retrospectively been claimed to be ought to reflect on the fact that Mill's own view of what had to be avoided at all costs was what he called the unhealthy condition of the large manufacturing districts, where an impoverished work force confronted a harsh, selfish and money-grabbing group of employers. If democracy and property were to be compatible, the distribution of property had to be such that it defused rather than provoked the class war.[65]

The second belief to which Mill subscribed, and which really follows on quite naturally from this, was that the working class would generally be ready to defer to middle-class opinion leaders. The fear that many political writers had always felt was that the mob, the masses, would simply run amok, abandon all restraint, and pillage their betters, if they were not kept down by the appropriate mixture of exhortation and police powers. Mill did not feel any such anxiety; the less well off would follow the lead of the rational middle classes, and would not be tempted into an orgy of golden goose killing. Given deference, and given a favourable distribution of wealth, democracy was nothing to be afraid of.[66]

As for the question which, I have said, Mill simply begged, it is not too hard to see that by 1820 the landed proprietor had lost credibility as a modern version of the Roman senator, full of *gravitas* and public spirit. The theory of rent in classical economics represented him as deriving an income simply by happening to be in occupation of intra-marginal land, and the classical emphasis on unproductive labour represented the landed nobility's servants

[63] Aristotle, *Politics*, p. 216 (1295b–1296a); S. M. Lipset, *Political Man* (Heinemann, London, 1960), pp. 48ff.

[64] Aristotle, *Politics*, p. 216 (1296a).

[65] Mill, *Essay on Government*, p. 90.

[66] ibid., pp. 89–91.

neither as potential recruits to the military nor as potential disturbers of the peace in a reversion to feudalism, but simply as a drain on the national product. Moreover, landowners had a vested interest in keeping up the price of wheat, and in making the bread of the poor dearer than it should have been. The senator was some way towards turning into the modern landlord, a figure not greatly admired in radical circles.[67]

It would be going out of our way to chase Mill through the arguments in which he further defuses the threat of democracy by diluting the extent of the democracy he proposes. The argument is simple enough though, and emphasizes the extent to which all arguments come back to a cost-benefit form. We need to have *enough* of an electorate to fairly represent the general interest and to vote down sinister interests; the vote is not, on this view, a natural right or any such thing; voting is a way of bringing power to control power.

So long as we have a good sample committed to the general interest and big enough to outvote opponents of the public interest, there is no call to enlarge the suffrage — if my interests are secured by my father's vote, I need not vote; if my interests are secured by my husband's vote, I need not vote; and since the non-propertied share no interests that they do not also share with the propertied, there is no harm in confining the vote to the propertied. Again, the contrast with Kant, and, as we shall see, with Hegel, emerges clearly enough. Where the upshot may *seem* to be the same, in that neither women nor the young nor the non-propertied get the vote in either account, the grounds of the exclusion are read very differently. In Kant it is personal dependence which is decisive, in Mill only that the interest in question will get looked after anyway.[68]

In none of this is there any of the concern for the social and cultural impact of the law which was a theme of the Scottish historians of the eighteenth century and an obsession from Hegel onwards. Nor do such notions as that wage labour is intrinsically insulting to the labourer ever appear above the horizon; the complex of anxieties gestured at by the term 'alienation' are nowhere in existence; we are not asked to be enraged at the thought that our skills, aspects of ourselves as they are, are for sale to the

---

[67] Spencer, *Social Statics*, p. 122.
[68] *Essay on Government*, pp. 72–5.

highest bidder; we are not asked to flinch at the way in which a market necessarily sets men at odds with each other. That I will let you have as little of my time as I can for the wage you pay is a brute and uncomplained of fact, and so it goes on. It is a nice joke in the history of social thought that the one place in which Marx ever wrote down what it would be like to produce in an unalienated way was in his notes on Mill's *Elements of Political Economy*. For of all the writers to whom any such notion is alien, Mill is the most obvious.

Since we shall soon see why Hegel, J. S. Mill and Marx were dissatisfied with the utilitarian account of property rights, their foundation in work, and their political consequences — one way and another they all held that it would not do to leave out history, to be quite so cavalier about the special claims of the labourer and quite so calm about the political implications of free enterprise — we need not make much of these deficiencies here. We may, however, observe how plausible a defence one could readily make of the doctrine.

In the first place, one could claim that the instrumental and utilitarian view of property comes easily, if not 'naturally' to many plain men as well as to philosophers. The view that the *point*, if not the origin, of rights of ownership lies in the way they do or do not increase general well-being by allowing appropriate areas of freedom of choice — from freedom to invest to freedom to paint your walls any old colour you choose — is the political common sense of the western democratic world. It is more commonplace than the natural right view, and it obviously allows argument to go on indefinitely about the best way to allocate and control rights over the use of a society's resources.[69] If it is not much use in framing hypotheses about how societies came to create property rights, which is still a contentious matter, it is a very useful hypothesis around which to organize change or resistance to change.

Moreover, its *unconcerns* seems to be widely shared *un*concerns. On the utilitarian premises, we should be concerned with the quantitative pay off to us, and to those whose welfare we value, and we should not worry about how it is achieved, nor whether the general structure of pay-offs is markedly egalitarian or in-

[69] This may be why the discussion of property rights in Ronald Dworkin's 'Liberalism', in S. N. Hampshire (ed.), *Public and Private Morality* (Cambridge University Press, Cambridge, 1978), pp. 128–32, is a good deal more awkward than Bentham's.

egalitarian.[70] The workers who feature in the industrial sociology of the past thirty or forty years seem to fit these requirements pretty well. Certainly, one cannot assume without further ado that their behaviour and their expressed opinions reflect the 'truth' about rational human behaviour; but one can say that a view much like Bentham's is part of everyday working reality.

It is also worth noting that in the hands of a more sociologically minded successor, like Maine, much of Bentham's fundamental framework remained intact.[71] This was partly because the legal positivism which was part and parcel of his utilitarianism seemed obviously right, and partly because the implicit account he offered of the scope and limits of government action and his explicit conservatism over the pace of change were so generally acceptable. Maine's hopes may have been for progress rather than utility, but the measure of progress was fundamentally utilitarian; he may have seen history as a movement from status to contract, but that, too, could be given a thoroughly utilitarian gloss in terms of the way property rights gradually got defined in the most useful way to encourage economically efficient activity. Maine feared democracy and Bentham did not because they disagreed about the actual inclinations of the bulk of the population.[72]

It was not a move out of Bentham's universe to hold that the way the universal desire for security would affect the poor would be by making them look for a new feudalism and making them reject the open society. Henry Sidgwick's *Elements of Politics* is an equally good example. Sidgwick was a more cautious and qualified thinker than Bentham, and he worried more about the way in which the property rights of existing owners must by definition curtail the freedom of the non-owner to use the objects in question. But the resolution of the problem runs along Bentham-like lines. Property *is* the creature of the law, but security *is* a very great good, and continuous redistributive unheavals would be mischievous. The state may, without impairing security, aid the non-propertied by providing them with education in order to give them a start in life and by creating a welfare safety-net beneath them.[73] How far the

[70] W. G. Runciman, *Relative Deprivation and Social Justice* (Penguin, Harmondsworth, 1972), esp. postscript, pp. 382–99.
[71] H. S. Maine, *Popular Government* (Murray, London, 1885), Preface.
[72] cf. ibid., p. 42 and Mill, *Essay on Government*, pp. 84–91.
[73] Sidgwick, *Elements of Politics*, pp. 142–68.

state can usefully go in these directions is limited by the need not to disturb security and incentive so much that the general welfare is lessened. What we find in Sidgwick is utilitarianism tempered by a reading of Herbert Spencer. A fully fledged, *laissez-faire* economy depends on people having the property rights they would have according to natural rights theory. None the less, these rights are the creatures of the law, and it is a utilitarian question how far we should go towards creating the economy dreamed of by Spencer.

One can, of course, complicate the argument in ways which embarrass the utilitarian. One can argue that it is technically impossible to assess any particular system of ownership against the utilitarian standard; one can deny that giving people property rights is a good way of solving the problem of co-ordinating everyone's productive activities and so make the pro-property solution seem less attractive. One can argue that the utilitarian edifice has to rest on non-utilitarian foundations; the working of ownership and contract depends on people just believing in an intuitive way that *pacta servanda sunt*, and being ready *suum cuique tribuere*. If people did not believe that each is entitled to his own and promises are to be kept without further question, there would be no arguing them into it on utilitarian grounds. But once we introduce these difficulties, we begin to enter the realms of pure moral philosophy; our more limited concerns entitle us to draw back.

# 5

# Hegel and Mastering the World

The move from Bentham to Hegel is hardly to be effected gradually, though I shall try in the course of this chapter to say something about the way utilitarian considerations find their way into Hegel's account of proprietorship, for, of course, they do find their way there. The project to which this chapter is devoted is to show how the Hegelian account of property, of its relation to work, and its consequences in politics is almost equally interesting as sociology and as philosophy.

As philosophy, it situates ownership within a general theory of practical freedom, which at the end of the day can, if Hegel is right, stand or fall only with Hegel's entire philosophy. This is, of course, implicit in Hegel's own assertion that the truth lies only in the whole. Freedom requires reason, reason requires a context in which to express itself; the adequacy of the context is to be judged by Hegel's wider philosophy of history and that in turn is, on Hegel's account of it, simply an aspect of philosophy generally.[1]

It is suggested in what follows that Hegel's widest philosophical aspirations can be detached from his account of work, property and politics, leaving the latter intact as sociology and the former as philosophy. And yet, it is for all that true enough that in a sense Hegel's whole philosophy is a labouring and a proprietorial philosophy. *Geist* or Spirit creates a world which is initially blankly alien or other, object not subject; this world, though it is the creation of *Geist*, is not seen to be such until it is wholly understood, until *Geist* has so to speak recapitulated in understanding its creative achievement and comes to see the world not as object but as subject.[2]

On this basis Marx interpreted Hegel's philosophy as a sort of coded message. Hegel's philosophy had in a way described the real meaning of the history of the world — the creation, alienation and

[1] Hegel, *Philosophy of Right*, pp. 2–3.
[2] G. W. F. Hegel, *The Phenomenology of Spirit*, tr. A. V. Miller (Clarendon Press, Oxford, 1977), pp. 10–11.

reappropriation of the world — but in a garbled form;[3] Hegel had discussed objects of thought, not real things, which were reappropriated by being understood, not by being physically taken and used. This chapter goes only half way along that path of interpretation. That is, I shall not try to show that Hegel's philosophy is really the Marxian historical saga in an obscure disguise. Rather, I shall argue that Hegel's account of the operation of a modern society and a modern state is *overtly* rather than covertly sociological. I shall also argue that its relation to Marx's own historical and sociological theory is interesting less because Marx supersedes Hegel than because he does not.[4] Hegel's philosophy supports his sociology in that the moral and intellectual vocabulary and the moral and intellectual aspirations couched in that vocabulary get their full sense from the philosophy as a whole. The unique colouring of Hegel's political theory stems from the way in which in his philosophy creative human intelligence is a model for and an aspect of creative intelligence in the world at large. When I say that Hegel's widest philosophical concerns are not, for all that, very directly implicated in his account of economic activity and proprietorial relations, I mean only to claim that it would be very difficult to show, say, that Hegel's account of absolute freedom inevitably implied, or was implied by, his account of the property law of restoration Prussia.[5] That Hegel's grounds for believing that men have the aspirations he claims they have are to be sought in his philosophy generally, is quite consistent with that.

Hegel discusses work and property in several places. He does so at great length in his early work on politics and economics, the *Jenaer Realphilosophie*, and gives a particularly engaging account of the genesis of work in the 'master-slave dialectic' of the *Phenomenology of Spirit*. The *Jenaer Realphilosophie* is interesting because in it Hegel is very much more alarmed by the divisions between property owners and the propertiless masses than he shows signs of being in his *Philosophy of Right*; and the 'master-slave dialectic' is interesting because it defends the view that *work* rather than enjoyment is the way to liberation. In the dialectic, Hegel

[3] Karl Marx, *Early Writings* (Penguin, Harmondsworth, 1975), pp. 385–6.
[4] cf. Charles Taylor, *Hegel and Modern Society* (Cambridge University Press, Cambridge, 1979), pp. 140ff.
[5] Z. A. Pelczynski (ed.), *Hegel's Political Writings* (Clarendon Press, Oxford, 1964), pp. 5ff.

envisages two competing consciousnesses, each of which wishes to reduce the other to dependence — in effect, each conscious agent starts, in Hegel's account, by wanting the world to be 'his' world, and everything in it to be dependent on his will; this includes other conscious agents.[6] The result of a conflict of this sort is that one consciousness submits out of fear of death, and becomes slave to the other.

The victorious consciousness is now able to enjoy the good things of the world without having to work for them, since the slave can do that. Up to a point, the 'master' is thus able to free himself from any dependence on the world, and to demonstrate that the world is 'his', that is, is there for him to enjoy. But Hegel thinks this is a historical dead end; the slave who does the work, though in a way dependent on the material world which can frustrate his efforts and make his work decidedly *hard* work, is the true bearer of freedom, because the experience of working on the world teaches him what his abilities are, and shows him how to transform both himself and the world.[7] It is in work rather than in consumption that human beings show their creative and intelligent capacities.

Here I shall concentrate on Hegel's account of the nature of property, its basis in work, and its implications for politics, as he gives it in *The Philosophy of Right*. There, our subject is so much Hegel's that after some introductory methodological remarks — among them his famous claim that political philosophy does not tell the state what it ought to be, but reveals only what it is[8] — Hegel begins his treatise by explaining the basis of property and contract in the section called 'Abstract Right'. Hegel begins his exposition of the rights of owners not from enjoyment or happiness but from freedom. This is not because he espouses any sort of natural law doctrine; he denounces natural law theories twice over, first for being tainted with a Rousseauian primitivism, and the foolish belief that men were happily law-abiding in some long vanished Golden Age, and secondly because he is hostile to the view that law is an 'organic' growth.[9]

Law is intelligently carved out of a non-intelligent natural environment, and although Hegel believed that he had overcome

---

[6] Hegel, *Phenomenology*, pp. 111–12.
[7] ibid., p. 118.
[8] *Philosophy of Right*, p. 11.
[9] ibid., pp. 15–18.

the separation of the 'is' and the 'ought' which was so striking a feature of Kant's philosophy, he was hostile to anything that seemed to collapse moral, legal or political obligation into the promptings of the natural self. The linking of 'is' and 'ought' in Hegel is achieved by making both of them aspects of 'must': because we are essentially rational creatures, we can see what we must rationally do, and this sort of necessity is so far from being *in*consistent with freedom that it is its highest expression.[10] A skilled chess player sees the move he has to make in a way the unskilled does not: his moves are made no less freely, indeed they are made more freely, since further analysis of what he is doing reveals no contradiction in his aims, and thus reveals him acting more completely as he wills.[11]

Hegel, therefore, sets out to analyse law as an expression of human freedom; the goal of law is the rational conduct of our lives, for only when our wills are directed by reason can they be directed in a determinate fashion and yet remain free. Happiness is rejected as altogether too subjective and shifting a goal, subject to the vagaries of taste and fashion; presciently, Hegel claims that most people's assessment of the quality of their standard of living is simply a matter of keeping up with the Joneses, not a self-contained evaluation of the good that their possessions do them.[12]

The starting point of Hegel's case is therefore not unlike Kant's except that Kant, working in the contractual mode, was bound to see property rights as the result of rules whereby we can mutually coerce one another and lose our external freedom without losing our *inner* freedom.[13] Hegel's view is anti-contractual — he does not merely reject the social contract as an account of the actual origin of states and the law, but as a model for legal relations too. Hegel sees property rights as implicit in our first and basic entry into the world as free agents; to be a free agent, or a *person*, however, involves being acknowledged as such by others, and in that sense the achievement of personality is a communal rather than a merely individual achievement. It is not a matter of agreeing to forgo as much of one's own liberty as everyone else will forgo of his; it is a

---

[10] ibid., §23, pp. 30–1.
[11] Martin Hollis, *Models of Man* (Cambridge University Press, Cambridge, 1977), pp. 165ff., defends a very similar view.
[12] *Philosophy of Right*, §191A, p. 269.
[13] Kant, *Philosophy of Law*, pp. 44–50.

matter of accepting and working with a system of rules which express one's commitment to living with them.

I have said often enough that Hegel's account of ownership takes possession seriously in a way no utilitarian theory can. We can now make good on that claim. Hegel contrasts the human agent as a *locus* of will, mind and reason with the stuff of mere nature, which is blankly material and, as it were, 'unoccupied'.[14] Things have no point or purpose of their own; if they are to have a point they must be given one by being occupied by human goals and purposes. This is a project with two aspects rather than one, for there is both the occupancy of particular objects to be considered, where, generally, it is the will of one person at a time that is involved; and there is the occupancy of the world at large, or the whole environment, by groups, or societies, or humanity in general.[15] Since, on Hegel's account, it is foolish to look for an international or supranational legal system, and property is sustained by law, there is rather a change of gear at the point where we move from individual to species appropriation. Mankind only 'owns' the world.

Still the main point survives; this is that individual appropriation is an aspect of, and is valued as, the general permeation of the non-mental by the mental, of the object by the subject. Somewhat like Kant, Hegel identified *taking in order to control* as staking the initial claim to ownership. The first taker does not have to justify his taking; the question we ask is negative, not positive, namely whether the thing is already occupied by a will which demands respect.[16] Superstitious people once thought trees and rivers were endowed with souls, but Hegel reckons it an unequivocal advance that the world has been de-animated, and shown to be wholly open to us to endow with our purposes. The only thing which can obstruct this taking is a will with prior claims. This seems to be an immediate bar to slavery, and up to a point it is, for when my will has fully taken possession of my body, I am a person and unownable. But Hegel is notably unwilling to issue moral complaints against previous epochs, so he does not say that slavery was always immoral. He contents himself with noting that a man

---

[14] *Philosophy of Right*, §44, p. 51.
[15] 'Abstract Right' is the realm of the individual legal personality and its demands (*Philosophy of Right*, §§34ff., esp. pp. 37–57), while 'Civil Society' displays the market and its workings as a sort of possession of all (ibid., §§187ff., pp. 126ff.).
[16] ibid., §44A, p. 236.

who accepts his slave status does come to be ownable; in effect he withdraws his will and leaves room for another. And he observes that slavery had a place in social life when a wrong could be right.[17]

Whatever the meaning of that, it is clear that Hegel does not believe that it can *now* be an open question whether slavery is permissible, and that he does not tackle the question in a utilitarian fashion. Within a system of law, persons and owned objects occupy exclusive classes. Hegel, indeed, condemns Roman Law for allowing fathers proprietorial rights over their children and denounces Kant for assimilating marriage to a property relationship. Marriage is not a contract at all, let alone one by which the possession of anything is transferred, or leased for use.[18]

Now, if the argument is to rest on the importance of what I loosely call the possessory relationship between will and object, so that the *Besitzwille* is to make all the important moral differences, we need to be clear on several points. One is on *how* things are occupied; another is on what makes something an occupiable 'thing' of the right kind; a third is on what the implicit goals of such occupation are. That is, as we shall see, one natural interpretation of Hegel is a rather romantic and individualistic one, which stresses the way in which an individual's projects for self-formation and self-expression are embodied in what he creates and owns.

On this view, the paradigm of a possessory relationship exists between a painter and his painting; the object he has created, though made of canvas and pigment, has no life at all except as *his* painting. What the materials show is what he has made of them; a more emphatic demonstration of the subservience of matter to mind could not be looked for. It would then be a matter of reproach against everyday economic life if most work could not provide artistic self-fulfilment; it would be a reproach against the system of property rights if the creator who was the *real* owner of the object he made had no control over its ultimate destination. And the commercial treatment of art in particular would be a scandal.[19]

Yet Hegel, as distinct from Stirner or the Young Hegelians or Marx, did not seem much moved by any such thought. Certainly he saw a weak connection between art and more humble forms of work, but he did not draw any radical conclusions from this. And

[17] ibid., §57A, p. 239.
[18] ibid., §75, pp. 58–9.
[19] Marx, *Early Writings*, pp. 375–9.

this, we shall see, is because he is ready to argue that the point of there being property rights is to be seen in a variety of ways in which people anchor themselves and their purposes in the world. There is no suggestion that each and every person can or should have certain sorts of property in order to be at home in the world — Hegel's is not a Rousseauian or a Proudhonian view; because Hegel moves easily from individual aspirations to the truth which lies in the whole, he only *seems* to be resting his case on the individualism of the romantics. The social role a man occupies can be *his* role, and can make him sufficiently at home in the world, so long as the rationality of the whole scheme is visible, and the various social stations and their duties are freely chosen by those who fill and fulfill them. No particular property rights seem essential — though rights certainly are.[20]

We have seen in the case of Kant how a theory which stresses control and occupancy cannot make labour an independent or basic title of ownership. Hegel goes along with this. Owning is having rightful control to the full extent allowed by the law; and this can be naturally acquired by merely taking whatever it is. Work reappears in the argument not to ground a title but to fix control. Hegel explains this *via* the concept of negation; freedom and negation belong together in the simple sense that a precondition of a free action is envisaging that the world can be what it is not, that the present state of affairs can be cancelled in favour of some other which we choose to bring about.[21]

This principle is even applied in a rather light-hearted fashion to the sheep merely nibbling grass; this is paradigmatically a case of consumption, a utilitarian starting-point for a theory of property rights, yet Hegel treats it as an instance — a low grade one admittedly — of the absolute dominion of mind over matter.[22] Even the sheep is one step higher than the flatly positive material world and her nibbling 'negates' the grass. The sheep, however, cannot be a candidate for either self-possession or the proprietorship of external objects, since it cannot treat itself as something with aspects to be negated. Human beings can and do treat their present goals as something they can change; they treat their present abilities as something they can modify, improve, and extend. This

[20] *Philosophy of Right*, §33, pp. 35–6.
[21] ibid., §44A, p. 236.
[22] ibid.

second order of negation is what makes us persons, for this is what it is to have a mind, a capacity to decide and to change one's decision for good reasons. That the mind needs embodiment and that we need determinate and consecutive characters is what makes property possible and necessary, and what rules some things out as candidates for proprietorship. Thus, on Hegel's analysis, I certainly possess my own body, but it is not my property; it is not property because if I negate, or destroy my body, I destroy myself, and so abolish the proprietor whose 'property' is at stake. The same argument applies to selling ourselves into slavery or selling one's civil and religious liberties.[23]

It takes no great astuteness to see that this argument is vulnerable to erosion; it may show that my *whole* body cannot be a form of property, but it does not show that any particular part with which I can dispense is not my property. It is clear Hegel would regard a contract to sell, say, one's left hand to someone who simply liked collecting left hands as disgusting and improper; but it is not clear that the apparatus of the distinction between what is external and what is non-external, or the notion of negation, can provide the whole story.[24] Still, it might be said in Hegel's defence that it is better to distinguish property and non-property and to allocate us and our liberties to non-property than to call them all property as Locke did, and then restrict what we may do with this 'property' so narrowly that it is hard to see in what sense they are property after all.[25]

But if negation is the key concept expressing the relation of proprietorship, the next question is: what is the most adequate mode of negation? That is, how is something most completely taken into ownership? The answer to this question is engagingly obscure, though the two poles of the argument are clearly enough motivated. One answer is that things most fully become ours when our work transforms them. We endow a thing with a new essence by working on it, and this new nature supersedes the original nature; naturally, therefore, labour gives one a solid title.[26] The image here again tempts one to see artistic creation as a paradigm case, but art is not the only one — the field where wheat now grows was once waste,

---

[23] ibid., §66, p. 53; cf. §70, p. 56; cf. *Two Treatises*, II, §6, and Kant, *Philosophy of Law*, p. 119.
[24] cf. Nozick, *Anarchy, State and Utopia*, pp. 58–9.
[25] cf. *Two Treatises*, II, §6, pp. 288–9.
[26] *Philosophy of Right*, §56, p. 47.

now it is a fertile spot. The fertility is a record of, and an embodiment of, the purposes, abilities and efforts of those who made it fertile. This line of thought rests on the notion that our aims *permeate* the results.[27]

Now one can see how utilitarian and non-utilitarian ways of thinking may join. We are, of course, driven to improve land for utilitarian reasons: to eat better and more reliably, and Hegel does not deny that — indeed he would be quite mad if he did. But what we end up with is not merely, and in the eyes of reason, not mainly, this utilitarian pay off. As Kant argued in his *Universal History* we have, in pursuing utilitarian goals, brought ourselves into moral and legal relations with others whose value is not utilitarian but absolute — it is they which now control our pursuit of utilitarian goals and give us standards by which to criticize and revise our view of our own and others' welfare.[28] Since Hegel's view of social life is so much less contractual and atomic than Kant's, his view of what this achievement comes to is correspondingly more elaborate, for he envisages a much more thoroughly communal existence developing on the basis of the rule of law. None the less, the doctrine has the same logical structure: we are prompted by utilitarian pressures into adopting a way of life whose *point* is not utilitarian.

Another aspect of this is that we live in a humanized environment; things are not merely natural objects any longer, but expressions of our achievements, and thus can be read as reminders of the culture to which we belong, of the goals and abilities we share. Needless to say, this is a two-edged offer; if history is a benign process, we shall no doubt feel an attachment to the record that we shall not feel if it is not, a point which Marx and Rousseau both took.[29]

If work is one way of anchoring our wills in things and so making them ours, the other paradigm case is where we leave the object untouched by everything save the simple, legally valid declaration that it is 'mine'. Hegel offers 'marking as ours' as the paradigmatic case of acquiring ownership of an object, and in a way quite rightly. When you receive three hundred shares in Ferranti from me, they become yours by a process which does not in the least involve your

[27] ibid., §57A, pp. 238–9.
[28] ibid., §20, p. 29; Kant makes much the same point in *Kant's Political Writings*, p. 74.
[29] Marx, *Early Writings*, pp. 395–6; Rousseau, *Social Contract*, p. 83.

having to go anywhere near Ferranti's factories or products or personnel. We may talk of your 'taking delivery' of the shares, as if in reminiscence of your having to enter on the actual physical piece of land to complete delivery of it; but all that really happens is that I cease to be entitled to claim a share of Ferranti's profits, cease to be able to demand a portion of the money realized at any dissolution of the company and so on, and you acquire these rights from me by transfer.[30]

Between us and the physical stuff which the company is engaged in creating and selling, there is an elaborate system of legal relationships — so elaborate that it is not true that the shareholder owns any of the company's machinery or buildings or products, even though the shareholders between them own the company which does own these things. For Hegel this control at extreme arm's length is a triumph of mind over matter. We can switch the destiny of things in the world not by pushing or shoving but by an affirmation of will. Even in the case of first acquisition, it is still true that the ability to put down a marker with your name on, in the knowledge that it will be taken by everyone as a sign of your ownership, is a triumph of the same sort. This is not to say that we should have invented such devices if we had not wanted to make use of things in a straightforward sense; it is also true, and Hegel says it, that society can only endorse such takings on condition they serve some social goal. But it is the fact of mastery rather than the utilitarian goal which interests Hegel.[31]

The same points reappear when we look at Hegel's justification of private, individual ownership and when we look at his account of exchange and money. So far as the opening arguments of the *Philosophy of Right* go, we can infer that it is *individual* ownership that is being explained and defended, either by reading Hegel in a romantic fashion — concerned with the way the unique individual stamps his own project on the outside world — or by simply assuming that the will is naturally embodied only in biological individuals, and that each biological individual is a natural focus of moral concern.[32] One can pour a good deal of cold water on both assumptions — for instance, by recalling that even when Hegel is in some fashion an individualist, he is more inclined to praise the

---

[30] *Philosophy of Right*, §§72ff, pp. 57ff.

[31] ibid., §44, p. 41.

[32] ibid., §35, p. 37.

individual for punctiliously doing his duty than for blazing his own trail, or by recalling that Hegel thinks the individual will only deserve recognition when backed by some social group. Why, then, isn't the family, the tribe, the state, the true focus of ownership?

The answer to this rhetorical question is complicated by the fact that Hegel does in fact say, when explaining the practical implications of his account of property, that when a man is head of a family, his assets, both real, and personal and intangible — such as his skills, say — belong to the family and are administered by him.[33] It is also complicated by the way Hegel takes two bites at the subject of entails, arguing in Part One of the *Philosophy of Right* that they are at odds with the concept of property, and are thus disappearing from the modern world, but arguing in the closing discussion of the state and its constitutional arrangements that entails can anchor a man to his place, his class and his culture, and in so doing render him more fit to exercise political authority by rendering him more stable, sober and reliable.[34]

However, Hegel is not in any doubt that property is, in essence, individual private property, and that as the modern world becomes clearer about this, so ownership becomes lodged in individual hands. Abolishing the estates of monasteries is no injustice, because monasteries no longer serve purposes which cannot be left to individuals or the state. Again, the modern state does not *own* anything, though it may tax anything and has eminent domain — so individuals are thus left as the sole true proprietors. This unfettered individuality, moreover, has a natural support in the fact that appropriating, choosing, making and so on are all of them relations between individual persons and the material world; where artificial persons and bodies co-operate to own things, it is only because individuals create them.[35]

We must not exaggerate Hegel's acceptance of individualism in economic and legal matters. When Hegel declares that feudal restrictions are vanishing because they are at odds with the truth about property, he is not defending the right of anyone to do exactly as he chooses with his property. Hegel's acceptance of Roman Law notions of property is heavily qualified, and although he takes for granted Roman Law assumptions of absolute

---

[33] ibid., §§169–71, p. 116.
[34] ibid., cf. §63A, p. 240; and §306, p. 199.
[35] ibid., §63A, p. 240.

ownership in the strict sense that someone or other can always be picked out as *the* owner, and all lesser interests attributed to his will, he has no time for the idea that we are absolute owners in the sense of being entitled to do absolutely anything we choose with what we own.[36] Capricious exercises of freedom, *contra* Bentham, simply are not exercises of freedom but of mere whim. A society may have to accept a certain amount of such behaviour as the price it pays for diversity and openness, but it is not itself an exercise of freedom.

English law seemed to Hegel to be utterly scandalous in this respect. The English had an uncontrolled chaos and cherished it as ancient liberty. So, in discussing testamentary disposition, Hegel is very emphatic that freedom does not involve being able to leave your property to absolutely anyone or anything you like; England struck him as a scene of family strife where fathers could bully children with the threat of disinheriting them, and where disappointed heirs had to waste their energies recovering their estates from lunatic charities.[37] But if the arbitrary individual will is not to be given much scope, Hegel was eager to give the non-arbitrary will of the present holder as much room as possible. Thus it is the careful head of the family who finds a prudent investment blocked by some antique feudal barrier to sale or purchase who has Hegel's sympathy, not the man who wishes to leave his money in trust for his favourite cat, nor yet the man who spots a good gamble on the stock market and wants to put his shirt on it. Hegel is bourgeois and anti-feudal, rather than individualist and pro-capitalist. It is because the modern world places so much emphasis on individual responsibility that private property is sacrosanct, rather than because *laissez-faire* makes for tremendous prosperity.

There is, though, no doubt that Hegel takes commercial society very much for granted.[38] For one thing commerce is implied in the concept of property from the very beginning. Hegel regards alienability as a mark of something really being property — which is why lives and liberties cannot be property. His reason is the same rather pictorial one that starts the whole process of appropriation. As a free agent, I rightly bring any and every external thing under control as 'mine'. Were men able to *take* but not *relinquish*, this

---

[36] ibid., remarks to §64, p. 52.
[37] ibid., §180A, p. 266.
[38] ibid., §65, p. 52.

freedom would be a bad joke — we would be much like the monkey who seized the sweets in the sweet jar, but could not extract his clenched fist when he had done so. If we could not get rid of what we had once acquired, we should be the prisoners of the world, not its governors.

Still, this does not do more than suggest that if there must be ways of marking the opening of my proprietorship, there must also be ways of marking its conclusion, so that others can see the difference between my taking off my jacket intending to put it on when I have finished washing up, and my taking off my jacket intending that whoever wants it can have it. The extension is natural enough; if I may abandon the thing, I may presumably abandon it on terms, and the result is then contract. The abandoning to one another of objects via barter is clumsy, which suggests the thought that money is a universal equivalent.[39]

Because Hegel conducts the whole argument in possessory terms, he has a problem peculiar to himself, but one whose solution is pregnant with future arguments. When I sell an object to someone else, and deliver it in advance of payment being made, I have lost actual possession of what I owned; yet if the buyer does not produce the payment, I can sue for my goods to be returned, and I can sue for breach of contract. On Hegel's view, this implies that we are all along owners of the value of the object, and that when we sell, we go on having a claim on the object's value even in the absence of the object itself.[40] If I agree to deliver the object on Friday for payment on Monday, I am still the owner of something over the weekend whether or not you pay up on Monday. This seems to Hegel to suggest that what we really own is not the thing but its value. This is a view we must resist for all legal purposes — if I steal your car, I am no less guilty of stealing if I leave you a cheque for its value, and a *forced* fair exchange is still robbery.

But even if we resist it for purposes of legal analysis, we may be tempted by it for purposes of social diagnosis. We may claim that what a man has bought when he buys a valuable, but to him quite unmeaning painting, is really no more than money to hang on the wall, and we may want, as Hegel did, to suggest that what the modern commercial owner owns is 'assets', that is, stuff whose only

[39] ibid., §80, pp. 62–3.
[40] ibid., §77, p. 59.

important quality is its monetary value.[41] Much of the old argument about the reliability of landed property and the unreliability of financial property picks up the same premises; it is not the bits of government paper to which the stockholder is attracted, but only the value they represent, and that value is not the sort of thing which is irreplaceably represented by one physical place or thing. Hence the view that financiers and the like are politically flighty, and their allegiance as mobile as their assets.[42]

Hegel, however, is much more philosophically imaginative than that. Later in the *Philosophy of Right* he does pick up these anxieties, and relies on them to argue for a political constitution which gives a special place to the owners of landed property. But he also turns the thought that what we really own is the *value* of the objects, into another link in the argument that in society we are confronted with a spiritualized rather than a flatly natural world; and for all that commercialization has its negative aspects, the rise of a monetary network is one more way of infusing things with human purposes. The transition, though, contains the seeds of trouble.

The attractions of Hegel's development of the concept of property depend on our everyday feelings about our need to identify with and express ourselves in things we make, control and use. There is no very direct connection between this and any particular form of ownership, though there certainly is a direct connection between this and ownership at all. There must be ways of allowing things to be enough 'mine' for me to be able to dispose of them as a gift, or how could I show friendship, enough 'mine' for me to be able to plan my life around their use, and so on. To argue for the claims of modern forms of property is to argue for the claims of modern men.[43]

But property is only one way in which modern man finds himself at home in the modern world, and Hegel broadens out the argument to a general consideration of the social support for and confirmation of, the individual's role, his ambitions and his political allegiance. To take an obvious example which cuts quite across the thought that property rights in the usual sense are

[41] ibid., §204, p. 132.
[42] Albert O. Hirschman, *The Passions and the Interests* (Princeton University Press, Princeton, NJ, 1977).
[43] John Charvet, *A Critique of Freedom and Equality* (Cambridge University Press, Cambridge, 1981), pp. 171ff.

uniquely effective as an anchorage, Hegel argues that civil servants should *not* own their official positions. He objects strongly to the British Army where officers could buy and sell commissions, and argues that such individual ownership is a feudal relic dying out as irrationality recedes, to be replaced by appointment by qualification and promotion on merit. What anchors the civil servant in his world is not the ownership of the office, but tenure subject to good behaviour and the public's recognition of his official status.[44]

This, though, reveals two things. One is that Hegel's argument, couched as it is in personalist or expressive terms, none the less implicitly contains a good deal of instrumental and utilitarian argument. For the modern world is quite largely a utilitarian world, and much of its rationality is utilitarian rationality. This is not to say that there is nothing distinctive in Hegel's account, for there certainly is — for one thing Hegel is concerned that we should think of our allegiance to our society and our state in *non*-instrumental terms; that we should not calculate the benefits of obedience and the risks of disobedience; not turn the relationship of allegiance into a contractual one.[45] All the same, what modern property rights express is a generally utilitarian view of the world. Nature exists to be *used*, and the extension of property rights and their elaboration and division is part and parcel of making nature more and more usable.

What is distinctively Hegelian in all this is the incorporation of these utilitarian considerations into a wider framework. Because *uses* are so various, the utilitarian standard cannot by itself distinguish good and bad uses, rational and irrational uses; even the felicific calculus cannot get far with that task. Hence Hegel's need to legitimize the sorts of use to which modern man puts the world — to serve the welfare of his family, for instance.

At this point we might fear that Hegel will go too far down that track, and the state will be asked to stand in as a kind of *curator bonis* to see that we act sensibly with what we have. To this, Hegel replies with a defence of the modern notion of individuality, a notion which is not biologically rooted — individuals are not just different physical entities — but which does incorporate some of the arbitrariness of nature. Much of our life will, properly, be

[44] *Philosophy of Right*, §294, p. 191.
[45] ibid., §258, pp. 155ff.

determined by our station and its duties. Some will, quite properly, hang on the accidents of what happens to each of us in particular. The individuation of ownership rights, the anti-feudal emphasis on the rights of the present against those of the past or future, hangs both on the thought that our modern sense of duty so emphasizes individual responsibility, and on the thought that we value diversity.[46]

All the same, and this is the second point, Hegel has a problem analogous to the utilitarian's problem of whether society is only a means to individual ends or the individual only a unit in calculating the social sum of utilities. Is the permeation of the world by purpose its permeation by individual purposes or by a social purpose? Does the individual really own his portion of the world, or is he merely a channel through which society's real ownership flows? Hegel evidently hoped to dissolve such oppositions. If there is a sense in which it is ultimately a matter of society owning its environment, that sense is not the same as that in which individuals own particular parts of it.

When he emphasized the individual's membership of the larger society, though, he did mean to emphasize that rights of ownership were not absolute, that they were licensed by the larger purpose of the whole society and could not be employed, as the idiom goes, to 'trump' them.[47] Conversely Hegel's sense of how much individual rights matter to the modern world was strong enough for him to believe that a state which arbitrarily or hastily or without compensation overrode individual proprietors and their purposes would be failing to live up to its own standards. In characteristic Hegelian style, we are invited to recognize that individuals could not sustain their own purposes unless these were legitimized by the larger purposes of their society, while the larger society could not realize its purposes except by realizing them in the multitudinous plans of separate individuals.[48]

Most critics of Hegel have tended to look with some distrust at the account he gives of civil society — what one might call social, economic and political life to the extent that they can be thought of

---

[46] ibid., §200, p. 130; cf. the discussion of 'internal teleology' in Charles Taylor, *Hegel* (Cambridge University Press, Cambridge, 1975), pp. 321ff.

[47] The expression is Ronald Dworkin's: *Taking Rights Seriously* (2nd edn, Duckworth, London, 1978).

[48] Taylor, *Hegel*, pp. 365ff.

without reference to the constitution of the state. Marx was so provoked by it that he took on Hegel's largest philosophical claims as well as his sociological claims, and abandoned traditional philosophy when he saw how far the facts of economic and political life were from Hegel's philosophically corrupted account of them.[49] I, however, shall content myself with a selective defence of some of Hegel's views, before drawing one or two conclusions about what they show about arguments over property rights.

Civil society, for Hegel, is essentially the market and its legal framework. It is the area of modern society where men meet only as proprietors and buyers and sellers. Within this framework, each treats every other as a means to his own ends; what, of course, makes this possible is that civil society is not *all* of society — laws limiting the way we may pursue our own self-interest are followed, but not merely out of self-interest; and in general the operations of the market place, which are in a limited way the operations of the state of nature, never become the full-scale state of war of Hobbes' *Leviathan* because of the moral and legal checks which it itself cannot — logically cannot — provide.

There are several points of interest in Hegel's account; here we shall concentrate — I hope not too fragmentarily — on his account of work, the question of poverty and the nature of social classes. Then we can see very briefly what this entails for Hegel's politics. The connection between these topics is plain enough. By the early nineteenth century, it was widely feared that economic advance would so intensify the division of labour that few people would do any but the most repetitive, mechanical, and mindless of jobs.[50] The pressure for this would come because of increasing competition; and this would also lead wages to be pushed as low as possible by employers; competition for employment among the unskilled was expected to be acute, especially since increasing mechanization would constantly be throwing people out of work.[51] On one familiar account, the result would be the division of society into well-off landlords, hard-pressed enterpreneurs, and impoverished

---

[49] Marx, *Early Writings*, p. 65.
[50] Adam Smith, *The Wealth of Nations*, ed. Edwin Cannan, 2 vols (Methuen, London, 1904), vol. II, pp. 734–5.
[51] cf. Marx's discussion of the generation of the reserve army of labour in *Capital*, vol. I, pp. 781–94.

labourers. Hegel's escape from this conclusion is not evasion, but an elegant and impressive piece of sociological thinking.

We have seen that for Hegel there is nothing suspect about wage labour. We may not sell *all* our time to another, for that is slavery and self-destruction, but we may sell a limited period of our services, for the part is 'external' to the whole. We have also seen something of the way Hegel's account of work as fixing our will in what we own seems to suggest that artistic creation is a paradigm of successful work. Now we have to fill out some of the sociological aspects of work, where Hegel accepts the bulk of Adam Smith's account of a market economy, in which the self-interested efforts of each are turned by the workings of the invisible hand into benefits for all.

Hegel is prepared to assimilate the fact of interdependence to property. The function of all assets is to allow us to secure our own and, more importantly, our family's welfare, by working on something for which there is a guaranteed need.[52] Now, in a market economy we can rely on the web of interdependence to ensure that our skills will find an outlet and bring in an income; this makes the system itself an asset. Hegel is by no means the last writer to assimilate guaranteed access to the means of earning a living to 'property' — C. B. Macpherson is a contemporary example of exactly this — but it is worth remarking that the assimilation is thoroughly suspect.[53]

A guarantee of employment may properly be said to be functionally equivalent in some respects to property strictly and legally construed, but it is not itself a property right, and there is no way in which it could be treated as one. Certainly one might call workers' skills a resource, and one could emphasize the way their value hinged on the network of relationships which guaranteed their employment. That does not mean they are property in the usual sense.[54] The point is one which is worth making, simple as it is, because it too crops up again in twentieth-century arguments about whether the so-called 'new class' in the Soviet Union should be said to own the means of production which it controls, and from

[52] *Philosophy of Right*, §199, pp. 129–30.
[53] Macpherson (ed.), *Property*, pp. 201ff., for his argument for redefining property.
[54] ibid., p. 204, admits as much.

which it derives privileges and consumer benefits. The clear answer is that it does not.[55]

On the face of it, what makes the 'new class' a *new* class is that it derives economic benefits not from ownership, nor a monopoly of skill, but from being politically licensed. Hegel's point is simply that modern man can, if fortunate, rely on the second nature of the economy where his ancestor relied on nature. As for the good that work does the worker, we finally get a defence of conscientious work rather than an assimilation of that work to artistic creation. The man Hegel admires is the man who 'hits the nail on the head' and does not flinch. In contrast to Rousseau's defence of the independent farmer who preserves his virtue by not entering into market relationships, Hegel again argues that we do not lose our independence and virtue when we enter these interdependent relationships. So long as people have secure and reliable social status, social stations whose duties they can perform, and contemporaries who can approve their performance, the market-place can support rather than threaten steadiness and reliability. The argument must not be over-worked – Hegel is quite aware that the market may *not* achieve this, and that wise political management will be needed.[56]

Thus Hegel was convinced that an *uncontrolled* market economy would cause poverty, misery, class conflict and political instability. He also feared its corrosive effect on old established ways of life; we find him complaining that in England one cannot tell the difference between a farm and a factory and that this is contrary to the nature of agriculture.[57] The belief that the natural trend in unrestrained market economies was to increased inequality and instability was a commonplace of the day and one which Hegel accepted. The upheavals in England after the end of the Napoleonic Wars seemed quite sufficient confirmation.

The discussion of these contemporary ills is one of the few places in the *Philosophy of Right* where Hegel seems quite uncertain what to conclude; he rather lamely says that overcoming the problem is one

---

[55] Leon Trotsky, 'Is the Bureaucracy a Ruling Class?' in *The Basic Writings of Trotsky*, ed. Irving Howe (Secker & Warburg, London, 1964), pp. 216–22, was no doubt overoptimistic about the future of the Soviet Union, but he was right to insist that apparatchiki do not meet the Marxist criterion of class membership, because their power and benefits are not based on ownership.

[56] *Philosophy of Right*, §§241–9, pp. 148–52.

[57] ibid., §203A, p. 170.

of the chief tasks of the future — a welfare state and colonization are vaguely suggested as possible remedies, but it cannot be said that Hegel is either very explicit or very convincing. Since many writers have made that point, comment here may be confined to two small issues. The first is that Hegel does not suggest that it is the existence of property that makes the poor poor; he is not an incipient Marxist, even if we note one or two pre-echoes of Marx's hostility to the division of labour in the argument. The existence of property does, as we have seen, entail *some* inequality, because freedom inevitably leads to results which reflect people's ability, energy, or luck, and these differ from one person to another, but it is only the modern economy which turns this into class inequality.[58]

The second point is that Hegel's concern is less with owners and non-owners than with the anchored and the non-anchored; because property is an anchor but not the only anchor, Hegel is committed to accepting some of the internal tensions of property — property anchors some, but the market shakes others loose — but controlling the results. Hence an emphasis on the way governments can control an economy and do not have to treat its operations as blind and uncontrollable forces of nature. Hegel's discussion of what he calls the 'police power' includes among other things governmental price fixing; there is no notion that property rights imply as a matter of logic or policy absolutely unimpeded free trade. Again, one might suggest that in this respect Hegel is not too far removed from the utilitarian, who, we saw, approaches the extent to which free trade is desirable in an entirely pragmatic fashion.

All this culminates in Hegel's discussion of the class structure of civil society. To call these elements 'classes' is perhaps misguided; Hegel calls them *Stände* or estates, which suggests the way they are rooted in economic life, but finally matter because of their political consequences.[59] Hegel half says that *Stände* are distinguished by the sorts of property they relate to, but it is more accurate to say that they are distinguishedd by social functions and life style or by their economic and political culture, and that the sort of property they have reflects and sustains that. So Hegel distinguishes three main *Stände* and a sort of anti-class. The three main classes are the agrarian estate, the commercial and industrial estate, and the

[58] ibid., §244, p. 150.
[59] ibid., §§301–12, pp. 195–203.

Crown's servants, the official estate.[60] Below these three estates lies the *Pöbel* — the 'rabble', who are not so much members of civil society as an unresolved problem for it.[61] The three major estates are labelled by Hegel in philosophical terms — the agricultural estate is 'substantial', the commercial estate 'formal' or 'reflective' and the bureaucracy 'universal'.

It is worth noting that Hegel does not divide his classes horizontally according to whether people have more property or less, or some property versus none. Presumably a skilled industrial worker, securely employed, cannot by any stretch of the imagination be put down as one of the 'rabble of paupers', even though he has no property; he must be a member of the formal or reflective class.[62] Hegel's division is in one case vertical, where he distinguishes an agrarian and an urban culture, and in the other case horizontal, in that the two unofficial classes look largely to their own interests, while the bureaucracy looks to the interests of all. That the division between classes cannot rest on property alone is plain enough from Hegel's insistence that modern civil servants do not own their positions.[63]

What Hegel is concerned with is the general stability and predictability of the lives of the members of these groups. Particularly, he contrasts the relaxed *Weltanschauung* of the agriculturalist, who plants the seed and waits patiently for the harvest in an attitude of trust and gratitude, with the busy-ness of the businessman, who constanly has to keep an eye on his assets to maximize his profits from them. Equally the agriculturalist is socially and geographically immobile; it is *this* place he lives in, cultivates and loves, and no other will do in exchange; it does not occur to him that he can employ different methods, grow different crops, get out into a wider world.[64]

Hegel, of course, knew that he was describing an ideal type and not the much more varied empirical reality. But it was enough to distinguish the traditionalist, communal, pious outlook of the countryside from the rationlist, self-centred and secular outlook of the town. Apart from anything else, here was Hegel's way of

[60] ibid., §202, p. 131.
[61] ibid., §244A, pp. 277–8.
[62] e.g., ibid., §252, p. 153.
[63] ibid., §277, §277A, pp. 179, 287–8.
[64] ibid., §203, p. 131.

making the old point that money breeds the world of easy come, easy go, while land stays put and its owner with it.[65] There is more, too, including a hint of the standard nineteenth-century English view that the ties of master and man in the countrty were paternal and caring on the one side and deferential and grateful on the other, whereas the callous cash nexus did not link employer and employee so much as set them at one another's throats.[66]

All this suggests that Hegel's main concern was with what in everyday terms of income or wealth we should think of as middle-class people. So I think it was. Hegel evidently feared that the commercial mind would apply its contractual and calculative schemes to every aspect of life. He was fearful that the independent, individualist, rationalist intellect would prove a powerful solvent of political loyalty; and when he did not fear that, he feared that any state in which the urban bourgeoisie held power would be one in which mean-spirited enterprises predominated, not those of a world historical kind.[67]

Military virtues as well as bourgeois virtues were wanted, and the meaning of life was not to be sought in a cash ledger. So we find Hegel after all defending the relics of the feudal order — guilds and corporations — as a device for rendering commercial spirits public-spirited; and we find him advocating a constitution which represents the landowners more directly than the commercial interests. This is not the place to defend or criticize Hegel's recipes. It is the place, though, to make one or two final comments on how Hegel proceeds, and how he illuminates our subject.[68]

Whereas Bentham looked to an independent, rationally evolved, moral standard to provide the critique of property rights, Hegel denies that we can so step out of our own times and standards as to discover such a thing. He looks rather to an explanation of how owning, acquiring, consuming, transferring, making and selling fit into our actual lives. It is not exactly a moral defence of property or the market or work, for there is no point at which Hegel sees his arguments ending in a moral exhortation. The assumption is rather that when we see our lives faithfully depicted, we shall simply go on

---

[65] ibid., §306, p. 199.
[66] ibid., §203A, p. 270.
[67] ibid., §324A, p. 295, appeals to the shining sabres of the hussars to remind the bourgeoisie that it is really true that man lives for something more than business.
[68] cf. Taylor, *Hegel and Modern Society*, for a sustained account of the contrast I rely on here.

living them, perhaps more at peace with ourselves, but not as a result of any moral conversion. This different conception of philosophical method is something Hegel shares with his greatest disciple and toughest critic. Marx thought that his condemnation of capitalism and the proprietary attitude to the world was not a *moral* condemnation, in just the same way that Hegel thought his defence of the bourgeois world was not a *moral* defence. Of course, Marx thought that once people saw clearly what capitalism was, they would realize they had to revolt against it rather than live at peace with it; but this would not be a moral decision − knowing what it was and what they themselves were, they would see what they *must* do.[69]

This is not to say that nothing in Hegel's vision of the world could be borrowed by writers who had quite other conceptions of the role of philosophy and the right of intellectuals to preach. The exuberant image of the will conquering nature in a pitched battle is employed to great effect by Carlyle in his account of Plugson of Undershot, as also is the quieter image of the way we can see generations of humble and unassuming care embodied in a green and smiling countryside; but Carlyle preaches unabashedly where Hegel would think it most unphilosophical to do so.[70] But in Bentham the thought that institutions may have a meaning with which their actual daily practice is at odds would find no foothold, while it is characteristic of Hegel that this is precisely how he works, though he, unlike Marx, sees practice as on the whole adequate to the underlying meaning.[71] Even a heretic must hold at least that much in common. When Carlyle complains of the cash nexus, it is because the *meaning* of work, which is the almost military subjugation of a recalcitrant nature, and which therefore demands expression in heroic, hierarchical and military forms of social organization, is misrepresented by contractual cash relationships.

This means that one cannot exactly 'compare and contrast' the views of Bentham and Hegel. One may, of course, say on particular points that Hegel comes to conclusions which Bentham would

---

[69] Karl Marx, *Writings of the Young Marx on Philosophy and Society*, ed. Lloyd Easton and Kurt Guddat (Doubleday, New York, 1967), p. 368.
[70] Thomas Carlyle, *Past and Present* (Dent, London, 1912), pp. 181ff., esp. p. 187.
[71] Taylor, *Hegel and Modern Society*, pp. 154ff. discusses the problem of what he calls 'situating freedom' in terms of this contrast.

reject — by 1818, we should not find Bentham defending the peculiar virtues of large landowners and entails as a way of locking them into their station and its duties. Nor would Bentham have thought the professional middle class so flighty as did Hegel — but then the English professional middle class did not make an 1848 revolution, where the Prussian professional middle class at any rate did its best to, so both might reckon to have been vindicated by events.[72] More generally, though, Hegel's vision of how work, property rights and politics were connected is at one level like Bentham's and at another level not.

The level at which it is like it is that both defend rationalized legal systems — tradition is for neither an independent source of validity — and both see a major part of government as administration; neither has any time for private interests dressed up as natural rights which their promoters try to place in the path of government action. Although Bentham treats modern, rational, utilitarian man as a fact of nature, where Hegel treats him as the product of the arcane purposes of history, both agree that neither the natural nor the social world can stand in his way, and that they must reflect his aspirations and his successes.

At this point the similarity ends. Bentham sees the constitutional problem as that of enforcing an identity of interest between rulers and people, where Hegel is obsessed by getting rational man to feel an adequate loyalty to his own state. Bentham, in a sense, stops at the point where politics secures that the government will maximize everyone's welfare, not that of its own personnel. He does not fear that we shall not be enough moved by its doing to be willing to sacrifice ourselves for our country, to remain loyal through thick and thin simply on the grounds that it is *our* country. This is no more than we should expect, given the initial contrast between a view of property rights which is concerned with a forseeable flow of benefit on the one hand, and a view which is concerned with our control of, and attachment to, a humanized world on the other.

# 6

# Mill and Marx and Socialism

A good deal of the justificatory and explanatory apparatus visible in my two final chapters has now been set out, and I shall not say more about it. Rather, I want to show it at work in contexts which are rather more familiar than those of the past few chapters — relying in so doing on the assumption that Marx and Mill and their sucessors are our contemporaries, and can be argued with as such. Mill and Marx can be seen as the two chief standard-bearers of political and economic reformism and revolution respectively. Methodologically and practically Marx was inclined to measure his own radical credentials by the inadequacy of Mill's; it is still true that to reforming liberals Mill's views come as easily as ever; equally, they are as much despised for their supposed thinness by Marxists as they were a hundred years ago.[1]

The usefulness of any comparison between Mill and Marx is sometimes doubted; Marxists who believe in the absoluteness of the break between Marxist science and the intellectual system of the bourgeois social theorist will certainly doubt it.[2] The point of the comparison here, however, is twofold. In the first place, what I argue throughout this chapter is that Mill and Marx were critics of capitalism and defenders of a socialist alternative to it not so much for reasons of welfare, but for the sake of freedom.[3] In the second place, though I make less of this, there is something very like a convergence of ideas between Mill and Marx on the nature of that freedom; so that in terms of the contrast I have been employing between instrumental and self-expressive or self-developmental categories of analysis, Mill and Marx are exemplary figures in showing what each mode of thought can incorporate from the repertoire of the other.[4]

---

[1] George Lichtheim, *Marxism* (Routledge & Kegan Paul, London, 1961), pp. xiii–xiv.
[2] Marx, *Capital*, vol I, p. 654.
[3] Graeme Duncan, *Marx and Mill* (Cambridge University Press, Cambridge, 1975) for a rather different view of their similarities and differences.
[4] ibid., pp. 293ff.

Naturally, I offer a very schematic account of both these substantial figures. In Marx's case, I rely very heavily on his indictment of property in his *Economic-Philosophical Manuscripts*, and explain his subsequent economic and political views in that perspective; I do not do much to justify this stance, but hope that what I say will be sufficiently convincing to take care of any doubts about the propriety of assuming that 'late' and 'early' Marx held much the same views.[5] In Mill's case, I rely on his statements about socialism in his *Chapters on Socialism*, and his *Principles of Political Economy*, but I also do something to explain why *Liberty* is a fundamental text for explaining what Mill meant by freedom, and is *not* a text in which he tries to justify the ownership of property by reference to the 'very simple principle' which the essay defends.[6]

Mill is notoriously hard to place among the critics and defenders of an economic system based on private property. Whether he was or was not a socialist is much debated, especially since there is no consensus as to what socialism *is*, and especially, though more trivially, because one popular view is that Mill briefly subscribed to socialism under the influence of Harriet Taylor and the 1848 revolution in France, before reverting to more or less orthodox support of capitalism.[7] We shall not settle the argument, but we may get clearer about what is at stake than most writers have managed. But behind this unclarity lies another.

This is the unclarity about the extent to which Mill was or was not a utilitarian; it makes a lot of difference to assessing the arguments Mill sets out for and against the individual ownership of land and capital whether he was a straightforward utilitarian or not. The argument of this chapter is that Mill's incorporation into utilitarianism of considerations of individual liberty, moral auto-nomy, and the culture of self-development complicates matters a good deal. It has the effect of making Mill more sceptical of the usual utilitarian arguments for individual ownership and free enterprise — the arguments from incentive and security that we have often mentioned — but it also gave him reasons for scepticism

---

[5] Louis Althusser, *For Marx* (Allen Lane, London, 1969) is the best known exponent of the view that between the young 'humanist' and the mature 'scientist' there is a complete epistemological 'break'.

[6] J. S. Mill, *Utilitarianism, Liberty and Representative Government* (Dent, London, 1910), pp. 150–1.

[7] Michael Packe, *The Life of John Stuart Mill* (Secker & Warburg, London, 1954), pp. 313–19, 488–91.

about the virtues of state ownership and control and reasons for opposing forms of property which would weaken the tie of responsibility between the individual and society. Mill found new and stronger arguments both against private property and for it; that, above all else, accounts for the dissension over his credentials as a socialist.[8]

The first thing we must explain is why Mill did not defend property rights as a corollary of the libertarian principle advanced in *Liberty*. The root of property is *not* our right to enjoy harmless liberty. It is true that a man who has a property right in something is free to use it in ways others are not, and it is true that if that right is removed, or limited in some way, his freedom has been limited. Mill, however, was an unflinching positivist and utilitarian about property rights.[9] Property rights are not natural liberties but social privileges, and we *have* only those property rights which the law gives us. The further question of what rights the law *should* give us is, in Mill's view, one to be settled on grounds of general utility, even if general utility can contain a large element of liberty promotion. That is, property titles are not to be defended by arguments from non-interference with harmless acts, which is what most arguments in *Liberty* are about. All the same, one argument for a particular set of property rights might be that it did not lead to so much interference thereafter as its rivals did; and one argument against an existing right being curtailed is that this would be an interference.

The greater part of *Liberty* is concerned to defend a view about the legitimate grounds for restricting a person's natural liberty, the famous view that it is only in self-defence that we may coerce others. This means that, *ceteris paribus*, I may stop you seizing what I have (but do not own), not because your aggression is an interference with my freedom, let alone proprietorship, in particular, but simply because my loss is a loss. By the same token, it would be in order for me in a civilized state to try to prevent harm to me and so stop a competitor opening a shop next door, or defeating me in an examination; what makes *ceteris imparibus* here is not a contractual or rights-based principle that I may not stop them doing

---

[8] Mill, *Principles of Political Economy*, II, i, 6, p. 986.
[9] ibid., II, i, 1–2, pp. 199–203; 'Chapters on Socialism' in *Essays on Economics and Society*, vols. IV and V of *The Collected Works of John Stuart Mill* (University of Toronto Press, Toronto, 1967), p. 753.

what I should myself claim the right to do, but a utilitarian argument for having a rule which stops us disabling the competition in this fashion.[10] Mill argues that the doctrine of *Liberty* has nothing to do with the defence of *laissez-faire*, and where non-intervention is the topic, he is plainly right.

For there are two distinct lines which Mill hoped to draw. One was the line between legitimate and illegitimate state or social intervention, the other the line within legitimate intervention between well- and ill-advised interference. Mill held that trade was a social act which fell into the category of activities legitimately controlled, whatever reasons there might be for a hands-off policy in practice. In so far as *Liberty* was concerned with freedom in the rather different sense of self-determination, the line between its concerns and Mill's economic concerns is thinner. It is clear enough that Mill's chapter on individuality in *Liberty* is very much of a piece with his account of 'the probable futurity of the labouring class' in the *Principles of Political Economy*. Still, the first point to establish is only that Mill's account of the nature of property rights is positivist, that the basis of legal right is not natural right, and that, crucially, there is no general argument to show that in the absence of the sort of private property system we now have, men would be less free.

In the absence of a natural right to property, the absence of property rights is not an absence of freedom, though it may be extremely difficult to imagine a world in which the freedom Mill is eager to preserve could survive the absence of analogues to private property, or in which men would not recreate such analogues. Would not people with the degree of free speech Mill envisages be likely to reinvent copyright and patents, say? Would they not combine in the sort of way which would demand something like the legal arrangements of the limited liability company? What makes property essential in Mill's eyes is the standard utilitarian considerations of incentive and security. In their absence no-one would do more than lead a minimally productive life, and the general level of well-being would be invariably low.

What makes Mill's account more interesting than that of his predecessors is that he was a sociologist with a conscience − or a moralizer with a sociological imagination. He said himself that until he encountered Owenites and Saint-Simonians he had taken

[10] *Utilitarianism etc.*, p. 150.

for granted existing English property relationships.[11] Nothing else seemed practicable — feudalism was a regime of force, traditional Indian and European tenures a tissue of exploitation and disincentive — and the dispensation of the societies of the north Atlantic littoral seemingly a uniquely rational property system. There was undoubtedly great inequality, but less than in most societies, and great poverty, but again less than in most societies; there was little reason to expect great benefits from wholesale reform, and many reasons to expect trouble.[12]

This did not mean that *no* reforms were worth making; the editor of Bentham and colleague of Austin was not likely to think that; but reforms were to be directed to making property more secure, and less encumbered by antique restrictions. There was much to be said for making it easier to break the restrictions on endowments, and for shaking up the organization of charities, many of which did none of the things for which they had been set up.[13] That, however, was the standard radical programme. For abstract schemes of common ownership, for the equalization of wealth or income, Mill initially had no time at all.

One reason, which is worth bearing in mind because it could pull in two different directions, lay in the supposed connnection between wages and population. The doctrine that wage levels reflected the size of the employers' 'wages fund' and the number of workers seeking employment — the average wage simply being the first divided by the second — suggested that one way in which workers could be made better off was by having smaller families. This could be a very conservative doctrine, placing all the onus of improving their lot on the workers. In Mill's hands it was better than that; he realized that prudence was not a virtue encouraged by poverty and ignorance, and that if the working class was to take the responsibility for its own improvement, a change in social attitudes and organization would be needed to provide an incentive for it to do so. As we shall see, it is an argument in favour of the workers' co-operatives advocated by Mill that they will demand just that self-control and foresight which population control also requires.

---

[11] J. S. Mill, *Autobiography*, vol. I of *The Collected Works of John Stuart Mill* (University of Toronto Press, Toronto, 1981), pp. 237–41.
[12] ibid., p. 239.
[13] J. S. Mill, 'Corporation and Church Property', in *Essays on Economics and Society*, pp. 193ff.

Self-management in industry is a complement to self-control in domestic life.[14]

Mill was clear that the economic arrangements of nineteenth-century Britain were grossly defective. Too many people worked long hours for low wages at very boring and disagreeable work.[15] This is not the place to go into Mill's economics in detail, but it is worth noting that Mill was an acute critic of those who thought wages automatically reflected the unpleasantness of a job. He saw that the labour market was not a perfect market, that class and background, not taste, determined what job a man did, and that low wages went with unpleasant work.[16]

His complaint against this is an objection from justice more than anything else, though arguments from freedom come into it. There was no proportionality between the effort a man put in, the sacrifices he made, and the reward he got. In economic matters, Mill relied more heavily on arguments from justice than one would expect. The only unequivocal property he thought anyone could claim was in what he had made by his own efforts. If here he seems to waver between thinking that this was an argument of desert, and suggesting that, since the thing would not have existed at all save for the creator's efforts, some strong personal bond exists between the maker and the made, it is generally desert which worries Mill; whence the contrast between a worker's deserts and a worker's income.[17]

Mill denied that anything like the Marxian tendency to immiseration existed; there was a steady downward pressure on wages, because employees would try to get all their factors of production as cheaply as possible. There was also a steady counteracting presure in a growing economy or anywhere labour was scarce; and in any case the cheapness of labour was a matter of a worker's productivity, and Mill thought high wages and high productivity went together.[18] The Marxian saga of workers always being replaced by machinery and always dropping from skilled to unskilled jobs did not seem to Mill to be an accurate *general* picture. Some trades at some periods were like this, but not the economy as

---

[14] *Principles of Political Economy*, II, vii, 3–4; pp. 765–9; *Chapters on Socialism*, p. 743.

[15] *Chapters on Socialism*, pp. 712ff.

[16] *Principles*, II, i, 2, p. 202; II, xiv, 1, p. 383.

[17] ibid., II, i, 3, pp. 207–8.

[18] ibid., II, xi, 2, pp. 338ff.

a whole. Mill never read any of Marx's economic writings, and his denials of the 'immiseration thesis' are directed against his French ally Louis Blanc — most of whose views Mill accepted, but whose immiseration thesis, 'une baisse continue de salaire', he denied — but Mill's objections are essentially those of later critics of Marx. They amount to saying that if competition can keep wages down, it can also keep wages up.[19]

What Mill did object to was the inequality which reflected no unequal merit or contribution, and beyond that he disliked the whole wage relationship. Although Mill did not share Marx's almost religious veneration of labour, Mill did share one of Marx's passions — a passionate dislike of the way industry was organized. That it amounted to a dictatorship of the managers over the managed was intolerable. It is worth insisting that it is the *manager-worker* relationship which is to Mill intolerable and not 'exploitation'. Theories of exploitation are couched in terms of the *capitalist* and the labourer, and what is represented as intolerable is the extraction of surplus value from the worker by the owner. In Mill's terms, however, most of what Marx discussed under the heading of exploitation would be better analysed in terms of the bargaining power of owners and workers, without invoking the theory of surplus value, and could be tackled by trade unions.[20]

The more distinctive issue is the political objection to industrial organization, the complaint that workers, seen as mere suppliers of labour, are put in a servile relationship with their employers. Their intelligence is not engaged, they have no say in setting the output, prices or profits of the firm that employs them; it is not true that they do not bear the risks of the company, for they do — if they lose their employment, they will suffer as much hardship as any of the investors, and more than the managers. But what they share is only risk, not responsibility. On Mill's view, though, it would not be enough to improve wages or even security. This would be well worth having, but it would still not be enough. What was needed was to put the workers themselves in charge of their own employment.[21]

There are several things to be noticed about this. In the first place, the argument is not directly about economic matters, nor

[19] *Chapters*, pp. 727ff.
[20] *Principles*, II, xiii, 2, p. 374.
[21] ibid., IV, vii, 4, pp. 766–9.

directly about ownership, though considerations closely akin to ownership considerations arise; and as soon as one starts working out in any detail what legal arrangments would be needed to implement Mill's hopes, we come to questions central to property at once — for instance, about what powers investors could or should have over a company, whether they should share in capital gains or only in profits and, equally pertinently, about the distribution of the proceeds from publicly owned enterprises.[22]

Still, it is not difficult to see that for analytical purposes, even if less plausibly in political practice, we can separate out issues of legal title and prescriptions for management. Either a monopoly central investment bank or a myriad of individual investors could supply the capital for an enterprise which would in the first instance satisfy Mill's test if and only if the workers in it managed it for themselves.

Mill's views on work as such are more loosely attached to this attack on the social relations of capitalist industry than are his views on what is and is not a morally acceptable form of organization. Mill certainly did have strong views about work, partly learned from Carlyle and Coleridge.[23] He complained that Bentham had no sense of the desire to work one's will on the world, no feeling for the poet's or artist's sense of order and power. For work in this sense Mill had the highest regard, and to judge by his favourite tag — 'work while it is yet day for the night cometh in which no man can work' — he had an acute sense of why work mattered.[24] Although Mill never liked the Hegelian jargon, he had a thoroughly Hegelian feeling for the way work anchored a man in a world which outlived him, and gave his purposes an objective life beyond his own.

What threatened this, though, did not seem to him to be the system of ownership nor yet the division of labour. It was more a whole social ethos, and it seemed to him to afflict the middle class just as much as the working class. Roughly, what Mill saw was a world in which getting on and money making were all that gave

[22] Alasdair Clayre (ed.), *The Political Economy of Co-operation and Participation* (Oxford University Press, Oxford, 1980), pp. 1–7, 185ff.
[23] J. S. Mill, 'Bentham', in *Essays on Politics and Culture* (Doubleday, New York, 1963), pp. 98–9; but it is worth recalling Mill's hostility to the brutality of Carlyle's belief in the Gospel of Work as it applied to Negro Slaves and the like. See Pedro Schwartz, *The New Political Economy of J. S. Mill* (Weidenfeld & Nicolson, London, 1972), p. 216.
[24] *Essays on Politics and Culture*, p. 98.

meaning — of an impoverished sort — to life.[25] It was this short-term, self-centred culture which did the damage. Forms of ownership and industrial technique seem to have struck Mill as more or less irrelevant. It is as well to say only more or less, of course, because Mill had no doubt that the great expansion of such an outlook was a result as well as a cause of the flourishing commercial economy of his day.[26]

The point, though, is that it is entirely conceivable that such an outlook could flourish under a system of public ownership, if less plausible that it would thrive in a society based upon handicrafts. It is wholly conceivable that in a system where industrial and commercial capital was owned by a state corporation, individuals would still measure their own success as human beings by no more elevated standard than how far up the managerial ladder they had climbed and how many consumable items they had acquired. A society could be 'consumerist' and selfish in the deplored way without the private ownership of capital.[27]

What Mill objects to, then, is the diffusion of selfishness, narrowness and a false standard of personal merit. The question of how great an evil he thought this was is not very easy to answer. He was too ready to see small events as evidence of very large defects and virtues. But it is familiar enough to readers of the *Principles* how drastically Mill revised his estimate of Yankee virtues and vices under the impulse of the Civil War — he quite reversed his abusive description of the men as dollar-hunters and the women as nothing but breeders of dollar-hunters.[28] Similarly, the English working class fell and rose in his eyes — the engineers' strike in 1852 seemed a mere conspiracy against the public; the cotton operatives' self-sacrificing support for the North in the Civil War showed the nobility of the working man. Like later liberals too, Mill was very quick to trace events to qualities in the characters and morality of the population, and less quick to give conditions their due weight.

None of this affects the main point, however, which is that Mill could not believe that in an age when politics was destined to become more democratic, industrial organization would not do so

[25] cf. J. S. Mill, 'Civilization', in *Essays on Politics and Culture*, pp. 45–76.
[26] ibid., pp. 45f., 48ff.
[27] Milovan Djilas, *The New Class* (Thames & Hudson, London, 1957) for one account, and Hedrick Smith, *The Russians* (Times Books, London, 1976), pp. 25–52 for a vivid description of their 'consumerism'.
[28] *Principles*, IV, vi, 2, p. 754n.

too. Whether he acquired the belief by reading de Tocqueville, or from some other source, Mill thought the tendency towards political and economic democracy was irresistible.[29] This being so, the only question concerned the form democracy might take. This was not an easy question to answer. The experience of France, where a democratic franchise had been exploited by Napoleon III to establish his dictatorship, was not reassuring. Britain was not likely to end up in quite that state, but the temptation to govern by a combination of paternalism and repression was one which British politicians would no doubt feel. So would British employers.

Mill did not think that employers had yet fully accepted even the contractual view of their relations with their workers; he thought that a feudal attitude was all too common. But he did not think it could go on surviving.[30] The argument behind Mill's conviction is not very clear, but in outline at any rate, the negative claim is that the workers would not defer to their 'superiors' very much longer; the positive claim is that once people acquire a taste for self-government, they will not relinquish it for any other benefit. The argument from self-government as an ideal, however, is not one which Mill directly invokes in his discussion of the probable futurity of the labouring class; it appears in its pure form in Mill's discussion of women's rights in *The Subjection of Women*, where Mill does appeal to the fact that no child, once free of parental authority, relishes returning to it, just as no nation come to independence would sell its independence for any degree of prosperity.[31] At all events, Mill thought it unlikely that workers would be content to serve as mere wage earners for much longer; only by being associated in the management of the enterprises in which they worked could they retain their sense of their own autonomy, dignity and responsibility for their own well-being.

The implications for legal property rights are indirect. That is, if self-management is the great goal, we clearly need to envisage a legal structure which allows it, or encourages it, but it is not obvious that only one system of property rights will allow it. As we have already seen, Mill's view of ownership makes it very important that people should have rights over what they make by

[29] ibid., IV, vii, 1–2, pp. 758–65.
[30] ibid., IV, vii, 1, pp. 759–60.
[31] J. S. Mill, *The Subjection of Women* in *Essays on Sex Equality*, ed. Alice Rossi (University of Chicago Press, Chicago, 1971), p. 237.

their own efforts, and this in turn suggests that there is no moral objection to contractual arrangements whereby people can exchange what they make just as they like with one another. And it suggests an explanation of profit which makes it morally acceptable in principle — that profit is a return for abstinence, a doctrine Marx detested, but one which is not implausible if the self-denying overtones of 'abstinence' are removed.[32]

If someone possesses a piece of machinery, either made by themselves or acquired by purchase or inheritance, those who want to work with it will have to contract with its owner. The owner's profits are simply what he ends with over and above what he has paid out for the machinery. A highly productive economy where capital equipment is much in demand will produce a high rate of return, though other factors will determine whether this will last, whether demand will be volatile, and so on. The point, however, is that Mill's way of looking at the relations between capital provision and the activities of workers explains what is otherwise hard to explain, namely his extreme casualness about the virtues of co-operators' capitalism versus co-operators' socialism.

Mill was perfectly clear that workers need capital goods to work with, but did not need capitalists to provide them. The case for the existence of the individual capitalist was, where it existed at all, partly managerial and partly entrepreneurial.[33] Although profit is not to be explained as managers' wages, the performance of managerial functions *is* the justification of an owner receiving anything above the going rate of interest. It is the rate of interest — with a margin for insurance — which measures the pure compensation for abstinence, that is, not employing funds in consumption; over and above that, the owner could claim something for management and something for entrepreneurial initiative.

If there is limited liability on a large scale, and the functions of ownership divide up in such a way that it is *managers* who spot the opportunities and run the firm, the moral claim of owners to whatever profits are made ceases to be a good one. Mill was here the begetter of an argument which became commonplace in the 1920s and 1930s, and which is the moral backbone of Tawney's *The Acquisitive Society*.[34] One might argue that there would still be a case

---

[32] *Principles*, II, xv, 1, pp. 400–2.
[33] ibid., II, xv, 1, p. 401.
[34] R. H. Tawney, *The Acquisitive Society* (Bell, London, 1921), pp. 96–104.

for paying shareholders different rates of interest for investments of different degrees of risk, and that that would replicate the existing notion that shareholders are legally entitled to the profits. But it does not really do that, for the higher and lower interest rates would only represent the greater and lesser chances of receiving payment at all. If the project succeeded, one would receive only a fixed return, the surplus, when it had been made, going to those who had made it.[35]

Mill in any event was a theorist of the 'stationary state' who anticipated an end to economic growth in the not far distant future. He was therefore not very interested in the entrepreneurial role in the capitalist economy, and was not therefore likely to explore very seriously the justifications for the individual capitalist which have been offered in recent years.[36]

One further point may serve to round off the argument. A view of the cycle from investment to profit and reinvestment which starts by visualizing a group of workers seeking a supplier of resources with which to mix their labour has already moved away from the image implicit in (what is also in Mill's analysis) the story which begins with the capitalist advancing wages enough to keep the workers alive while they work on his machinery and in his factory. I do not want to make much of this; obviously, whichever way we look at it, we can ask the crucial question, which is what the balance of bargaining power is between workers and capitalists.[37]

All the same, as Marx probably felt, the contractual picture implied by Mill seems to imply that the workers are united, well enough fed, and in no great hurry to find someone to supply them with resources, while the reality was that a capitalist, who had all the time in the world to wait for the workers to accept his terms, faced unorganized individuals who were permanently on the verge of starvation. Mill, up to a point, can be accused of writing in an equality of bargaining power that in his day hardly existed outside the USA and perhaps not often even there.

At all events, in a non-growing economy and one in which the old system of ownership and management have ceased to coincide, associations of workers owning their own firms, or borrowing capital from elsewhere, emerge as morally equivalent and equally

[35] ibid., pp. 87ff, 98ff.
[36] e.g. George Gilder, *Wealth and Poverty* (Basic Books, New York, 1981), pp. 47ff.
[37] *Principles*, V, xi, 5, p. 932.

practicable.[38] The matter does not rest there, however. There is the question of how all this is to work in areas other than industry, and there is the question of how much inequality the arrangements invisaged by Mill will allow, and how far they permit the transmission of such inequality from one generation to the next. Finally, there is the question of how the market-place enters the picture.

We have seen already that utilitarians do not see property rights as 'natural'; but if one can distinguish degrees of unnaturalness here, we may say that the ownership of land in outright freehold is especially unnatural. Arguments from incentive cannot directly apply, since land cannot be created; land can, of course, be improved, but that is an argument for giving the improver a right to the value of his improvements, not an argument for the existence of freeholds.[39] Arguments about security of tenure, and about the importance of personal connection, do apply, of course, but they apply in all areas, and neither peculiarly to *land* ownership, nor peculiarly to *ownership*. The absentee owner of the freehold cannot claim personal connections with his land — his tenant has a much stronger case than he — and arguments in favour of not disappointing expectation apply to tenants, to employees who hope to go on doing the same job and who fear dismissal, and generally.[40]

If there are good reasons for not giving workers a freehold in their jobs, the same reasons imply that the freehold ownership of land is anything but sacred. Mill was perfectly willing to see landlords who were a barrier to improvement bought up by compulsory purchase, so that their land could be resold, or leased, to tenants who would thereby get an incentive to improve their property. The target of Mill's concern now makes little impact, since the Irish question — in that respect — has been answered.[41] But the basic argument applied to more cases than the need to get English landlords off the backs of their Irish tenants. It applies in any case where the value of a tenant's improvements accrues to the landlord, and where the landlord has insufficient commercial

[38] J. Vanek, *The General Theory of Labour-Managed Economies* (Cornell University Press, Ithaca, NY, 1970) shows indeed how few welfare differences there would be so long as the market was preserved.
[39] *Principles*, II, ii, 5–6, pp. 227–30.
[40] ibid., II, ii, 6, pp. 230–1.
[41] ibid., II, ii, 6, pp. 229–30; II, vi, 1, pp. 252–4.

incentive — or insufficiently commercial habits — to make the improvements. To compare lesser with greater, the relationship between the tenants of council housing and their landlords is equally to be condemned on these considerations, and it is not difficult to see how the run-down state of much public housing is to be explained by analogy with the run-down state of nineteenth-century Irish farms.[42]

The twist in Mill's argument, of course, is what it commonly is in Mill's work, and that is his eagerness to promote the moral improvement of all parties. Landlords under threat of compulsory purchase would become more vigorous and wide awake, and tenants who replaced those evicted would similarly be energetic, prudent, innovative and imaginative. It is perhaps characteristic of liberal thinking to be at one and the same time insufficiently attentive to the way people are now at the mercy of institutions which individually they have no realistic hope of changing, and exaggeratedly hopeful for the effects of institutional change. One can see this in Mill's reaction to such things as the Northcote-Trevelyan report of 1854, which Mill seemed to think might cause a sea change in working-class attitudes to work and responsibility — now, it seemed, the average manual worker was astonishingly narrow, selfish and irresponsible; with the introduction of competition into the selection of recruits for the civil service, he might become enlightened, practically over night.[43]

To the twentieth-century eye, it is not only this tendency to swing from condemnation of the present to utopian optimism about the future that is particularly striking. Another striking feature is Mill's casualness about the legal details altogether. He seems not to consider the anxieties which nowadays do much to explain trade-union hostility to co-operatives, especially the fear that a person may have all his or her savings in the company he or she works in, and therefore be absolutely ruined if through no fault of his or her own it goes broke.[44] One might suppose that Mill gave little thought to this because by comparison with the plight of the nineteenth-century worker absolutely at the mercy of his employer's

[42] cf. ibid., II, ii, 6, p. 229, on what happens when the owners have no money for improvements and the tenants no stake in the property and therefore no incentive to risk their own money.

[43] Alan Ryan, 'Utilitarianism and Bureaucracy', in G. Sutherland (ed.), *Studies in the Growth of Nineteenth Century Government* (Routledge & Kegan Paul, London, 1972), pp. 53–4.

[44] Clayre, *Political Economy of Co-operation*, pp. 1–8.

competence and honesty, the co-operator would not be badly off. Mill's belief in the imminence of a no-growth economy may also have led him to underestimate the speed with which financial disasters can strike.[45]

One further consideration, however, which is worth bearing in mind is that Mill's attitude to the market was essentially that of a moralist. Mill's motives for defending competition are not the same as those of most economists. It is true that Mill appeals to some of the considerations that any economist would have done, when, for instance, he denies that competition always lowers wages. That is, Mill argues that just as competition among workers can drive down wage rates, so competition among employers can drive wages up; but there is little emphasis on competition as a force for economic growth or as a means of enforcing efficiency. Mill does assume that competition makes for efficiency, not uniquely, but perhaps more reliably than, say, unreinforced public spirit would.[46] All the same, Mill is much more eager to see justice secured than to see efficiency for its own sake. The connection between justice and competition demands that the workers should understand the role of the market. In assessing workmanship, the market must be made to reinforce the desire of the scrupulous workman to demand neither more nor less than the worth of his work.[47]

Whether we can visualize the market being so transformed from a competition in which each tries to beggar his neighbour into one where each tries to emulate the best achievements of his neighbour, is not an easy question to answer. Critics may say that it is obviously foolish, inasmuch as the market only operates *because* each agent in the market-place pursues his or her own selfish interests without regard to any more elevated consideration than the bare legality of the proposed line of action; to alter the agent's motivation is to abolish the market.

One might defend Mill by appealing to an analogy which moved him. An army exists to fight the enemy, and its standing aim is no doubt to kill as many enemy as possible while suffering the minimum of casualties itself. Yet, within its own ranks there will be

---

[45] *Principles*, IV, vi, pp. 752–7, where Mill not only predicts the stationary state, but encourages us to bring it to pass sooner rather than later.

[46] ibid., V, xi, 5, pp. 941–2 contrasts private and governmental undertakings along these familiar lines.

[47] ibid., IV, vii, 7, pp. 794–6 makes both the moral and the technical case.

a rivalry among its members to show themselves brave, generous and self-sacrificing. The example of Sir Philip Sidney, who sacrificed his last drop of water to comfort a dying enemy, will be held up as the ideal, not the career of some character who worked out the cost-effective balance between risk to himself and danger to the enemy. Mill was anxious to capture for economic life something at least of the military virtues, and the analogy suggests that he was not simply wrong to think it could be done.[48]

Is this enough to make Mill a socialist? The question is too vague to be given an unequivocal answer. In a sense he certainly was, since he envisaged something like the abolition of the distinction between workers and capitalists, and one reasonable test for socialism would be the aspiration for a classless society. If Mill was thus far a socialist, he was more nearly in the syndicalist mould than in anything else, for one of the ways in which Mill was unlike both Marx and his Fabian successors was his hostility to government.[49]

Marx, of course, visualized the role of the state in paradoxical ways — the state will control production and distribution only until they have been so socialized that the state withers away, and what administration is left will not be political at all. The Fabians generally visualized something like perpetual management boards, politically appointed, essentially on the grounds of expertise, gradually getting more and more of economic life under efficient control.[50]

Mill wanted none of this. He was not hostile to government activity as such; nobody in his position in the East India Company could have been so silly. Nor did he think governmental activity necessarily less efficient than private, self-interested activity. What he did think was that the habit of placing more and more matters in the hands of the state was inimical to progress. All the arguments for experiments in living to which *Liberty* is committed reappear in the discussion of the principles of government intervention in book V of the *Principles*; talent should be spread about, not monopolized

[48] J. S. Mill, 'Auguste Comte and Positivism', *The Collected Works of John Stuart Mill*, (University of Toronto Press, Toronto, 1969), vol. X, p. 341.
[49] ibid., V, xi, 6, pp. 942ff., almost suggests that the better government gets at running things, the more important it is to restrict its activities for the sake of giving the population at large plenty to do on its own behalf.
[50] Which is why Beatrice Webb disliked producer co-operatives; cf. Ken Coates (ed.), *The New Workers Co-operatives* (Spokesman Books, Nottingham, 1976), pp. 28–30.

by the bureaucracy, and although central government could properly intervene in all sorts of cases where market failure was likely — the provision of public goods, control of monopolies, setting standards where consumers had no real power to do so — the way it chose to intervene ought to be with a view to developing the capacity of the society for self-management.[51]

Governments were uniquely placed to collect and hand out information, to co-ordinate voluntary effort, and to provide a legal framework for what their citizens wanted to do; but this made it all the more important that they should assist and not compel, and that where compulsion was needed that it should be applied with as light a touch as possible. The sort of thing Mill had in mind is readily illustrated in the field of education; governments could legitimately compel parents to have their children educated, but should refrain from telling them how or where to do so. None the less, parents could not be expected to be able by ordinary market pressures alone to keep up high standards in schools, so governments could legitimately enforce standards of competence, perhaps by examining students, and perhaps by providing benchmark schools as an example.[52] Defenders of private property as the only basis of political and other liberties would no doubt think that some more strenuous prohibition of government intervention is needed, and that only by firmly placing the onus of providing education on parents and private schools would diversity, high standards and due regard to parental choice be secured. Mill, in contrast, thinks that the 'freedom' offered to those without resources is illusory, and that only a public and effective concern for freedom and diversity could really be relied on to secure them.

Mill, then, is a rather ambiguous figure. His concerns wear well, since the flexibility of his approach to the role of competition, the duties of government and the attractions of self-management means that his conclusions are not too tightly tied to the historical conditions under which he actually wrote.[53] Mill's doubts about the justice of private property remain live ones. For example, Mill sees that the considerations which suggest that we ought to

---

[51] *Principles*, V, xi, 6, pp. 942–3.

[52] *Utilitarianism etc.*, pp. 347–8, where Mill's *Representative Government* applies the principle to relations between central government and local bodies.

[53] cf. Schwartz, *New Political Economy*, pp. 235–41.

recognize private property resulting from a person's own efforts tell against recognizing anything like an unrestricted right of inheritance. Neither incentive nor justice dictates that a person should be able to begin life at too great an advantage over everyone else; but there is much to be said for the view that we should do as little as possible to interfere with the lifetime choices of the owner of property.[54]

The position that Mill espouses is that we should look to accessions taxes rather than death duties to spread wealth around more equally: the present owner may leave his property as he likes, but in the knowledge that he will do no good to anyone already well endowed. Mill anticipates twentieth-century discussions even more markedly than that — he points out that a taxation system like this will only work properly if introduced in a climate of opinion friendly to equality rather than to the activities of tax avoidance experts, and that there will have to be exceptions to the policy of spreading wealth around in such cases as the ownership of great estates like Chatsworth, where the estate is as much a public resource as it is private property. If Mill's concerns wear well, and his solutions to some difficulties anyway seem to be persuasive, not everything about the discussion strikes so up-to-date a note. Mill shows little sense of the dynamism and rapidity of change which characterizes modern industrial economies, and no suspicion that new technologies may all but dictate the organization of their employment. That is part and parcel of his belief that he lived in an economy soon to reach a stationary state, and one of the background causes of the moralizing tone which strikes a twentieth-century ear rather oddly.

I have already said that Marx measured his own revolutionary virtue against the imperfect radicalism of Mill. The contrast between them, however, is not captured by observing that Marx was generally more in favour of revolutionary upheaval than was Mill. Indeed, it is hard to believe that Marx and Mill would have been far apart on most practical issues — they both admired the communards of 1871, but knew all along that they were doomed; neither would have encouraged the communards before the event, though both defended the commune against its detractors, and Mill was, if anything, more hostile to Napoleon III and his empire than

[54] *Principles*, II, ii, 3–4, pp. 218–25.

was Marx.[55] Mill was inclined to deplore loose talk of 'revolution' when English working men indulged in it, and inclined to think it a peculiarly French weakness — but Marx said much the same.

The contrast we would do better to explore is the contrast between the philosophical inheritances of Marx and Mill. To put it somewhat peremptorily, Marx's work displays everywhere its origins in what I have called the German self-developmental and self-expressive tradition; this means that a concept such as that of alienation, which is rather awkwardly translatable into the terminology of utilitarian ethics, is central to Marx's account of the evils of private property and capitalist economy.[56] Moreover, it is because Marx begins in this philosophical mode that he denies all along that his complaints against capitalism and private property are *moral* complaints.[57] Unlike Mill, who was a legal positivist when it comes to analysing what property *is*, and who applied an expanded utilitarianism to the question of what property rights there *ought* to be, Marx denied from the beginning that there was the sort of cleavage between *what is* and *what ought to be* which most theories of ethics supposed. Hegel had closed any such gap between analysis and prescription.[58]

But whereas Hegel's mode of analysis presupposed that in the last resort the philosopher could show that things were — in some sense — as they should be, Marx's presupposed that there would be genuine and unresolved contradictions in the real world. Marx could claim that his condemnation of private property was not a *moral* condemnation because he believed that the condemnation sprang from, and was implicit in, any serious analysis of the division of labour, the market, private ownership and profit. This is not to say that Marx's work begins and ends with the *Economic-Philosophical Manuscripts*, and it is not to say that there are no significant changes in Marx's outlook between 1844 and the publication of *Capital*. It is plausible to see Marx shifting from a

---

[55] Mill wrote to the general council of the International Working Men's Association to declare his unreserved approval of Marx's first address on the Franco-Prussian War of 1870; 'there was not one word in it that ought not to be there.' Henry Collins and Chimen Abramsky, *Karl Marx and the British Labour Movement* (Macmillan, London, 1965), pp. 178–9.
[56] Marx, *Early Writings*, pp. 322ff.
[57] Marx, *German Ideology*, p. 47.
[58] Paul Walton and Andrew Gamble, *From Alienation to Surplus Value* (Sheed and Ward, London, 1972) give a plausible, if sometimes high-pitched, account of how Marx's views both developed and yet preserved a consistent and distinctive philosophical focus.

more romantic concern with self-expression in work in his early essays to a more utilitarian concern with our general enjoyment of the world in his later work.

All the same, in something of the same way that Mill might be said to stretch the concept of utility in taking so much account of freedom and diversity as sources of happiness, and yet to remain a utilitarian for all that, so Marx's attention to the detailed workings of capitalism, his concern for simple overwork, poor diet or poor housing − attention to issues of 'welfare' − is couched within a theory in which freedom is the great goal and 'alienation' the key term of disapprobation.[59]

We have seen how Hegel explained property in terms of men's fixing their wills in the world by appropriating, transforming and consuming things in the outside world. Marx's analysis turns this inside out. That is, Marx's strictures on property entail that Hegel's positive claims for private property, work and the market are all of them the reverse of the truth. So far from affirming ourselves in working, owning and exchanging, we deny ourselves, suffer loss, behave in a thinglike and non-human way.[60]

The argument in outline is this. Human beings do indeed have a need to form projects which they implement in the objective world. Marx claims that Hegel's great merit was to see that this urge to work is essential to humanity, and his failure was to confine his attention to one form of work, namely thought.[61] This is not wholly plausible − the more important difference is that Hegel looked for something other than human activity to explain human activity, the work of *Geist* or Spirit, where Marx had no such hankerings after the transcendental. Still, what is central is Marx's view that men are defined by their capacity to work, and are distinguished from all other creatures by what Marx calls their ability to produce *freely*.[62] Other creatures may build nests or hives on an instinctive basis; man alone is free to consider his own needs, to change them, to envisage ideal objects and to proceed to realize them. Aesthetic creation is a paradigm of free production, for here there is no limit or constraint on what we can create, though there are, of course, non-constraining standards of success.

[59] Marx, *Early Writings*, pp. 324–34.
[60] ibid., p. 326.
[61] ibid., p. 387.
[62] ibid., pp. 328–9.

So central to Marx's thinking, in his early years at least, is this picture of man as essentially a creator that he even writes of enjoyment and consumption in terms of the creation and appropriation of objects.[63] Thus the spectator who really appreciates a painting is held by Marx to have taken part in creating an object of beauty, which as an object of beauty is appropriated by the aesthetic sensibility.

We therefore have a picture of a human world in which we create and appropriate objects in two senses, one the most literal sense in which the painter paints in oil on canvas and therefore creates a new physical object, which we can then take and put where we want, the second the more philosophically interesting sense in which the painter creates the beauty as an object of appreciation, and one which we do not appropriate by taking the physical painting and hanging it where we want, but by enjoying it *as* beauty. Marx held that just as a blind man cannot see the visual properties of things, which therefore do not exist *for him* as visible objects, so the man with no aesthetic sense cannot see the beauty of a painting, whose beauty therefore does not exist *for* him.[64]

This enables Marx to argue that what happens under the reign of private property or capitalism is that work and enjoyment are both dehumanized, and in the same way; and it also allows him to argue that property is, paradoxically, a form of failed appropriation — we only acquire the external, non-human aspects of things, and fail to acquire their richer substance. The richer we become in conventional terms, the poorer we really are.

Man as a creator needs to create and enjoy; sometimes this is no more than to say that we need to produce food and eat it, build houses to live in, and so on.[65] But human beings, in doing this, do more than merely maintain their own physical fabric. Ideally, they also weave a pattern of social interaction which expresses their deepest attachments to one another and the world. A meal is not a mere exercise in stuffing chemicals through a hole in the face; it is an occasion in which emotional ties can be affirmed and celebrated, skills can be displayed and admired, a platform provided for conversation. What Marx maintains is that under capitalism work and consumption are devalued, rendered non-human.

[63] ibid., pp. 352–4.
[64] ibid., p. 353.
[65] ibid., pp. 327–8.

This operates in two ways. In the first place, work becomes purely instrumental, as, for most workers, does consumption. In the second place, the whole system of production and exchange escapes from human control, and takes on a life of its own, hostile to the human beings who, paradoxically, both created the system and run it still. That work becomes purely instrumental is not to be wondered at; with the advanced division of labour the worker does only a fragment of a job, and never organizes the whole process of creation from seeing a need, through design, and on to production. What he does is perform some small, repetitive operation. Such skill as is involved is generally built into the machine, so his work is minimally human, and its pace is dictated by the machine's requirements, not his.[66]

Worse yet, he has no choice in *what* he helps to produce; if the goods are shoddy, or dangerous to health, he can do nothing about that — all he is is an instrument in the production of whatever the capitalist who employs him has decided to produce. As if this was not enough, the organization of the labour market ensures that those with whom he works are his sworn enemies, since competition between workers for employment means that everyone else is a threat to one's own livelihood. When Marx describes all this as 'alienation', this is to seize on the contrast between the *human* qualities which work might display and its reality under capitalism; we are co-operative, rational, innovative, sociable beings, who are forced to work against one another, unintelligently, repetitively, and in hostility. Everything we create in these conditions is marked with the horrors of its origins — it is as if every good in the market-place wears a label saying 'this was wrung from the forced labour of its makers; they do not care whether it gives you pleasure or good service, for all they care is that you should pay as high a price for it as you can be got to pay.'

Before carrying on the story to matters of consumption, we ought to notice that Marx's objections to the uncontrollability of production, the unchosenness of what is produced, the disconnection between the needs it satisfies and what is produced, and the horrors of the division of labour, do not imply that the capitalist is more able to control what goes on than is the worker.[67] It is

---

[66] ibid., pp. 325–6.

[67] cf. *Capital*, vol. I, Marx's preface, p. 92; Marx's slogan is that capitalism embodies the tyranny of things over men; the individual capitalist is merely the agent of the process; see too the appendix to *Capital*, vol. I, pp. 989–90.

property as capital which is in control, and its owners are at its mercy — which is the chief reason for saying that on Marx's account the Hegelian emphasis on the human sovereignty over the inanimate world is exactly the reverse of the truth.

The owner of capital is forced to maximize profits; if he produces what he enjoys without regard to profitability, he simply loses his money to the man who does maximize his profits. Since maximizing profits involves pressing forward with the division of labour, replacing skilled work by unskilled, employing advanced machinery, selling whatever he can for all it will fetch, he is the instrument of the power of capital in dehumanizing the workers, not an independent agent.[68] This is not to say that Marx really thought that capital had a life of its own in the sense in which Hegel's *Geist* is the ultimate driving force of social life and social change: but he did have a strong sense of the way in which men can contrive a social order which then confronts them as if it is a force independent of *all* their wills.

Because work is so repulsive, men inevitably flee it like the plague. Instead of it being a demonstration of human freedom in action — co-operative, innovative, and invigorating creation — it is drudgery, not to be borne a moment longer than necessary. Free time is non-work time. Work is engaged in purely to secure the means of survival. Here too, however, we find the system has turned against its creators. The capitalist has no concern with his workers except when they are at work. He cannot afford to starve his workers to death, since that would mean nothing was produced and no profit was made; short of that, the less he paid them, the higher his profits would be.

The effect of this is to force down the workers' standard of living; but for Marx this is not only a question of reducing their welfare in the sense in which most economists would employ the term now. It is also a question of turning human enjoyment into mere animal survival. Food, drink and shelter are reduced to the bare elements of what would keep the worker alive at a level where he can work for the capitalist and live no life beyond that.[69] Marx's argument is that the human use of the animal necessities is impossible under those conditions; they do not provide an occasion for distinctively human interaction or skill or taste, but reduce human life to the

[68] *Early Writings*, pp. 299ff.
[69] ibid., p. 327.

crudest kind of animal behaviour. This necessarily infects the whole environment, for working-class housing will inevitably be mean and squalid, factories ugly, filthy and dangerous, and working-class consumption goods of the lowest possible quality.

Marx relies here on a distinction between the human and inhuman — or dehumanized — area of things which it is hard — unless one is a Hegelian — to describe as anything other than a moral distinction. Human beings are, in the terminology of Marx's early work, 'species beings', creatures whose membership in the human species is an important part of their emotional concerns. We are, in the idiom of a later time, culturally formed; it is our nature to live in a culturally complex world. Human beings do not merely eat 'food'. We are simultaneously omnivorous and exceedingly selective; our culture tells us what to enjoy and what to find disgusting, and food and drink form the raw material of social life as well as fuel for the physical machine.

Marx claims that the workers' food and drink is reduced to mere fuel. This is a cultural matter, too — the food is not merely scanty and of poor quality, it is loaded with cultural meaning to the effect that it is not meant for celebration, not meant as the basis of family gaiety, but meant only as fuel. The worker is in one sense shut out of a human culture and forced into a merely animal life, and in another sense shut into a culture of poverty where he can only see himself in such a light.

Things are not very much better, though they are doubtless more comfortable, for the bourgeois, the owner of capital. Whereas the worker is reduced to the status of merely exemplifying 'labour', the capitalist is not at all enriched by being reduced to an exemplar of 'capital'. He learns that what he must eat, drink, wear, live in and live among all have the standing of a sort of credit guarantee.[70] What he consumes is not fuel for his physical frame, but proofs that he has money. Too bad if he is tone deaf, he must go to the opera; too bad if he is colour blind, he must hang Old Masters on his walls; he cannot afford not to buy expensive food and drink even if his ulcer prevents him eating or drinking any of it.

So capitalism stands condemned at work and in consumption; neither owners nor workers control its operations or really enjoy its products. The plight of the worker is vastly the worse of course — the owner of capital may be even more cut off from the ideal of free

[70] ibid., p. 377.

co-operative creation than are the workers, that is, more alienated than they, but he runs no risk of starvation, less risk of illness, his children are less likely to die in infancy, and he himself is more likely to live to a ripe old age.

It is a plausible view of Marx's and Engels' work that sees them becoming more and more concerned with these welfare disparities as they grew older. But it would be wrong to suggest that they lost interest in, or touch with, the initial analysis of the alienated condition. There are some obvious connecting threads between *Capital* and the *Economic-Philosophical Manuscripts* — a familiar one is the analysis of the 'fetishism of commodities' where Marx analyses the delusive character of orthodox economics, which treats economic activities — relations between men — as if they are the activities of goods — relations between things.[71]

In a manner of speaking, economics *is* about relations between commodities, but only because we have created a social order — the market — in which we exchange products in ways we have allowed to escape our control. There are also what one might loosely term 'moral' connections between *Capital* and the early essays — the emphasis on freedom, the contrast between a world out of control and one under the control of freely associated producers, for instance. No doubt *Capital* belongs to social science in a more obvious fashion than the *Manuscripts*, which may be said to belong to speculative social theory; but one can hardly say that a treatise like *Capital*, which spells out the economic impact of a system whose spirit had already been delineated in a speculative way in the *Manuscripts*, is a *break* with those speculations.[72]

The movements in Marx's ideas do, however, force on us some questions about what he supposed the connection to be between political and economic transformations, or, to put it rather differently, where he thought we were going and how we might get there. We have seen that Mill supposed that public debate about the moral rights and wrongs of the existing order could lead to peaceful change. Advanced groups of workers and their middle-class allies could create co-operatives and hope to encourage others to develop; time would help as the arrival of the 'stationary state' lessened the attractions of ordinary entrepreneurship; and the process would be politically self-reinforcing — such workers would

[71] *Capital*, vol. I, pp. 163ff.
[72] Especially in the light of appendix to ibid., pp. 988–91

arouse fewer reasonable fears in the bosoms of the existing political classes, and where they met with unreasonable resistance, they would be able to wear it down without violence; practice of this kind would make them better at industrial self-government, and so we might reasonably hope not for continuous tranquillity, but for a tolerably quiet transition to social democracy.[73]

The picture is in many ways a 'rationalist' one; reasonable men ought to be able to develop a common sense of justice, a common taste for freedom, and then to govern themselves in the light of it. This makes the assumption that notions of legitimacy can be rationally discussed by the owners and non-owners of capital, that morality is rather more than ideology. It certainly assumes that both the owning and non-owning classes can get to the point of seeing that existing patterns of ownership are not what a concern for freedom and justice would license, and that this would lead to peaceful change rather than panic-stricken attempts to hang on to privilege on one side and outright revolt on the other.[74]

It is these assumptions which Marx rejects more or less *en bloc*. For the remainder of this chapter I shall try to explain why, and with what consequences for his account of what a socialist society would be like. Since, on my view of it, the central questions about the political theory of work and ownership can be summed up by, 'Why have both Mill and Marx turned out to be wrong?' — at any rate so far — I leave much of the criticism until the next, concluding chapter.

The intellectual charm of Marx's social and political theory stems in part from its appearance of systematic rigour — even rigidity; the internal determinism which Marx ascribes to the capitalist mode of production is very impressive. We get the impression that *everything* that goes on in a capitalist society can be linked to the demands of its central feature — the creation of surplus value.[75] It is not merely that Marx insists that there are strict limits to what sorts of social arrangements can coexist — we might all agree that feudal land tenures are unlikely to survive the arrival of capital-intensive, profit-maximizing farming — so much as that he holds that all other social arrangements have to

---

[73] Duncan, *Marx and Mill*, pp. 291–4.
[74] ibid., pp. 288–91.
[75] G. A. Cohen, *Karl Marx's Theory of History* (Clarendon Press, Oxford, 1978), defends the most plausible version of this claim that I know of.

accommodate themselves to the creation of surplus value in such a way as to *promote* its creation and realization. Of course, they only do so for a limited time. After that they become fetters which have to be burst asunder.[76]

Still, in spite of this appearance, Marx's account of capitalism and its demise leaves plenty of room for different interpretations. It is likely that he would have been pretty scornful of disciples who tried to turn an intellectual commitment to leaving as little as possible unexplained into a rigid dogma.[77] On the connection between ownership and politics and on the related issue of how much hope there is of a peaceful reform, Marx plainly kept his options open. The political essays he wrote at the same time as the *Manuscripts* concentrate on defending what he calls 'true democracy' against Hegel's account of rationality of the modern constitutional monarchy described in his *Philosophy of Right*. Here, the target against which much of his argument is directed is Hegel's account of the virtues of the bureaucratic or 'universal' class. But the *Communist Manifesto* says nothing about bureaucracy, and is concerned only to make the general point that the modern state is a committee for managing the common interests of the bourgeoisie.[78] Quite how far this is done is obviously variable, and in *The Eighteenth Brumaire of Louis Bonaparte* Marx even allows for the possibility of a state which somehow floats above its social basis and promotes its own interests. Engels' much later gloss on Marx's theory, *The Origins of the Family, Private Property and the State* wavers between the view that the state is a *condition* of there being property, classes and exploitation, and that it simply *reflects* them.[79]

At Marx's funeral Engels claimed that Marx had been above all else a revolutionary.[80] It can be tempting to suggest that what matters about Marx's account of politics is not the analysis of how the economic power of classes relates to their political power, but the simple clarion call to the proletariat to revolt against its oppression, and that we should not look for greater coherence in Marx's theory than that task demanded. This is too defeatist. It is

---

[76] *Capital*, vol. I, pp. 928–9.

[77] 'De omnibus dubitandum' was supposed to be his favourite tag.

[78] Karl Marx, *The Revolutions of 1848* (Penguin, Harmondsworth, 1973), p. 69.

[79] Friedrich Engels, 'The Origins of the Family, Private Property and the State', in *Selected Works of Marx and Engels in Two Volumes* (Foreign Languages Publishing House, Moscow, 1962), vol. II, p. 263.

[80] Engels, 'Speech at the Graveside of Karl Marx', in *Selected Works*, vol. II, p. 168.

not very difficult to give an account of the politics of a capitalist state which is true to the spirit of Marx's analysis, and which leaves dangling only those loose ends which Marx left dangling. That several different sorts of state apparatus are consistent with the capitalist mode of production is not a cause for surprise, nor ruled out by Marx; he agreed that each country was to some extent the creature of its own history, and that how it faced the exigencies common to all capitalist societies might well be idiosyncratic.

What we can say quite straightforwardly is that the chief 'task' of a state in capitalist society is to ensure by a combination of coercive power and ideological suasion that the bourgeoisie can continue to extract and pocket the surplus value created by the workers.[81] For our purposes, the main thing that this entails is negative: there cannot be real democracy. If there was real democracy, the workers would simply outvote their oppressors and abolish the private property system which allowed them to dominate and exploit them. Moreover, if real democracy was firmly instituted, there could be nothing like the legal and political system we now see in operation, since that simply exists to allow the appropriators of other men's labour to carry on doing so.

That real democracy abolishes 'politics' as usually understood is no cause for surprise; once men associate freely to decide what to produce, how to produce it and what to do with it, the conflicts which call for a state to resolve them will have vanished.[82] So will the distinction between a political arena in which we are called upon to act unselfishly and according to principle, and an economic arena in which we may act as selfishly as we like so long as we do not break the law. More surprising, but not inexplicable, is the suggestion that morality will also disappear; the explanation is that morality for Marx inescapably bears a connection with ideas of justice, of people's rights, of what they may *demand* from one another.[83] Once there is no scarcity, once nobody has privileged access to power or to wealth, there will be no question of demands or rights, no conflict of will or even of opinions.

Between the present and such a state of affairs the gulf is

[81] cf. Ralph Miliband, *Capitalist Democracy in Britain* (Oxford University Press, Oxford, 1982), pp. 1–2.

[82] *Early Writings*, pp. 188–91.

[83] Steven Lukes, 'Marxism, Morality and Justice', in *Marx and Marxisms*, ed. G. H. R. Parkinson (Cambridge University Press, Cambridge, 1982), pp. 177–205.

enormous. There are many obvious questions about its political accessibility, its empirical plausibility and even about its logical coherence. The simplest view seems to be this. Under capitalism the workers cannot but become politically stronger, even if they are all the time deterred by a combination of threats and blandishments from employing that power fully. To some extent their assault on the system can be slowed down or appeased by concessions here and there. But the inner logic of capitalism pushes the capitalists and their political helpers more and more into a corner; crises, the pressure of competition, whether national or global, leave less and less room for manoeuvre.

Eventually there has to be a revolutionary transformation of mock democracy into real democracy. This is unlikely to happen without a struggle, since the owners of capital have little to gain by giving in gracefully, though they may do so. In any event, Marx is more than half inclined to believe that a revolution provides good exercise in shaking off the muck of previous ages, and in inducing the appropriate solidarity and courage in the workers.[84] Where there has not been even a pretence of democracy, as in Germany or France under Napoleon III, revolutionary upheaval is inevitable.

In either case, what supervenes as a political form can only be 'the revolutionary dictatorship of the proletariat'. This is a radical democracy with one major aim only, to hasten the transition from what the *Critique of the Gotha Programme* defines as the 'lower stage' of socialism to the 'higher stage' where the narrow horizons of bourgeois right are transcended and all contribute according to their abilities and receive according to their needs.[85]

During this period, the salient features of capitalism are discarded. Although workers are paid according to what they produce, there are no capitalists taking a share of the proceeds, so even if there is inequality there is no exploitation, and each person receives back over a lifetime the value of what he has put in — not in the form of wages alone, of course, but in wages, education, health care and a pension. This stage does what capitalism cannot do, and that is live up to the standards of justice preached by capitalism. People receive the value of their labour and nobody

[84] Marx, *German Ideology*, p. 86.
[85] Karl Marx, 'Critique of the Gotha Programme', in *The First International and After* (Penguin, Harmondsworth, 1974), p. 347.

receives an income without earning it — nobody who *could* earn an income that is.[86]

This lower stage is a system in which moral principles are operative, since the aim is to secure that people are rewarded according to their efforts. Capitalism had always claimed, but falsely, to operate according to this principle; the lower stage of socialism therefore marks no sharp moral break with capitalism. It does mark a sharp break in how seriously that morality is taken, however. Equally, there will be continuity with the moral basis of democracy, in that each citizen will have a certain kind of political equality with every other. Achieving this may involve dramatic institutional breaks with the old order — we cannot have professional politicians or professional administrators who arrogate to themselves the power which the ordinary man cannot lay hands on. Almost at once, however, the distinctively *political* aspect of politics will begin to disappear, and the role of morality will also diminish since conflicts of interest will diminish, and the control of production will become a *practical* rather than a moral business.[87]

At the end of the road lies the stage of full socialism. There is no question of our arrival here needing a new revolution or a new political convulsion; the claim that the state will 'wither away' plainly implies gradual change. But withering away is not all there is to it. If Marx is coherent, it must be possible to envisage people steadily becoming very different in belief and temperament — not *wanting* power, finding immediate satisfaction in being useful to others in their society, enjoying their work, and looking forward to the satisfaction which their products will give. Only if this happens will we really have dissolved the opposition of individual interests and the general good. And only then can we have a wholly non-alienated life in which everyone expresses his social nature in free co-operation with his fellows.

Is this a coherent picture? Even if it is, we shall have to discuss next chapter's question — why has the programme gone so wrong? If it is not, we would be some way, though not all the way, towards answering that question — of course an incoherent programme will go wrong, and the native wit of the plain man will sooner or later sniff out its incoherences. The answer is not clear. To my mind, there are incoherences in the picture of ultimate socialism,

[86] ibid., pp. 345–6.
[87] *Early Writings*, pp. 189–90; *First International and After*, pp. 336–7.

stemming from incoherences in the theory of alienation. Even if this claim is resisted, it can hardly be denied that there are simply great gaps in the picture, and that their subsequent filling in has aroused endless controversy.

This is not to tackle Marx on the familiar ground of vulnerability to experience. Marx's claim that 'administration' would replace 'politics' roused Bakunin to accuse him of proposing a 'pedanto-cracy', a tyranny of professors of economics and industrial relations, and the idea that the Communist Party would, uniquely, be uncorrupted by power now looks like a bad joke.[88] But the point at issue here is different. Marx's picture of what will happen upon the abolition of private property raises two crucial questions: how will decisions be taken and on what basis?

The theory of alienation points in two different directions. In so far as it insists on the lack of *rational* decision-making under capitalism, it suggests that centralized and co-ordinated cost-benefit calculation ought to replace the market. This, though, is quite at odds with others of Marx's views; his stress on the malleability of our desires, and on their social causes and social objects goes badly with any reliance on people's subjective assessment of their own cost-benefit schedules. To ignore them, though, would be to espouse dictatorship, and would be equally unwelcome. It would be foolish to chide Marx with not seeing in addition the complexities introduced by Arrow's so-called 'im-possibility theorem', but it is not foolish to complain that when he said that individual labour would be at the same time immediately social labour, he was running away from a difficulty he had no business evading.[89]

The incoherence, though, lies not so much within the rationalist cost-benefit picture as in the tension between it and the more romantic 'self-expressive' picture more obviously associated with the theory of alienation. Here there is no stress on the efficient adjustment of means to ends, only on the adequacy of social life to express our emotional attachments. The trouble Marx faces is that he hopes to fully satisfy us on this score while we live in a large-

[88] Which is why Marx's notes on Bakunin's *Statism and Anarchy*, in *The First International and After*, pp. 333–8 look too much like an attempt to answer real doubts with definitional answers — that is, by reiterating that what people will have under socialism will not be political power, to which the only reply is, 'so what?'

[89] J. P. Plamenatz, *Karl Marx's Philosophy of Man* (Clarendon Press, Oxford, 1975), pp. 462–5.

scale, socially varied, industrial society, while the only examples we can rely on to make sense of what he hopes for, are drawn from small-scale, or even family life. The mother who knits a sweater for her son really does express her love for him in so doing, and part of the value of the sweater to him is just that that was her reason for doing it. But this is not a relationship we can generalize. Their knowledge of one another has a special intimacy by *contrast* with the everyday world; her knitting the sweater picks him out as the subject of special attention, and his gratitude is to her because it is *she* in particular who knitted it. It is a tautology but a useful one that not *all* relationships can be special. The self-expressive side of the theory of alienation relies on the thought that somehow they might be, that we might achieve a unified economy through mutual love.[90]

Together, the two views produce an uneasy effect. Common sense suggests that in any society some behaviour will be fairly well explained and indeed justified as being rational in cost-benefit terms; efficient planning to minimize costs and maximize benefits would be what rational men would engage in. But to give the planning anything to bite on, the costs and benefits have to be individual, self-interested costs and benefits, since otherwise decisions would be locked in an indeterminacy like that which besets two polite people each trying to get the other to go through the door first.

Equally, common sense suggests that in any society where such things are felt at all, people *will* value the expressive features of work, and the relationships implied in work, just as Marx does. But not *all* of their motivation can possibly come from such a source; sweaters must have other and primary purposes before they can serve as media of emotional expression and communication.[91] The common-sense version of Marx's vision would then boil down to the hope that the proprietary rights of the owners of capital could one way and another be abrogated to whatever extent made it possible to increase the amount of emotionally engaging and interesting work, and made it possible to organize the production of material benefits as efficiently and unwastefully of human effort as techniques allowed.

Common sense would also expect there to be some trade-off

[90] *Early Writings*, pp. 277–8.
[91] Jon Elster, *Sour Grapes* (Cambridge University Press, Cambridge, 1983), pp. 97–100.

between these two goods, and would also doubt whether it would be at all *obvious* what method of decision making would best replace the disorder of bargaining between independent owners of capital or labour power. But common sense would be amenable to the thought that a society in which class conflict had diminished, and reasonable good will prevailed, could afford to find its way by trial and error. The trouble is that this common-sense view is not Marx's. In spite of denouncing almost all his opponents as utopians, he never does more than claim that all these oppositions and contradictions will solve themselves.[92]

His readers feel inhibited in denouncing him in turn as as wild an utopian as his opponents because they feel, I think rightly, that the common-sense view is very attractive, and, I think wrongly, that Marx must really have meant to put it forward rather than the project for utopia. The truth, I fear, is that Marx relied on a 'cost-benefit rational calculator' view of human nature, but failed to suggest how he might calculate what to do; he relied on a view of man as essentially concerned to express his social nature in creating and exchanging his products, but did not suggest how this could be done in an inevitably anonymous society. And in relying on both views, he did not explain how they could be squared with one another.[93]

---

[92] Plamenatz, *Karl Marx's Philosophy of Man*, pp. 463ff.
[93] ibid., p. 472.

# Why Are There So Few Socialists?

I am rather conscious that this last chapter represents something of a flying leap over a century of intellectual history, and that the perspective from which it is written is unfailingly that of the male, 'first world' affluent worker. I am conscious, too, that it says little explicitly about the concerns of the first five chapters of the book. To anyone anxious about this there are two things to say. The first is that it would of course have been a pleasure to write about Morris and Bellamy, to say something serious about Durkheim and Weber, and to tackle the issues raised by Berle and Means and many others; but, it seems to me that doing this would not have disturbed the assumptions on which this last, very brisk look at some large issues is based. That is, a slower and more scrupulous tracing of the route from 1883 to 1983 would not have disturbed the view that both Mill's reformism and Marx's revolutionism were very plausible in their day, and have in many ways continued to be plausible, and yet have turned out inadequate predictions of what the working classes in developed countries would actually demand. This also must excuse my male, and first world bias; Marx and Mill looked for the impetus for a transition to socialism to come from the developed countries. It is no part of my case to suggest that first world capitalism poses no problems for third world countries — it is evident that it poses innumerable problems; and it is no part of my case to suggest that within first world countries politics ought to be a male preserve — only that as a matter of fact it largely is such, and only that as a matter of fact the male worker's wishes determine the policies of labour-oriented parties. I ask why those on whom Marx and Mill relied for the transition to socialism did not respond to what Marx and Mill supposed was the case for socialism — not whether they were the only possible bearers of the task, nor whether this was the only case. I take for granted that they were not and it is not.

Secondly, and in the same vein, I have not tried to underline the fact that the 'family-centredness' of industrial workers not only makes them more accepting of the capitalist order but does so for reasons which Hegel would have understood; I have not tried to emphasize that Locke, Rousseau and Hegel would all have agreed that the moral conviction that we ought to go to work to support our families is a securer basis of psychological and social peace than a narrowly self-interested calculation of the benefits to each of us individually would be. I have not tried to ask whether the affluent worker's liking for televisions and home computers represents a desperate attempt to shelter from the emptiness of civilized life which Rousseau diagnosed — on the whole, I take it for granted that it does not, but I do not try to argue the point at length. I have not tried to discuss whether the secularization of our society renders us as morally rudderless as Locke would have feared. And so on. It is not that I think such questions meaningless or pointless; and it is not that I have no views on the answers to them. It is simply that I have concentrated my attention on one question, in the hope that readers who have borne with me thus far will be willing to make some other connections for themselves and be ready to defer other questions to other places.

It is somewhat glib, but quite useful, to frame this final chapter round the question of why neither Mill nor Marx turned out to be right. A slightly different way of putting it would be to reframe Sombart's question and enquire 'Why is there no (voluntarily accepted) socialism practically anywhere?'[1] A third way of putting the same point would be to observe that so long as property is a central concern of political theorists, it is simply assumed that many of the miseries of capitalism are to be laid at the door of private property — whence it is assumed that the state can and will wither away when it is no longer employed by the capitalists, that work will become interesting and meaningful when the power to make it anything else has been removed from the hands of the capitalists.[2]

What has happened in the hundred years since Marx's death is that partly by internal erosion and partly by external impact the

---

[1] Werner Sombart, *Why Is There No Socialism in the United States?* (Macmillan, London, 1966), pp. 61–119; it was his memorable observation that socialist Utopias were wrecked on the reefs of American roast beef and apple pie; there was much more to it than that, but unheard of affluence by European standards must be part of the answer to his question.
[2] Marx, *Early Writings*, p. 395.

belief in the centrality of property institutions has been replaced by
something more eclectic, while the moral position implicit in both
Mill's and Marx's views — that the right or the power to determine
work and production should be determined by the social function of
such rights and powers — has become a commonplace except
among libertarians.[3] The result is not, of course, that there is any
consensus on the virtues of socialism or capitalism, only a
consensus that 'it's his' invites the further question, 'What good
does its being his do for everyone else?'

But the existence of this consensus is partly suggestive of the
displacement of arguments about property rights from the centre of
political debate. There are two aspects of this which I shall tackle.
One is the lack of demand for socialism in developed capitalist
democracies where the working classes have the political ability to
push through almost any changes they are agreed on, and yet show
no signs of agreeing on anything very radical. The other is the
intellectual dissolution of the belief in socialism — the increasing
doubt whether any amount of tampering with the ownership of
firms would make work meaningful, the state less oppressive, or the
economy more manageable. The two are connected.

One cause of the lack of demand for socialism is, obviously, the
plain man's disbelief that it can produce the goods, either moral or
material; and one cause of the loss of the intellectual faith in
socialism is, equally obviously, the feeling that the degree of
commitment and competence which the average man would have
to bring to the building of socialism will not be forthcoming.[4] Marx
and Mill anticipated that some sacrifices would be needed to build
socialism, but neither would have thought it made any sense to
offer working men a hundred years of one-party rule, bureaucratic
muddle and tyranny, and constant moral bullying with only the
faintest prospect of genuine self-government at the end of it.[5]

The lack of demand for socialism has several different aspects,
and is a subject which would decently occupy a long book. In the
context of this book's concerns, we can concentrate on three points
only. The first is that if property rights are thought of in a purely
instrumental fashion, justified in terms of the welfare of people at

[3] Tawney, *Acquisitive Society*, pp. 87–104.
[4] S. N. Hampshire and Leszek Kolakowski, *The Socialist Idea* (Quartet Books, London, 1977), for a gloomy, but unhostile round-up.
[5] ibid., pp. 1–17.

large, capitalism has turned out to be very much more successful in producing material well-being than anyone in the mid-nineteenth century expected.

No doubt, the connection between the property rights characteristic of capitalist economies and their prosperity is extremely contestable; no society in the late twentieth century operates a pure market economy in which all firms are price takers, nor price setters; no society ties ownership, management and entrepreneurship together in the way Adam Smith assumed they were tied together, and in which both Mill and Marx observed that with the rise of the joint stock company they were not.[6] Some of the co-ordination which the market cannot provide is now provided by governments attached to indicative planning, and some is provided by simple collusion between large corporations, but this hardly impinges at all on property rights in a legally recognizable sense.

One might say, as any reasonable Marxist would say, that what this shows is that capitalists are willing to concede governments whatever powers they need to keep the golden goose laying. This is no doubt true, but the effect is that the working class of developed industrial societies has nothing against capitalism *so long as* it is prosperous, and it has been sufficiently prosperous thus far to ensure that there is no great demand for socialism.[7]

This view is, of course, denied by a good many socialists, who point out, and quite rightly, that even if there is a good deal of general prosperity, it is spread very unequally, and that some people live predictably insecure and impoverished lives — unskilled workers in declining trades, poorly educated young people from ethnic minorities, the long-term sick, and so on. But in terms of providing much social pressure for socialism, these groups are negligible.

This is not to say that it is morally acceptable to ignore their avoidable sufferings; the view that we have duties only to those who could cause us trouble is simply disgusting. What is true is that to most people these deprivations look like a failure of humanity or governmental organization; what they need is more efficient welfare-state capitalism, not socialism. As for the more general inequality, striking in income and much more striking in wealth, that we can observe in any capitalist economy, most people

---

[6] J. K. Galbraith, *The New Industrial Society* (André Deutsch, London, 1972), pp. 86ff.

[7] Daniel Bell, *The End of Ideology* (The Free Press, Glencoe, Ill., 1960), pp. 273ff., 369ff.

do not spend their time envying those with incomes ten times their own, but only those with incomes ten per cent greater for much the same sort of work.

Three men digging in the same hole to locate gas, water and electricity mains will be acutely aware of differentials in their pay; about the wealth of Lord Cowdray they neither know nor care.[8] This is not because they have made the sort of calculation John Rawls or F. A. Hayek asks them to make, and have concluded that they do as well as can be done out of the system;[9] rather, so long as they do not feel too hard up they do not begrudge other people what they happen to get. Being Lord Cowdray is like winning the pools — good luck rather than legally licensed robbery. No doubt, if they were worse off, they would be more inclined to wonder if it wasn't legalized robbery — the point is that prosperity prevents such questions being asked.

It can be argued that much of this is the result of constant moral and political indocrination, that the ideology of welfare-state capitalism is nicely adjusted to getting the working class to see the world in these terms. There is no doubt that readers of popular newspapers, watchers of television and cinema, do receive a good deal of propaganda, some crude, some subtle, some intended, and most of it not — all social systems do a good deal to keep up the illusion of their own naturalness and inevitability. But it would be foolish and insulting to think that people simply absorb what they have thrown at them. There are more readers of the *Sun* who vote Labour than Conservative, though the paper does its level best to suggest that to vote Labour is the act of a knave and a madman. Equally, the ideological climate in which working people live is one in which it is claimed that the owners and managers of big business *deserve* their incomes, wealth, capital gains and the rest; but is it very doubtful that any of this cuts much ice with a working-class audience.[10] By and large the working class acceptance of the wealth

---

[8] W. G. Runciman, *Relative Deprivation and Social Justice* (Penguin, Harmondsworth, 1972), ch. 2, pp. 10–41, for an explanation of the idea that our sense of grievance or contentment is very largely a matter of our 'reference group' and that that is usually a group to which we are 'close'.

[9] Rawls, *Theory of Justice*, pp. 278–9; F. A. von Hayek, *The Mirage of Social Justice* (Routledge & Kegan Paul, London, 1976), p. 131.

[10] Frank Parkin, *Class Inequality and Political Order* (MacGibbon and Kee, London, 1971), pp. 88–96.

and power of the owning and governing class comes from nothing more than the belief that some are born lucky.

In addition, a point to be stressed again in explaining the intellectual dissolution of socialism, this acceptance rests on a shrewd sense that the existing owners and managers, and their political allies, have had some considerable practice in running the industrial and political system. Their *right* to their wealth and power is less as issue than the unlikelihood that we could replace them at all quickly and cheaply with anything better. The curious mixture of loyalty and contempt with which the English working class regards its trade-union leaders seems to stem from this source; they lack the polish and plausibility of their establishment opponents, they are, anyway, often in sectional opposition to any given group of workers — leaders of skilled workers are frequently at odds with leaders of unskilled workers over the narrowing and widening of differentials — so while they will be supported to the death on appropriate issues, they will be deserted on general political issues without any compunction whatever.[11]

Prosperity, then, has been enough to allow the capitalist economic order to survive. Some further features of this prosperity have also been important and ought to be mentioned. One is that the belief in the homogeneity of working-class life has turned out to be false. The proletariat in the nineteenth-century sense has vanished; unskilled manual workers make up barely one sixth of the work force; white-collar jobs have vastly expanded, as have jobs in a new — that is, non-domestic — service sector.[12] The effect of this is to offer many people a way — or the illusion of a way — out of the least prosperous sectors of the economy, and to give many more people a degree of security in their prosperity that contrasts very powerfully with, say, the condition of a docker at the turn of the century. There is no longer a *common* interest in change for the sake of prosperity, for many workers must regard it as very doubtful whether they would gain from a change. Even when they had got their share of the gains from expropriating the expropriators, they

---

[11] The very low support for the Labour Party among trade unionists in the British General Election of June 1983 is one illustration of the political rift between leaders and rank and file; but even when trade unionists voted Labour in larger numbers, a majority disapproved of the political ties between the unions and the Labour Party. Goldthorpe *et al.*, *The Affluent Worker*, vol. III, p. 178.

[12] A. H. Halsey, *Change in British Society* (2nd edn, University Press, Oxford, 1981), pp. 24–6.

might be net losers by what they had to share with those worse off than themselves.

A second thing is that political theorists have underestimated the impact of the family on people's outlooks. Bacon's dictum that he who hath wife and children gives hostages to fortune, and is thereafter less apt to projects of great good or great evil, is very important.[13] On the whole most people are selfish on behalf of their families, rather than on behalf of themselves, and more cautious about putting their families at risk than about themselves. Hence, take-home pay is tremendously important, and there is no upper limit to how much of it a worker might reasonably want, but it is not true that the logic of the theory of games applies with full rigour to his behaviour, leading him to seize even a *small* chance of a large monetary gain. Rather, he values security very highly indeed. It is this which makes the existence of the welfare state so important and stops taxation being resented.

A third thing relates to the sort of consumption which has been made possible. There has been any amount of nonsense talked and written about the politically narcotic effect of consumer durables — as if the housewife would have gone out and studied the elements of Marxism–Leninism had she not been mesmerized by watching her washing whirling round in the washing machine. But what is important is the way in which the welfare of the nuclear family has been increased; the drudgery of washday, the boredom of winter evenings, and the health of women and children are more seriously discussable subjects than narcotization.[14]

No doubt, people may have warm, well-lit homes, plenty of food and drink, any number of consumer durables, and still not be happy — however well off you are, you may have a broken heart, a deplorable sex-life, and children who take hard drugs. But most people seem to concur in the view that happiness is very loosely connected to the world's goods, and that as between unhappiness with comfort and unhappiness with poverty, a rational person chooses comfort.

This leads on to a different subject. We have distinguished between welfare-minded and 'expressive' theories of property, and have seen expressive theories concentrated on the demand for meaningful work and industrial self-government. The next and

[13] Goldthorpe *et al.*, *Affluent Worker*, vol. III, pp. 181–4.
[14] ibid., p. 184.

final aspects of our analysis of the lack of demand for socialism, then, are the seeming unconcern of working people for the quality of work on the one hand and for self-management on the other.

It seems to be empirically true that working people do not regard more interesting work as worth losing money for.[15] Job enrichment programmess have a rather mixed record of success in improving productivity, reducing absenteeism, and doing the other good things hoped from them. On the other hand, it plainly cannot be true that working people do not care whether work is more or less interesting, or that they take no interest in their work. The man who leaves his factory with a cry of 'thank God it's Friday' may well go home and rewire his house, build shelves for his wife or a bedroom unit for his daughter, or dig till his muscles ache to get the ground ready for his leeks; he is not a person who finds all work intrinsically repulsive. Why, then, does he not demand a more interesting time at work?[16]

The first thing to observe is that most workers are perfectly clear whether their jobs are intrinsically dull or intrinsically interesting; there may conceivably be some workers who enjoy repetitive assembly-line work, for its own sake, but few of them show up in survey data, and in general there are few surprises about what people find interesting or the reverse. This is not to say that the data are wholly consistent − only that they are not very hard to interpret.[17]

A factory or a mine, or any other place of work, is an elaborate social system, not just a place where various physical activities go on, and what people go there for is more varied than Marx or Mill gave them credit for. The boringness of a job may be very much less objected to if there is plenty of social exchange of an enjoyable kind going on; again we all possess resources for simply ignoring the intrinsic dullness of what we are doing − so long as the work does not demand too much attention, we can daydream to our heart's

---

[15] ibid., pp. 54ff.

[16] Ken Coates, *Essays on Industrial Democracy* (Spokesman Books, Nottingham, 1972), pp. 43–5.

[17] Goldthorpe *et al.*, *Affluent Worker*, vol. III, p. 55n. insists on the objective nastiness of most assembly-line work; although Clayre's informants, *Work and Play* pp. 184–7, perhaps found more consolations at work than did the Luton workers on whose responses *The Affluent Worker* is based, they do not disturb the basic thought that they sold their time in a hard market for the benefit of their families.

content, and may be quite happy to do so.[18] Those of us who are fortunate enough to have interesting occupations may still find that by the end of the day our minds are wandering a good deal. To have even a fairly boring task to perform is for many people better than having nothing at all to do; standing by an assembly line is at least better than standing by a wall picking one's teeth.

Two other things matter as much. The first is that people come to work with expectations. If they are family-centred, they will necessarily — and rightly — be money-minded. We cannot take home our job satisfaction and employ it for the benefit of husbands, wives and children; they *can* share the income we bring home, they cannot share our enjoyment of the job. Now, this opens up some interesting questions about the extent to which money-mindedness may have got out of hand, and may not be so obviously rational as I suggest. Someone who enjoys his or her job may well go home a happier and a nicer person than someone who does not, and the family will surely benefit from that. A man who tries to buy off the demands of his family by earning a lot of money, but who is never at home except when he is tired and ill-tempered, is plainly being quite irrational in his own terms and theirs.[19]

Two things seem immediately obvious. One is that this sort of irrationality *might* be less likely under socialism, since monetary rewards would not play the same role as now — though it is all too easy to imagine equivalents — but it is not by any means inevitable outside socialism. In so far as anything is unequivocally a question of individual psychology, this is. At all events, it is scarcely a powerful motor for change. The second thing is that a firm is now a good device for providing one with money income, and not a very good device for providing much else. It is perfectly sensible for someone to sell forty hours a week of boredom for a decent wage, especially if there are few alternatives to so doing.[20]

This may all sound deplorably acquiescent in the status quo. But it is not quite as bad as that. Not only do most people have a great many interests outside work; they have a great deal more time to

---

[18] But Goldthorpe *et al.*, *Affluent Worker*, pp. 64–5 insist that the workplace community offers a pretty thin social life and one which does not provide any basis for outside sociability — 'mates' are not 'friends'.

[19] Barbara Ehrenreich, *The Hearts of Men* (Pluto Press, London, 1983) produces a daunting list of reasons why men get into this state and frequently end up bolting from their families as a result.

[20] Goldthorpe *et al.*, *Affluent Worker*, vol. III, p. 184.

pursue them than they had in the middle of the nineteenth century. There is a world of difference between working twelve to fourteen hours a day six days a week, and working seven and a half hours a day in a five-day week. None of us in his right mind would much begrudge spening an hour or two a day doing the household chores, even if he or she would flinch from the life of a *plongeur* or dustman; on a larger scale, shortening the working day really is a liberation from tedium.[21]

This is not to say that a shorter working day has created the unalienated man of Marx's vision — we do not find our working lives such a central part of our lives as Marx had hoped — but that the horrors of what Marx called an alienated life have been vastly reduced. Domestic existence is by no means merely seizing food, shelter and sexual comfort in an animal fashion; work is not servitude to a machine for all the hours our strength lasts out. And as hours have been reduced, so has the unpleasantness of the work. Positive concern with life-enhancing work may be limited, but a concern to reduce the burden of toil is not. Some work is still brutalizing in its harshness, some simply dirty and unpleasant. But in general the amount of sheer toil has been steadily diminishing.[22] Marxist critics point out, and perhaps rightly, that this is not all gain — sometimes work becomes less skilled as it becomes lighter, and sometimes workers become more tightly controlled in how they work as the work itself gets easier. All the same, in terms of our question — why have the working classes not revolted against their working conditions? — part of the answer is that the work is easier and there is less of it.

This still leaves the third aspect of the argument untouched. Mill, it will be remembered, thought the desire for self government, once aroused, would be unstoppable; Marx, all his life, believed that being the object of other men's decisions was intolerable. It is plain that in some sense we *could* have had some degree of workers' control in countries like Britain, and yet no such thing has happened. Moreover, it is also clear enough that even if most trade-union leaders are firmly convinced that management cannot manage, they would not themselves accept the industries they

[21] Karl Marx, *Capital*, vol. III (Lawrence & Wishart, London, 1974), p. 820.
[22] Daniel Bell, *The Coming of Post-Industrial Society* (Heinemann, London, 1977) on the rise of non-manual labour; but see Harry Braverman, *Labour and Monopoly Capital: The Degradation of Work in the Twentieth Century* (Monthly Review, London, 1975) on the horrors of 'deskilling'.

bargain for as a gift. There are certain exceptions — the National Freight Corporation is one — but it would be more than difficult to give British Leyland to the workers, let alone the coal industry or British Steel.[23]

The explanation, though it hardly amounts to much more than a restatement of the facts, is that the working class has never acquired a taste for self-government in its own right. Neither Mill's view that self-respect and a desire for responsibility would require it, nor psychological theories like Abraham Maslow's about the need for self-actualization by controlling the world, have turned out to be much of a guide to practice. To put it somewhat vulgarly, so long as the cow has been producing plenty of milk, nobody has been very excited about who decided when to milk her.[24]

It is important not to adopt the wrong tone of voice about all this. Middle-class intellectuals telling the lower orders to adopt middle-class moral ideals make an unattractive sight at the best of times. To say that the working class has 'let down' Mill and Marx invites the obvious retort that nobody ever asked Mill and Marx to work out the moral ambitions of the workers for them. Saying that the working class has settled for prosperity rather than hegemony sounds much too like an accusation that the 'swinish multitude' has lolled about in luxury instead of behaving like self-governing creatures blessed with reason and free will. Seeing that most people life in something far from luxury, and are kept exceedingly busy doing their best for themselves and their families, any such imputation would be sheer cheek.[25]

Oscar Wilde complained, famously, that what was alarming about socialism was that it would encroach too far upon our freedom to spend our evenings as we chose. An ordinary worker, faced with the thought of having to run the firm he works for is almost bound to feel either that Oscar Wilde is right, and that the idea of attending a committee on investment or finance or whatever on top of his job is too wearing to contemplate, or else that he

---

[23] For perfectly good reasons, if Brian Chiplin and John Coyne, 'Can Workers Manage?' (Institute of Economic Affairs, London, 1977) are even half-way right.

[24] Abraham Maslow, *Motivation and Personality* (Harper & Row, Evanston, Ill, 1970), pp. 97–104.

[25] Goldthorpe *et al.*, *Affluent Worker*, vol. III, p. 184 express what seems to me the proper degree of hostility to *de haut en bas* moralizing.

simply would not know *how* to run the company if it was proposed that he should do it full time instead of his current job.[26]

Even if self-government amounted only to electing a board of directors, or appointing top management, he might well think that he had no opinion worth giving on the matter. Mill, of course, had in mind firms with twenty or thirty employees at most, where it is not implausible to think that the workers could rather easily run the firm themselves, and that administration in the general sense would occupy only a hour or two a week, rather in the way it does in something like an Oxford or Cambridge college. Whether anything of the sort could be done in parts of ICI or General Motors is an open question; but they are not an environment which *invites* the experiment.

One final point in this connection will lead on aptly enough to the intellectual dissolution of the ideals of socialism. One deterrent facing workers who might want to experiment with workers' control is the poor record of the best known co-operatives in Britain. The poor record largely results from the fact that setting up a co-operative is often the last throw of a bankrupt concern, and if the bankruptcy is the result of there being no market for its goods, nothing anyone does about changing its ownership or management will make any difference. But this point, valid as it is, does not do much to shake the popular association of co-operatives and economic failure. So, it is hardly to be wondered at if working people do not feel inclined to experiment with a prosperous company, and only reluctantly become self-governing.

In none of this does the orthodox trade-union movement give a radical lead. Unions are happy with a role in an oppositional system which they know how to operate; management is expected to be on the lookout for profit, and the union's job is to see that management pays as much as possible for the workers' co-operation.[27] It is a view of the world which has the advantage of appealing equally to radicals who hope that eventually the whole capitalist order will collapse and to conservatives who devoutly hope it will not. The radicals need not be implicated in profit making; the conservatives, who believe in the rights of the existing

---

[26] Michael Walzer, *Radical Principles* (Basic Books, New York, 1980), pp. 128–38 discusses 'a day in the life of the socialist citizen' with a lighter touch than most.

[27] Goldthorpe *et al.*, *Affluent Worker*, vol. III, pp. 165ff. on the 'instrumental collectivism' behind workers' siding with union efforts on their behalf.

owners and managers, are happy to sell what they have — control of the labour power of their members — for as good a price as they can get. What neither wants is to experiment with workers' control. Whether there could be much of a shift without a prior shift in political outlook is rather dubious; as things stand, radicalism is associated with a belief in Marx's 'general crisis of capitalism', and since, like the Last Trump, nothing absolutely forbids belief in it, it is not likely that the radicals will move, and quite certain that the conservatives will not.

All of this, it should be said, amounts to the claim that the working classes on the whole *accept* the existing order. It does not imply that they embrace it with any great conviction. Indeed, the thrust of what has been said is precisely that large convictions are not to be looked for. Welfare-state capitalism can call on a limited loyalty, but capitalism is not, in spite of some heroic recent attempts, morally very engaging.[28]

Max Weber's account of the Protestant Ethic made the reason quite clear — life might gain a *meaning* as an attempt to follow one's calling, to demonstrate one's consciousness of one's duty to do what one would with God's gifts, and in the process one might be a successful capitalist. But being a successful capitalist is not the sort of thing which gives life meaning. The ordinary person does not lead a meaningless or an amoral or an apathetic life; but the meaning of his life, what engages his moral energies and his attention, are largely domestic concerns. If welfare capitalism falters badly or for long, it will not be able to rely on our loyalty to save it since we feel very little.

The last influence on the working classes' failure to demand the overthrow of capitalism which I have yet to mention is socialism's intellectual disintegration. This, too, is a story worth several books;[29] but again it is not impossible to sketch its main features. All of them imply that ownership is *not* our crucial concern; and we can plausibly summarize them in a series of propositions. The first is the claim that power and property are less closely connected than either Marx or Mill supposed; this was the great claim of Weber, and the great lesson taught by the Russian Revolution. That is,

---

[28] George Gilder, *Wealth and Poverty* strikes me as heroic — but implausible.
[29] Hampshire and Kolakowski, *The Socialist Idea*, pp. 18–44; Lewszek Kolakowski, *Main Currents of Marxism*, vol. III *The Breakdown* (Clarendon Press Oxford, 1978) chronicles the mixture of political and intellectual corruption which went into the decay of Marxism.

Marx, though not Mill, tended to think that the reason why states existed, and why they developed bureaucracies, elaborate legal systems and the power of police and army to enforce their provisions, was because the owners of property needed to be defended against the propertiless.

It seemed to follow that once private ownership of industry had been abolished, there would be no need for political domination. But once it is admitted that men may have an interest in domination for other than material reasons, and once it is admitted that they can satisfy their material interests without actually *owning* anything, it becomes clear that socialism is wholly consistent with tyranny, with inequality of welfare on the grand scale.[30] Under the Stalinist revival of wage differentials in the 1930s, socialism proved to be consistent with wider differentials than capitalism in the USA. Those who possessed power did not need to appeal to those who 'owned' the means of production for resources; those who could call upon the instruments of coercion could also demand whatever resources they needed to sustain their grasp on the instruments of coercion.

The attempts of some writers to describe the Soviet Union as 'state capitalist' rather than as a 'deformed workers' state' make no great difference.[31] Either what we see *is* socialism, and it is consistent with tyranny, because tyranny stems from the monopoly of the means of violence — and in this area, the disparity between governments and their subjects has grown enormously since the days of the Commune — or else what we see is not socialism, because there exists a ruling class able to extract and enjoy the surplus produced by the workers, and what we have found is that our former view of property was inadequate, and we do not really know after all *how* to abolish private ownership.[32]

In either event, what we know is that what we formerly supposed to be the way to abolish oppression is nothing of the sort. In

[30] Milovan Djilas, *The New Class*, pp. 45ff. argues that they do own the means of production, as does Tony Cliff, *Stalinist Russia, a Marxist Analysis* (Michael Kidron, London, 1955), pp. 134–43, though both of them accept that the sort of 'ownership' involved is a matter of *de facto* control rather than de jure proprietorship.

[31] Trotsky, *Basic Writing*, pp. 216ff., argues that they do not own the means of production, cannot bequeath their power and therefore cannot be a class; my own view is that what makes them a 'new' class is simply that the features that make them a class are not related to what they own and do not own.

[32] Perhaps we don't: cf. Kolakowski's gloomy view of the abolition of civil society in *The Socialist Idea*, ch. 1, pp. 18ff.

passing, however, it is worth noting that the negative conclusion is the only one we can safely draw. The example of Nazi Germany is by itself enough to show that there is no reason to think that private ownership is a reliable defence against tyranny either. What is, is a question which lies outside our scope entirely, but it is clear that it has rather little to do with ownership.[33]

The second claim is a corollary of the first, and amounts to saying that since power and property are more separate than are supposed, a ruling class can exist under socialism. One face of its existence we have already noticed. The other, perhaps even more daunting, is the face of non-tyrannical bureaucracy. If a class is defined in terms of its members possessing a common interest which they jointly pursue, in part by forming a solidary social order resistant to antagonistic classes, then a bureaucracy is always at least liable to form a class.

It may not be tyrannical, and it may rely rather little on its access to the means of coercion, but it will surely emphasize its own virtues — technical competence and orderliness, access to the secrets of government, responsibility for the maintenance of rules, for example — and try to restrict access to its ranks, while securing for its members whatever material privileges it can. And if esteem is to count as a privilege, it will no doubt do its best to secure that too.[34]

This, however, brings us to the central claim against socialist ambitions, produced by Weber and made much of by Schumpeter. The central figure of the modern world is the bureaucrat. Rational management rather than ownership is what Weber seized on as the central element in capitalism, and the rise of the bureaucratic form of administration is, so far as anything is, one of the unstoppable social forces which propel Weber's social theory.[35]

To writers in this tradition what matters is not the relations of owners and workers, but the power of managers. In modern capitalism the key figure is not the owner, but the manager; once the joint stock company had been transformed into the modern limited liability company, with its share capital spread among thousands of 'owners', the real power over the company and its employees lay in the hands of managers, the day-to-day experience

---

[33] Becker, *Property Rights*, pp. 75–80, 117.
[34] Anthony Giddens, *Capitalism and Modern Social Theory* (Cambridge University Press, 1971), pp. 232ff.
[35] ibid., pp. 181–3.

of the worker was not one of either confronting or co-operating with an owner, but that of fitting into a bureaucratic hierarchy — at the bottom. But since the owners were thus removed from the scene, how different would socialism be? The answer seemed to be that it would be little or no different. The functionalist assumption that in a rational age only the most efficient form of management and organization would survive implied that if efficiency dictated a bureaucratic structure for industry, that is what it would get.

There are innumerable questions which all this raises. The most obvious is how much difference it makes whether the managers are answerable to shareholders concerned with profit or to a state authority which need not be. But here again the thought is that a government concerned with efficiency would want some measure of the 'profitability' of its enterprise, since otherwise resources would simply be wasted by being employed sub-optimally. In that case the government could hardly help behaving very like a share-holding body under capitalism. It would be like a pension fund or a bank holding investment funds which it can shift in search of the best rate of return.

If this is true, the attractions of socialism further diminish, since it is also true that anything which can be done by a government under socialism can apparently be done by a government under capitalism, when it operates via the tax and welfare system.[36] There seems little room for workers' control or creativity in such a picture, and that is because workable socialism looks distressingly like a system of rational, technical calculation, the arena of the all-powerful expert rather than the liberated common man, and in looking like that it looks like tidied-up welfare-state capitalism too.

Is this an inescapable outcome? Plainly no simple answer is compelling, but one reason for saying it is rests on the connection between the inevitability of bureaucracy and the growth of technology. If it is held, as it is in Galbraith's work, that the decisive features of modern technology are enormous economies of scale and very long periods between planning and production, the modern enterprise has to be very large and have a well-planned future. It is no use spending a billion dollars and fifteen years developing a jet engine and finding nobody ready to buy it, so characteristically there has to be an exceedingly unfree market in such things, dominated by firms which spend a great deal of time

[36] Rawls, *Theory of Justice*, pp. 265–84.

planning and predicting their own futures, and getting each other to fit in with their plans for the future. In short it has to look more like a government department than the nineteenth-century firm with twenty employees. Once again, it is not clear how socialist ownership would make any difference to this result.[37]

Each of these points suggests that ownership is not decisive. It is not merely a matter of pointing at the USSR and observing that it provides neither prosperity nor self-government nor meaningful work. That is an argument of very great vulgarity — though it is not a weak argument. Rather it is a matter of pointing out that the forces which work against these things under capitalism also work against them under socialism, and that whatever palliating device is available under socialism is no less available under capitalism.

The area in which this is perhaps most obvious is that of the restoration of meaning to work. As an empirical matter, it is plain enough that people will often enjoy work and find it meaningful so long as they are sure it contributes to a worthwhile goal. No doubt *many* Chinese were cynical about the exhortations they were deluged with during the Great Leap Forward and other mass campaigns, but some doubtless felt the Chinese equivalent of the puritan conviction that a man who sweeps a room for God's sake makes the room and the action fine. But in everyday routine, uninteresting work emerges as uninteresting, and the question of how the really boring elements can be palliated or embedded in something *socially* attractive re-emerges too. The crucial disenchanting slogan then is: what makes work drudgery owes more to technique than ownership.

This is a claim which, like all the rest, deserves long and careful thought. Technique is more elusive a notion than it looks, since techniques have to be worked by people with skills and attitudes which make all the difference to their working or not. The idea that we can readily read off organizational demands from technique is much too simple — for one thing different accounting methods may make a lot of difference to whether a technique is held to be cost efficient or not. Still the basic thought is simple and hard to resist. It is no accident that industrial techniques resemble each other world wide. Efficiency is suffiently culturally neutral to achieve that at least. The effect, though, is to make a lot of work boring and alienating, regardless of ownership patterns. Working for Ford may

[37] Galbraith. *New Industrial State*, pp. 21ff., 98ff.

be awful in many ways, but they are mostly very like the ways in which working in the Togliatti plant in the USSR is awful.[38]

In so far as the dreariness of industrial labour is getting less — and it seems that it is — that owes nothing to ownership, a little to control, and much to technique. It owes a little to control because there is ample evidence that work forces, even in totalitarian states, are not wholly compliant. Unless labour-lightening innovations are made, productivity drops and absenteeism rises; the Japanese may employ robots first, but the USSR will not lag all that far behind. Crucially, though, Taylorism, beloved of Lenin, is only a faintly lunatic extension of what almost everyone agrees on, that the horribleness of industrial work is very much the result of a search for efficiency, with the consequent subordination of everything else to increased productivity. If the search for efficiency now offers to lead us out in less dreary and constrained work, that is a bonus and a happy one. It is, however, not a socialist bonus.[39]

If, then, we conclude that socialist ambitions have been eroded by the internal difficulties of the socialist ideal itself, are we to conclude too that everyone discussed in the previous chapters and pages was simply wrong, either about the importance of property rights or about the need for meaningful work, or about the importance of self-government? The answer is evidently not. Property rights are still important, because it is still true that what you own, how much you own, and what you can do with it makes a lot of difference to your well-being and security — and not only in capitalist societies; owning a car in the Soviet Union is plainly a matter of some consequence for your happiness and self esteem.[40]

But property rights are nowadays important because they are *rights* rather than because they are *property* rights. In the past a good deal now achieved by quite other means than the creation of property rights was necessarily achieved differently. Moreover, inequalities once connected almost entirely with property are now not — save in the very loosest sense, where we might count the unique talents of Mick Jagger or Ursula Andress as 'property' in their own persons. The issues which arguments about property

[38] Huw Beynon, *Working at Ford* (Penguin, Harmondsworth, 1973).
[39] William Blauner, *Alienation and Freedom* (University of Chicago Press, Chicago, 1964), pp. 182–4; later research does not confirm that process workers are notably less alienated.
[40] Smith, *The Russians*, pp. 25–51.

were always arguments about are live issues still — security, prosperity, citizenship, making a mark on the world.

Marx and Mill and a lot of nineteenth-century writers may have been wrong about the way industrial society would develop — overestimating the pressure of hardship or moral autonomy or solidarity; but they were not wrong about the importance of the subjects with which they were dealing. That their concerns now agitate economists, political scientists, moral philosophers and industrial sociologists only shows that they tackled more than one man would nowadays be wise to do — and that they have left plenty to think about.

# Index